POETS TRANSLATE POETS

POETS TRANSLATE POETS

A *Hudson Review* Anthology

EDITED BY **PAULA DEITZ**

With an Introduction by Mark Jarman

Syracuse University Press

First Edition 2013

13 14 15 16 17 18   6 5 4 3 2 1

∞ The paper used in this publication meets the minimum requirements of the American
National Standard for Information Sciences—Permanence of Paper for Printed Library
Materials, ANSI Z39.48-1992.

For a listing of books published and distributed by Syracuse University Press, visit our
website at SyracuseUniversityPress.syr.edu.

ISBN: 978-0-8156-1027-4 (cloth)   978-0-8156-5247-2 (e-book)

Library of Congress Cataloging-in-Publication Data

Poets Translate Poets : a Hudson Review Anthology / edited by Paula Deitz. —
First Edition.
     pages cm
   Includes index.
   ISBN 978-0-8156-1027-4 (cloth : alk. paper) 1. Poetry—Translations into English.
I. Deitz, Paula, editor of compilation.
   PN6101.P58 2013
   808.81—dc23   2013025708

Manufactured in the United States of America

In memory of

Frederick Morgan

(1922–2004)

Founding Editor of the *Hudson Review*

PAULA DEITZ has edited the *Hudson Review* since 1998. The journal was founded in New York in 1948 by Frederick Morgan, Joseph Bennett, and William Arrowsmith and is, according to the *New York Times*, "one of the most prestigious literary journals in the country." Paula Deitz is also a cultural critic who writes about art, architecture, and landscape design for newspapers and magazines in the United States and abroad.

MARK JARMAN is a poet and Centennial Professor of English at Vanderbilt University and an advisory editor of the *Hudson Review*.

CONTENTS

German   *121*

Russian   *303*

Spanish   *353*

PREFACE

Paula Deitz

While the name of the *Hudson Review* denotes the magazine's local origins in a makeshift office in lower Manhattan a block from the Hudson River, like the city in which it was founded in 1948, its outlook from the beginning has been international. Frederick Morgan, a founding editor who had majored in romance languages and literatures at Princeton University, reminisced in a 1997 interview about a conversation he had early on with Ezra Pound in which "he opened my eyes . . . to the possibilities of publishing translations from foreign literatures." Though Pound, he continues, "was very strongly focused on the Mediterranean tradition . . . that particular strength of his happened to mean a lot to me at that moment."[1]

Along with letters from London and Paris and literary criticism about writers abroad from the classical to modernist periods highlighted in early issues, the first translation of poetry appeared in the Volume 1, Winter 1949 issue: three French poems translated by W. S. Merwin, at that time a graduate student at Princeton University. Since then, translation has remained for the *Review* a cherished literary and cultural tradition, providing our global readership with an engaging worldview. Since 2000 alone, the journal has published an entire issue featuring works translated from eight different

---

1. Michael Peich, "The *Hudson Review*'s Early Years: An Interview with Frederick Morgan," *Hudson Review* 51, no. 2 (1998).

languages as well as special issues devoted to French- and Spanish-language literature.

Like many editorial decisions, this anthology originated in a simple perception that while the poets translated in the *Review*—from Homer to Russia's Dimitri V. Psurtsev—constitute a history of world literature, the translators themselves are among our most distinguished American and British poets and that these poems belong as much to them as to the original authors. In keeping with this spirit, the poems were initially organized by translator, so that the section, say, of W. S. Merwin's translations would read almost like a small collection of his own poems. In the end, however, for greater clarity of our purpose, the poems are arranged by language, but we urge readers to make use of the index to read one translator's work, often from several languages, straight through to experience a different and cumulative effect.

This selection from a much larger group comprises seventy-seven known and several anonymous poets, who wrote in twenty-five original languages, and sixty-one translators. All of these translations made their first appearance in print in the *Hudson Review* prior to book publication, as is our policy. A reader may wish to keep this in mind when reading, for example, Richmond Lattimore's excerpt from Homer's *Odyssey* or, more recently, scenes from Corneille's *Le Cid* in Richard Wilbur's translation. Added to the experience of reading the poems as literature is the knowledge of the cultures that produced the original authors, from the imperial court of China to the political upheavals of twentieth-century Europe—knowledge that can be gleaned from the biographical notes.

Grateful appreciation is due my colleagues for their invaluable assistance in selecting and preparing this anthology: Mark Jarman, an advisory editor since 2003, also for his masterful introduction; managing editor Ronald Koury; associate editor Zachary Wood; assistant editors Madeleine Fentress and Zoë Slutzky; editorial assistant Scott Bartley; and student editorial interns Christian N. Desrosiers, Ricky D'Ambrose, Rebecca T. Hawkins, and Becky Tseytkin. We are particularly indebted to the National Endowment for the Arts and the New York State Council on the Arts for supporting issues of the *Hudson Review* in which many of these translations originally appeared, and to the Florence Gould Foundation and Michael A. Boyd, whose generous gifts have made this anthology possible. Our special thanks to the authors, translators, and copyright holders of these poems for their gracious cooperation. Finally, to our publisher, Syracuse University Press, and its editors for bringing this book to life for all to read and enjoy, we express our gratitude for understanding our vision since our initial contact.

INTRODUCTION

Mark Jarman

Since 1948, when it was founded, the *Hudson Review* has published nearly five hundred poems in translation from more than thirty languages. Two of the magazine's founders, Frederick Morgan and William Arrowsmith, have themselves made significant contributions as translators from ancient and modern languages. Poetry in translation has been such an important feature of the *Hudson Review* in part because of the influence, direct and indirect, of the great modernist poet Ezra Pound. In the journal's early days, Pound offered the *Hudson Review* a steady stream of editorial advice from his residence in St. Elizabeths Hospital in Washington, DC. The magazine published major translations by Pound from Sophocles and from Confucius. Pound's approach to translation was to turn the poets he translated into new creations and to break new ground for poetry in English. His translations recalled the languages and cultures of their origins, but as they were understood by Pound. His transformative practice of "making it new" is one of the two major traditions of translation found in the *Hudson Review* and in this anthology. The other, no less valuable but more self-effacing, seeks an appropriate form that preserves as much of the original as possible, including its literal meaning, while still making a good poem in English. The master of this tradition, Richard Wilbur, also published important translations in the *Hudson Review*, and many of the translations in the anthology reflect his approach.

These two traditions derive from one that begins in the Renaissance and combines both Pound's emphasis on transformation and Wilbur's attention to the original form. When English poet Thomas Wyatt translated Italian poet Francesco Petrarch in the sixteenth century, he introduced the Italian sonnet to English literature while making poems we think of as purely Wyatt's. In subsequent centuries, we can see how John Dryden turned Virgil into a writer of iambic-pentameter couplets and how Alexander Pope did the same with Homer, in both cases making the translated sound very much like the translator. Samuel Johnson transformed Juvenal into yet another maker of witty iambic-pentameter rhyming pairs. Because translation from classical languages was an elemental part of English education throughout the Renaissance, it is possible to imagine William Shakespeare in his grammar school in Stratford doing early miracles with Ovid and Catullus. We know for sure that Ben Jonson did so in London, because he disparaged Shakespeare's grasp of classical languages and boasted of his own. Part of a poet's training in craft was by turning a hand to translation. The more gifted the poet, the more valuable the translation and the more likely that the translation would be a new addition to the poetic art.

In Pound's version of this tradition, translation is meant to transform one literature into another. A good poem translated should become another good poem—one belonging as much to the translator as to the original author. A good poet is probably the best catalyst for this metamorphosis. Pound innovated in translation in ways that exacting scholars of the languages he translated have found troubling, not to say exasperating. One of Pound's most ambitious experiments with translation is included in this anthology. It is his translation of Sophocles's, or, as he has it, Sophokles's, drama *Women of Trachis*. When the translation was first offered to the *Hudson Review*, the strongest editorial response to this extended work of Poundian chutzpah was from William Arrowsmith, who protested to Frederick Morgan, "I'm afraid this kind of thing challenges every good wish I have for the classics." Arrowsmith also speculated that Pound was either mad or ignorant. But eminent translator and poet Robert Fitzgerald (represented here by translations from Sophocles's *Oedipus Rex*, Catullus, and Horace) responded more tolerantly, though not without a certain ironic humor by saying that it was "pure Pound, but Pound deep in the Greek and out the other side." It is possible that the same could be said for any of Pound's translations, deep in the Provençal, Chinese,

French, Italian, Latin, Greek, yet always pure Pound. If you consider the stages of Pound's career, through his fascination with romance languages, ancient Greek and Latin, and ultimately with Chinese, his translations charted the development of his poetry.

In a sense, the Pound tradition of translation is a way of making new the Western tradition of translation. Dryden and Pope turned the Greek hexameters of Homer, the verse records of heroes, into heroic couplets. This form with its potential for the epigrammatic worked especially well for Pope, so well that it is a defining poetic style of his age. Still, Pope and Dryden employed a mode they believed was the most accurate way of representing the Greek verse. Chapman in translating Homer had tried heptameter couplets, the foundation of common measure, two hundred years before but hardly with the same success. Pound, especially in his Chinese translations, created a verse as valuable as the heroic couplet—the cadenced free-verse line, which we can hear in Carolyn Kizer's translations from the Chinese in this anthology. Yet it has to be admitted that the literal meaning of the original language, important to Dryden and Pope, who could actually read Latin and Greek, was not of crucial importance to Pound. Pound saw the image but was after an altogether new measure for English verse.

Pound is both an influence and an example of doing otherwise to the two members of his generation, two of the great modernists, who are also included here, William Carlos Williams and Marianne Moore. Though Williams turned to translation at the suggestion of Pound, whom he met when both were students at the University of Pennsylvania, for Williams the act was in some ways a retrieval of first languages. He grew up in a multilingual household, in which the language he spoke at the table was his mother's native Spanish, though she herself preferred French. Williams translated poems from Spanish throughout his career, and two of his marvelous translations, from Eugenio Florit and Pablo Neruda (Neruda's famous "Ode to My Socks"), are here. The only other translator in this anthology working in what might be called a native or home language is Rhina P. Espaillat, who brings a similar sensitivity to her translations of poetry from Spanish.

And there is Marianne Moore translating the fables of La Fontaine. The three herein were published in the *Hudson Review* in 1954, the year Moore published her collection of La Fontaine's fables. According to her biographer Charles Molesworth, Moore had worked on these fables, translating only the best of them, as Pound advised her, for at least a decade. And just as La Fontaine himself turned Aesop into the seventeenth-century French master La Fontaine, so Marianne Moore turned La Fontaine into a poet who reads as much like Marianne Moore as La Fontaine, although according to her biographer scrupulous accuracy was always her aim, which should not surprise us. One more thing, surely an influence of Pound, that characterizes her translations and indeed all of the translations here is that the tradition of modern translation has been to speak in a natural tone, formal when necessary and colloquial when possible, without any attempt to re-create former rhetorical modes that would sound artificial and antiquated. Pound is especially insistent on this in his translation of Sophocles, perhaps to a fault. But that attempt to give us an English of our time, even when translating from twenty-five hundred years ago, is what makes these translations readable today.

Ezra Pound's importance as an exemplary translator is clear in the translators of the same generation as Frederick Morgan and William Arrowsmith, notably Galway Kinnell, Carolyn Kizer, W. S. Merwin, and Louis Simpson. The tradition of Ezra Pound is one in which translators employ translation to make further discoveries of style, so that one way of understanding the stage of their development is to see how poetry emerged out of their translations at different times. W. S. Merwin's next step as a poet can always be inferred from his work as a translator. The translations Merwin did of medieval European poets, particularly from the Provençal, reflect the young Merwin's interest in the traditional lyric forms he was working in in the 1950s. So we have him translating Richard I, de Peitau, de Vaquieras, and a Renaissance French poet like du Bellay in the elegant lyric forms we find in Merwin's first two books, *A Mask for Janus* and *The Dancing Bears*, and then turning to modern French poet Jean Follain and his gnomic free-verse portraits, and two giants of modern Russia, Osip Mandelstam and his hermetic symbolism and Sergei Essenin and his nostalgic narratives. These latter modes would come to characterize Merwin's collections from the 1960s and 1970s, like *The Moving Target*, *The Lice*, *The Carrier of Ladders*, *Writings to an Unfinished Accompaniment*, and *The Compass Flower*. Ultimately, in his Quechua translations, the last of his translations to appear in the *Hudson Review*, we can hear the appeal of this minimal incantatory style from the Andes as it emerges in Merwin's work of the past twenty years, rather like a return to what he was trying to produce among his elegant formal lyrics of the 1950s. As a translator, a poet as prolific as Merwin generously allows us this panorama of the Pound tradition of translation.

There are others we can see entering into a dialectic of translation and translated work and producing a synthesis often of great beauty, and in retrospect giving us insight into a stage of the translator's own development as a poet. Like his Princeton classmate W. S. Merwin, Galway Kinnell not only shows his sympathy for modern French poet Yves Bonnefoy's early work but also finds in "On the Motion and the Immobility of Douve" a way into the sequential form, which would carry Kinnell out of the traditional metrics of his first two books and into the many remarkable poems of the later 1960s, culminating for him in *The Book of Nightmares*. Louis Simpson, one of the major translators in this assemblage of masters, shows us how much poets as different as the Medieval French François Villon and the modern French Valery Larbaud and Philippe Jaccottet have in common with the author of *Adventures of the Letter I* and *Caviar at the Funeral*. We see Simpson making his way from his early traditional formalism into the free-verse narrative style of his mature work with the translations of Larbaud and Jaccottet, though when translating a ballade by Villon he sticks with traditional English verse. Carolyn Kizer reveals the coming of her distinct style by her translations of the Medieval Chinese Tu Fu, closest of all to the work Pound himself did with Li Po. Her translations seem to be of a piece with Pound's Cathay poems. Charles Tomlinson's sinuous style and flexible free-verse rhythms, learned in part from William Carlos Williams, are given fresh life in his versions of poems by Italians Giuseppe Ungaretti and Lucio Piccolo. But Tomlinson can turn from the legato arias of those Italians to something more jagged, elliptical, and discontinuous in the verse of Mexican poet Octavio Paz and the neater quatrains of the Spanish Antonio Machado. Finally, Frederick Morgan, whose work always moved easily between traditional and free verse, turns the ambiguous twelve-syllable alexandrine couplets in French symbolist Stéphane Mallarmé's "Afternoon of a Faun" into a kind of vers libre, employing end rhyme occasionally and unpredictably and keeping to a loose iambic-tetrameter line.

When poets translate poets, both are transformed. Though Robert Frost claimed that poetry is what is lost in translation, and Galway Kinnell made the counterclaim that poetry is what is found in translation, I would argue for a synthesis of these two theses. A poem in translation becomes a new poem. Though the original language and its poetic effects may indeed be lost, the new language provides a new originality. A good translation is less an imitation (though Robert Lowell used this word for his translations) than an homage. Pope and Dryden and translators like them, whom we might say are as much a part of the Richard Wilbur tradition as the Pound tradition, perceive verse measure and rhyme and feel obliged to produce a facsimile.

Although it can be exciting and historically illuminating to watch these masters turn others into themselves, just as remarkable are those translations—and aside from the ones by Merwin, they predominate—by poets of remarkable formal gifts who have found a way to put their mastery of tradition at the service of another tongue. The greatest of these poets is without a doubt Richard Wilbur, whose translation from Renaissance French poet Pierre Corneille's *Le Cid* is included here. The seventeenth-century French alexandrine becomes, in Wilbur's voice, echoed perfectly in the English heroic couplet. John Frederick Nims works a similar magic with Goethe's "Trilogy of Passion" but matches the German rhyme scheme and meter almost exactly. R. S. Gwynn defers his typical mordant humor to translate romantic French poet Victor Hugo's tender and visionary "So Boaz Slept," a retelling of the book of Ruth from the point of view of Boaz, forefather of David and Jesus, choosing iambic pentameter for the alexandrine, as Wilbur does, and observing the envelope rhyme scheme of Hugo's quatrains—no mean feat. The secret to these translations as to all of the others gathered here is to sound as natural as possible in English no matter how closely the translator has chosen to follow the original.

The translators of passages from epic—the *Iliad*, the *Odyssey*, Lucretius's *On the Nature of Things*, *Beowulf*, and *Sir Gawain and the Green Knight*— have all worked in the Wilbur tradition, finding a measure to represent the original prosody. William Arrowsmith for his version of a section of book 3 of the *Iliad*, "Helen on the Walls," and Richmond Lattimore for his version of the unforgettable opening of the *Odyssey*'s second book have both written a loosely iambic and anapestic hexameter for Homer's Greek hexameters. A. E. Stallings in her passages from three of Lucretius's books from *On the Nature of Things* ("Against the Evils of Religion," "Against Passion," and "On the Development of Civilization") has created sprightly heptameter couplets for the Roman poet's dactylic hexameter (itself an imitation of Homer's meter). Alan Sullivan and Timothy Murphy translating the Anglo-Saxon *Beowulf* give us the hero's last speech before his fatal encounter with the dragon, or "fire-drake," and do so in the alliterative form of the original, something that W. H. Auden demonstrated could be done in modern English in *The Age of Anxiety*, but they have also included the distich form created by the caesura that divides the line in Anglo-Saxon poetry. And John Ridland, in his translation of *Sir Gawain and the Green Knight* and the crucial episode in the castle of Bertilak before Gawain faces the Green Knight's ax, has preserved the alliterative line of the original as it alternates with the rhyming bob-and-wheel stanza. Ridland has also given us modern English for the Pearl Poet's own fourteenth-century English dialect.

In fact, the most valuable translations here may be in the tradition of Richard Wilbur. The Wilbur tradition, making an accurate translation of poetry in a form that honors if not duplicates the original of the poem, while also doing so in modern English with little or no attempt to replicate the rhetoric of the original poem and its period, is as much a part of the Western tradition as the Pound way of translating is, and in fact probably closer to it. "Make it new," Pound's famous declaration, clearly equates artistic excellence with novelty. The Wilbur tradition recalls Robert Frost's preference for "the old-fashioned way to be new." If you think of the way so much of Wordsworth, Keats, and Coleridge is translated into the American vernacular of Robert Frost, you can also understand why Frost believed poetry is what is lost in translation—from one language to another. But as Galway Kinnell implies, when poetry is found in translation, frequently it is a new form of the old-fashioned way—for example, Greek hexameters coming back as iambic hexameters, French alexandrines as blank verse or heroic couplets.

One of the remarkable achievements of the Wilbur tradition of translation in this anthology is Charles Martin's version of nineteenth-century Roman poet G. G. Belli, whose poems in Romanesco dialect—earthy, vulgar, obscene when necessary, sweet when called for, irreverent almost always—made him one of Italy's most beloved poets and a Roman icon. Martin's translations into an equally colloquial and irreverent English, without being arch, mannered, or tinny—that is to say, without creating a translatorese—are an impressive transformation. At the same time, Martin's versions hew in form and expression closely to the originals. All sonnets, in fact Italian sonnets, Martin's poems bear comparison with an earlier attempt to capture Belli in English by Anthony Burgess in his wonderful, little-known novel about the death of Keats, *ABBA ABBA*. Keats and Belli were contemporaries, after all, though Belli enjoyed a much longer life. Belli himself more resembles Robert Burns, in his Scottish dialect poems, than he does Keats, but even Burns who could write a wonderfully ribald, profane, and obscene lyric is not beloved for these very qualities as is Belli.

Charles Martin is one of our finest translators, known most widely as a translator of Catullus, Ovid's *Metamorphoses*, and the Bhagavad Gita. In this anthology, he also contributes with Johanna Keller translations from the Medieval French of Christine de Pisan. With just the right touch of inversion, formality, and the almost archaic word, Martin and Keller capture the world of de Pisan and her attempts to challenge the antifeminine tropes of the period as she frankly praises the sexual gratification of her lover who loves her "well," enjoys her solitude when her lover is away, and debunks the male protestations and whining of the Petrarchan tradition. But again, though the translation reminds us of the courtly tradition in Europe from more than six hundred years ago, alien as that tradition may seem, the English diction of Martin and Keller's translation makes it seem less alien and more familiar.

Another gem of the Wilbur tradition of translation is Emily Grosholz's of Yves Bonnefoy (a poet she translates superbly) and his homage to the great English contralto Kathleen Ferrier. In the French, his poem "To the Voice of Kathleen Ferrier" consists of four quatrains, with rhymes occurring only in the third and fourth quatrains, and possibly the first. Bonnefoy, usually not constricted by the alexandrine, departs from that meter only in a couple of lines. His sense of Ferrier's voice is hauntingly accurate, calling it a voice that is "blended with gray" and also combining qualities of crystal and mist. Grosholz has preserved his quatrains but provides an audible pentameter line (the French metric is based only on syllables, the English on accents and syllables). Some of her translation reflects Bonnefoy's Gallic exactitude, "I celebrate the voice blended with gray," while at the same time preserving the English mood of reserve appropriate to Ferrier—for example, when Grosholz translates the French "brume" or "mist" into the less poetic "low clouds." For Bonnefoy's exclamatory "Ô lumière," "Ô cygne," and "Ô source," we have in Grosholz's version "O light," "True swan," and "Source." One of the most beautiful renderings she gives us is of Bonnefoy's description of Ferrier's voice, "Qui hésite aux lointain du chant qui s'est perdu" as the voice "That falters in the distances of singing." I do not know which I prefer, that in Bonnefoy's poem the hesitating voice is ultimately lost in the distance, thus elegizing the singer's early death, or that in Grosholz's version it simply "falters" there. One of the beauties of translation at this level is that we are given not only a version of the original in our language, but also a poem in its own right. Emily Grosholz in translating Bonnefoy's homage has given us an English elegy for an English singer.

There are many examples in the anthology of poets whose natural inclinations of style find their kinship in the poems they are translating. Charles Tomlinson hints at this sympathy between translator and translated in his version of Ungaretti's "Little Monologue":

> Poets, poets, we have put on
> All the masks; yet one
> Is merely one's own self.

Surely, this is true of translation, yet the self in its "mereness" does become more greatly developed, exposed, ramified, and hatched like a seed or an egg.

Rhina Espaillat's kinship with the poets she translates from Spanish, as a native speaker of the language she translates into English, finds a particular resonance with the Chilean poet Gabriela Mistral. Mistral's traditional formalism corresponds with Espaillat's own, so that we can hear in Espaillat's translation of Mistral's "The Death Sonnets" a music of meter and rhyme in

English that echoes the Spanish. Still, there are subtleties to the Spanish that cannot be brought over into the English, like the connection between dusting and dust in Spanish, *espolvoreando, polvo,* and *polverado,* which in Espaillat's poem become *sprinkle, dust,* and *mist.* The Spanish insists audibly on the return of the body to the earth, but the English, while not so insistent on the aural connections, maintains an imagistic one. The English also introduces an earthier, even grittier edge with its monosyllabic and Anglo-Saxon rhymes (*sleep / deep, alone / bone*). Poetry may have been lost in translation, but poetry has also been found.

Choices about how to translate Russian poet Anna Akhmatova, a poet of complex forms, have often dispensed with all effects except imagery and expression. Thus, in Judith Hemschemeyer's Akhmatova we have the great poet of the senses as they are ignited in charged but enclosed spaces, so that even a street or time of day can seem packed with explosive potential. This mode is the way Akhmatova is often successfully translated. So to have Jennifer Reeser's translations that come as closely as possible to the prosody of the Russian originals while also capturing that invigorating embrace of the senses is valuable.

Modern Greek poet C. P. Cavafy translates well into English, as W. H. Auden claimed, due to the distinctiveness of his voice. But like Akhmatova's, many translations into English have turned Cavafy's poems, often complexly and subtly formal, into free verse. There is no doubt that a poem by Cavafy could not be anyone else's, but it appears to be because of his two distinguishing subjects—the ordinary lives and homoerotic affairs of young men in early-twentieth-century Alexandria and the large and small doings of the classical world, from the Caesars through the Byzantine emperors. Still, one of his best recent translators, Daniel Mendelsohn, has hinted at the nuanced rhyming of Cavafy's poems, especially in two short lyrics here, "Longings" and "Prayer." And Cavafy's own sense of the meters appropriate for song or story also emerges in Mendelsohn's translations. In this way, he captures that distinctive voice Auden speaks of, along with the subjects that lovers of Cavafy regard as uniquely his.

Like Constantine Cavafy, modern Argentine poet Jorge Luis Borges has a distinct set of subjects, including historical and contemporary Buenos

Aires, the romance of gaucho life on the pampas, and the nooks and crannies of world history and literature. Who else but Borges could ask if a recent dream of a white deer had come from his reading of English or Persian literature? Like Cavafy's, his voice is distinct, though I think more so in his prose than in his poems. Often Borges is summoning the voices of historical figures, rather than exposing their secrets via gossip and anecdote like Cavafy. Borges, however, does not seem to have a colloquial style to mix with a more formal approach, as Cavafy does. He is always literary, even as his literariness can be another mask, as it so often is in his stories. He has the benefit of two excellent translators in the work of Emily Grosholz and Robert Mezey. Grosholz gives us both one of his fervent lyrics, recalling the passionate garden of St. John of the Cross, and also a cold-eyed blank-verse sonnet summing up his career, beautifully and pitilessly, in Buenos Aires. The translations by Mezey also give us a sense of the entire scope of Borges's poetry and include a prose poem and the almost unbearably poignant "The White Hind," which shares a motif central to Borges's fiction: that the dreamer is himself being dreamed.

Zbigniew Herbert, a member of the Polish Resistance during World War II and afterward a despiser of Communist rule in Poland, is at his best when he plays the role of subversive in his poems, whether it is to ironize classical history or to suggest, often in his prose poetry, the deadening rule of the totalitarian state, especially via censorship and the corruption of language. His work, like the poetry of most Eastern European poets during the Iron Curtain years, is in free verse, and his experiments with the prose poem have been widely influential in the West. From this perspective of history, because he avoided the status of émigré, though he traveled as much as he could outside of Poland, he looks like the greatest political poet of Europe since Yeats. Peter Dale Scott, himself a political poet during the Vietnam War era, seems ideally suited to translate Herbert. Irony like Herbert's always translates well, since it occurs on a symbolic level in which the terms are recognizable as they make the transit from one language to another. It would be hard to miss the allegorical and political import of the two prose poems here, "The Wringer" and "Episode in a Library," in which a laundry and a literary analysis take on the overtones of the repressive and ideological state apparatus. Yet Herbert is never overbearing or obvious. And this point too is clear from the translations. He works playfully with apparently literal images so that you can imagine an obtuse state censor missing the point entirely.

These major figures of the twentieth century, early, middle, and late, are all well represented and rightly so. But one of the pleasures of any anthology is the isolated poem that, usually not part of a larger selection of a poet's work, becomes one to return to, for its uniqueness and quality. This anthology is no different from others in that respect. Denise Levertov's translation of "The Cricket" by Bulgarian poet Krassin Himmirsky celebrates the survival of the natural world and the durability of poetry. William Arrowsmith's translations of three poems by Medieval Japanese poet Hitomaro include the lovely free-verse imagism of "Grief at the Mountain-Crossing of the Prince," which reminds us of the value placed on the humanity of all throughout world poetry, including those individuals separated from the rest of us by noble birth. The stringent political subtext of nineteenth-century German Christian Morgenstern's "Maids on Saturday," translated by Lore Segal and W. D. Snodgrass, foreshadows the later songs of Bertolt Brecht and Kurt Weill, especially one like "Pirate Jenny," from *The Threepenny Opera*. Jerome Rothenberg's translation of twentieth-century German Erich Kästner's "Autobiography" gives us Europe between the world wars with a gleam of black humor in straight-faced rhyming quatrains. Influential Hungarian poet Attila József's inimitable take on the pleasures and pains of daily life is reflected in Michael Paul Novak and Bela Kiralyfalvi's translation of "To Sit, to Stand, to Kill, to Die." Horace's "Prayer to Venus," translated by Craig Watson, expresses that desire for revenge on an estranged lover that is as fresh today as in the heart of any ancient poet. And finally there is tragic Russian poet Marina Tsvetaeva's tour de force, "Poem of the End," translated by Mary Jane White, with its ironic title considering the poem's length and its endlessly microscopic examination of how two lovers break apart and their relationship slowly dissolves.

All of the salient interests of English and American poet-translators of the past sixty-five years and more are here in *Poets Translate Poets*: classical Greek and Latin; Medieval Chinese; Old and Medieval English; Medieval,

Renaissance, and Modern European; and Southeast Asian. A complete anthology of poems in translation from the *Hudson Review* could supply a book three or four times the length of this one. But this selection has been made according to the advice Ezra Pound gave to Marianne Moore when translating La Fontaine, and is an attempt to include only the best.

POETS TRANSLATE POETS

BULGARIAN ▶

KRASSIN HIMMIRSKY *(ca. 1939)*

The Cricket

In vain we tried to banish him.
The roar of engines did not drive him away,
nor the asphalt with which we covered the fields.
We put up steel fences, walls of cement
                              and concrete.
Darkened the air with gas fumes
and shut ourselves in highrise buildings.

But he, like a password,
crossed every barrier unharmed.

And when we claimed victory
in the shade of a leaf, unseen
his fine string music started again.

Its tone reeled off our forgotten friends,
                    our forgotten homes,
                    our souls.
It recalled to mind
the world's forgotten beauty.

Then we looked for him,
meaning to speak in friendship at last,
but in vain.

He was nowhere visible.
And only within us
still rang and rang his refrain.

                              Denise Levertov, 1983

CHINESE ▸

TU FU *(712–70)*

Adviser to the Court

Working All Night in Springtime

When day begins to darken
Flowers along the wall
Merge into the shadows.
Skyward the birds chirp softly
Searching for a roost.

Ten thousand common households
Are illumined by the stars.
The firmament of Heaven
Is drenched in all the moonlight
Of this most brilliant night.

So quiet! I hear keys turning
In gold locks of the Palace doors.
The wind, a faint jingle, sounding
Like the Imperial horses
As they shake their pendants of jade.

I must present a memorial
To the Throne-room, in the morning.
Sleepless now, whether I work or not,
All night I measure the hours
Of all night, in my mind. . . .

Reply to a Friend's Advice

Leaving the Audience by the quiet corridors,
Stately and beautiful, we pass through the Palace gates,

Turning in different directions: you go to the West
With the Ministers of State. I, otherwise.

On my side, the willow-twigs are fragile, greening.
You are struck by scarlet flowers over there.

Our separate ways! You write so well, so kindly,
To caution, in vain, a garrulous old man.

On the Way Out

Last year I rejoined the Emperor by this road
When the barbarians swarmed over the Western suburbs.
I'm so far from having recovered from my fear
That shreds of my soul still dangle in the air.

Dangling and wandering, as I do now,
Close to the Throne, yet I am driven away
To a vast, distant province! Surely His Majesty
Could not have intended this. What, I, betrayed?

Ruin! As talent fails and I grow old.
My steadfastness in trying times has aged me.
I pull on my horse's reins, and pausing,
Gaze for a final time on the Palace walls.

Banishment

Too Much Heat, Too Much Work

It's the fourteenth of August, and I'm too hot
To endure food, or bed. Steam and the fear of scorpions,
Keep me awake. I'm told the heat won't fade with Autumn.

Swarms of flies arrive. I'm roped into my clothes.
In another moment I'll scream down the office
As the paper mountains rise higher on my desk.

Oh those real mountains to the south of here!
I gaze at the ravines kept cool by pines.
If I could walk on ice, with my feet bare!

Reunion

Joy in this meeting grieves our two white heads
Knowing they greet each other a final time.
We nod through the long night watches, still resenting
The speed with which the candle shrinks and pales.

I dread the hour the Milky Way dries up forever.
Let us fill our cups and drain them, over and over
While we can, before the world returns with dawn
When we blot our eyes and turn our backs on each other.

Carolyn Kizer, 1964

OLD ENGLISH ▶

ANONYMOUS

The Fire-Drake, from *Beowulf*

Lines 2510–2709

Now Beowulf spoke   his last battle-boast:
"In boyhood I braved   bitter clashes;
still in old age   I would seek out strife
and gain glory   guarding my folk
if the man-bane comes   from his cave to meet me."

Then he turned to his troop   for the final time,
bidding farewell   to bold helmet-bearers,
fast in friendship: "No sword would I wear,
no weapon at all   to ward off the worm
if I knew how to fight   this fiendish foe
as I grappled with Grendel   one bygone night.
But here I shall find   fierce battle-fire
and breath envenomed,   therefore I bear
this mail-coat and shield.   I shall not shy
from standing my ground   when I greet the hoard-guard,
follow what will   at the foot of his wall.
I shall face the fiend   with a firm heart.
Let every man's Ruler   reckon my fate:
words are worthless   against the war-flyer.
Bide by the barrow,   safe in your byrnies,
and watch, my warriors,   which of us two
will better bear   the brunt of our clash.
This war is not yours;   it is meted to me,
matching my strength,   man against monster.
I shall do this deed   undaunted by death
and shall get you gold   or else get my ending,
borne off in battle,   the bane of your lord."

The hero arose,   helmed and hardy,
a war-king clad   in shield and corslet.
He strode strongly   under the stone-cliff:
no faint-hearted man,   to face it unflinching!
Stalwart soldier   of so many marches,
unshaken when shields   were crushed in the clash,
he saw between stiles   an archway where steam
burst like a boiling   tide from the barrow,
woeful for one   close to the worm-hoard.
He would not linger long   unburned by the lurker
or safely slip   through the searing lair.
Then a battle-cry broke   from Beowulf's breast
as his rightful rage   was roused for the reckoning.
His challenge sounded   under stark stone
where the hateful hoard-guard   heard in his hollow
the clear-voiced call   of a man coming.

No quarter was claimed;   no quarter given.
First the beast's breath   blew hot from the barrow
as battle-bellows   boomed underground.
The stone-house stormer   swung up his shield
at the ghastly guardian.   Then the dragon's grim heart
kindled for conflict.   Uncoiling, he came
seeking the Stalwart;   but the swordsman had drawn
the keen-edged blade   bequeathed him for combat,
and each foe confronted   the other with fear.
His will unbroken,   the warlord waited
behind his tall shield,   helm and hauberk.
With fitful twistings   the fire-drake hastened
fatefully forward.   His fender held high,
Beowulf felt   the blaze blister through
hotter and sooner   than he had foreseen.
So for the first time   fortune was failing
the mighty man   in the midst of a struggle.

Wielding his sword   he struck at the worm
and his fabled blade   bit to the bone
through blazoned hide: bit and bounced back,
no match for the foe   in this moment of need.

The peerless prince   was hard-pressed in response,
for his bootless blow   had maddened the monster
and fatal flames   shot further than ever,
lighting the land.   No praise for the warlord's
prowess in battle: the blade he brandished
had failed in the fray   though forged from iron.
No easy end   for the son of Ecgetheow:
against his will   he would leave this world
to dwell elsewhere,   as every man must
when his days are done.   Swiftly the death-dealer
moved to meet him.   From the murderous breast
bellows of breath   belched fresh flames.
Enfolded in fire,   he who formerly
ruled a whole realm   had no one to help him
hold off the heat,   for his hand-picked band
of princelings had fled,   fearing to face
the foe with their lord.   Loving honor
less than their lives,   they hid in the holt.
But one among them   grieved for the Geats
and balked at quitting   his kinsman, the king.

This one was Wiglaf,   son of Weostan,
beloved shield-bearer   born in Scylf-land.
Seeing his liege-lord   suffering sorely
with war-mask scorched   by the searing onslaught,
the thankful thane   thought of the boons
his kinsman bestowed: the splendid homestead
and folk-rights his father   formerly held.
No shirker could stop him   from seizing his shield

of yellow linden   and lifting the blade
Weostan won   when he slew Eanmund,
son of Othere.   Spoils of that struggle,
sword and scabbard,   smithwork of giants,
a byrnie of ring-mail   and bright-burnished helm
were granted as gifts,   a thane's war-garb,
for Onela never   acknowledged his nephews
but struck against both   of his brother's sons.
When Eadgils caught   the killer of kin,
Weostan fled.   Woeful and friendless,
he saved that gear   for seasons of strife,
foreseeing his son   someday might crave
sword and corslet.   He came to his kinsman,
the prince of the Geats,   and passed on his heirlooms,
hoping Wiglaf   would wear them with honor.
Old then, and wise,   he went from the world.

This war was the first   young Wiglaf would fight
helping the king.   His heart would not quail
nor weapon fail   as the foe would find
going against him;   but he made his grim mood
known to the men: "I remember the meadhall
where beer-swillers swore   with many a boast
to the lord who   lavished these rings on his liegemen.
We promised to   pay for princely trappings
by staunchly wielding   sword-blades in war
if need should arise.   Now we are needed
by him who chose,   from the whole of his host,
twelve for this trial,   trusting our claims
as warriors worthy   of wearing our blades,
bearing keen spears.   Our king has come here
bent on battling   the man-bane alone,
because among warriors   one keeper of kinfolk
has done, undaunted,   the most deeds of daring.

But this day our lord   needs dauntless defenders
so long as the fearful   fires flow forth.
God knows I would gladly   give my own body
for flames to enfold   with the gold-giver.
Shameful, to shoulder   our shields homeward!
First we must fell   this fearsome foe
and deliver the life   of our weathered lord.
Is it right that one man   be wrathfully racked
for his former feats,   fall in this fight
guarding the Geats?   Helm and mail-shirt
shield and blade,   we both shall share."

So speaking, he stormed   through the reek of smoke,
with helmet on head,   to help his lord.
"Beloved Beowulf,   bear up your blade.
You pledged in your youth,   powerful prince,
never to let   your luster lessen
while life was left you.   Now summon your strength;
stand steadfast.   I shall stand with you."

After these words   the worm was enraged.
For a second time   the spiteful specter
flew at his foe,   and he wreathed in flames
the hated human   he hungered to harm.
His dreadful fire-wind   drove in a wave,
charring young Wiglaf's   shield to the boss,
nor might a byrnie   bar that breath
from burning the brave   spear-bearer's breast.
Wiglaf took cover   close to his kinsman,
shielded by iron   when linden was cinder.
Then the war-king,   recalling past conquests,
struck with full strength   straight at the head.
His battle-sword, Naegling,   stuck there and split,
shattered in combat,   so sharp was the shock

to Beowulf's great   gray-mottled blade.
He never was granted   the gift of a sword
as hard and strong   as the hand which held it.
I have heard he broke   blood-hardened brands,
so the weapon-bearer   was none the better.

The fearful fire-drake,   scather of strongholds,
flung himself forward   a final time,
wild with wounds   yet wily and sly.
In the heat of the fray,   he hurtled headlong
to fasten his fangs   in the foe's throat.
Beowulf's life-blood   came bursting forth
on those terrible tusks.   Just then, I am told,
the second warrior   sprang from his side,
a man born for battle   proving his mettle,
keen to strengthen   his kinsman in combat.
He took no heed   of the hideous head
scorching his hand   as he hit lower down.
The sword sank in,   patterned and plated;
the flames of the foe   faltered, faded.
Though gored and giddy,   Beowulf gathered
strength once again   and slipped out his sheath-knife,
the keen killing-blade   he kept in his corslet.
Then the Geats' guardian   gutted the dragon,
felling that fiend   with the help of his friend,
two kinsmen together   besting the terror.
So should a thane   succor his sovereign.

Alan Sullivan and Timothy Murphy, 2000

MIDDLE ENGLISH ▶

Anonymous Fourteenth-Century Poet

From *Sir Gawain and the Green Knight*

Part IV: The Meeting

Now as the New Year was drawing nigh, and the night before it passed,
Daylight was driving the dark away, as the Lord above commands.
But a wild weather was working up in the world outside their doors:
The clouds emptied their cold contents keenly down on the earth,
With cruelty enough from the north to torment the naked flesh.
The snow fell snittering sharply, nipping the wild creatures;
The whistling wind whipped down upon them shrilly from the heights,
And filled the hollows of every dale up full with heavy drifts.
The knight was listening closely to this as he lay awake in his bed,
And though he locked his eyelids shut, he got very little sleep:
From each cock crow throughout the night he could tell what hour it was.
Hurriedly he got out of bed before the break of day,
For there was light enough from a lamp that was glowing in his room.
He called out to his chamberlain, who promptly answered him;
He bade him bring his chain-mail shirt, and saddle up his horse.
The man obediently got up, and fetched the garments for him,
And began to get Sir Gawain dressed, in most resplendent style.
First he put on his warmest clothes, which would ward off the cold,
And next he brought the armor out that had been carefully stored:
Both the belly piece and all the plate polished bright and clean,
The rust on the rings of his costly chain-mail shirt had been rubbed off,
And all gleamed fresh as when first forged, for which he was keen to thank
                              Them all.
            When he had donned each piece—
            All had been polished well;
            Unmatched from here to Greece,
            He said, "Bring my steed from his stall."

While the noble knight was being arrayed in his most handsome clothes—
The surcoat draping over his armor adorned with the pentangle badge
Stitched onto velvet, framed around with precious, potent stones
Inlaid along the embroidered seams, setting it off so well;
And on the inside the coat was beautifully lined with the finest fur—
Yet he did not leave the lace behind that had been the lady's gift;
That present Gawain did not forget, for the good of his own self.
After he had belted the sword above his powerful hips,
He wrapped the love-token carefully two times around his waist;
Quickly that knight, and delightedly, wound it about his middle.
The girdle woven of green silk well suited that splendid man,
Against the royal red of the cloth, which looked so rich in itself.
But he wasn't putting this girdle on because of its costliness,
Nor out of pride in its shiny pendants, however polished they were,
Nor even for the glittering gold that glinted upon the fringe,
But in order that he might save his life when he was obliged to submit,
To face, without dispute, what he would take from the sword's or knife's

Sharp stroke.

Once the brave man was set,
He hurried out and spoke
His thanks to all he met,
To all the noble folk.

Then Gringolet was made ready to ride, that was an enormous horse
That had been stabled comfortably and in a secure fashion:
That proud horse, due to his fit condition, wanted to gallop now.
The knight walked out to where he stood, and gazed on his glistening coat,
And soberly he said to himself, swearing it on his oath,
"Here inside this moat is a company setting their minds on honor:
May joy come to the lord who maintains and manages them all;
And as for the delightful lady, may she have love in her life!
If out of charity they can receive and cherish a guest so kindly,
And offer such hospitality, may the Good Lord reward them
Who holds the heavens up on high—and also all of you!

And if I should stay alive on earth, for any length of time,
I would quickly pay you some recompense, if I were able to."
Then the knight stepped into the stirrup, and swung astride the horse;
His servant offered him his shield, which he settled on his shoulder,
And he dug his spurs into Gringolet, kicking his gilded heels,
And the horse started forward over the stones, no longer standing still,
To prance.

> His man was mounted then
> Who bore his spear and lance.
> "This castle I commend
> To Christ against mischance!"

The bridge was let down for him to pass, and the broad gates in the wall
Were unbarred, swung open without delay, all the way back on both halves.
The knight rapidly blessed himself and passed across the planks,
Thanking the porter who kept the gates, who knelt before the prince—
He wished the knight "Good day" and prayed that God would save Gawain—
And he went on his way accompanied by a single guide
To teach him the turns by which to reach at last that perilous place
Where he was destined to receive the grievous, terrible stroke.
They bent and stooped beneath bare boughs along the hillside slopes;
They clambered along below the cliffs where the cold was clinging close.
The heavens were holding high above, but were threatening underneath;
The mist was mizzling on the moor and melting on the mountains;
Each of the hilltops had a hat, a huge mantle of mist.
The brooks were boiling and foaming, bursting over their banks,
White water shattered against the sides, as they made their way downhill.
The route was wild and meandering that they followed through the woods,
Until it would soon be time, in that season, for the sun to break
From night.

> They were on a high hilltop;
> On all sides snow lay white;
> The guide with him called, "Stop!"
> Abruptly, to the knight.

"For I have brought you here, sir, at the appointed time,
And now you are not far at all from that noteworthy place
That you have sought and asked about so very particularly.
But I shall tell you the truth, my lord, since now I know you well,
And you are one man on this earth whom I regard most highly:
If only you'd act on my advice, it would be much better for you.
The place you are pressing forward to is held to be perilous;
A man lives in that wasteland, the worst man in the world,
For he is strong and stern and grim and above all loves striking blows,
And in his massiveness more of a man than any other on earth;
His body is bigger than four of the best and biggest knights to be found
In Arthur's house—he is bigger even than Hector or any other—
And he is in charge of all mischance that happens at the Green Chapel,
For nobody passes by that place, however proud in arms,
But he will batter him to death with a blow from his strong hand,
For he is a man without restraint, and has no use for mercy:
Whether it be a churl or a chaplain that's riding by the chapel,
Whether a monk, or a priest who says Mass, or anybody else,
He thinks it as fine to murder a man as to stay alive himself.
Therefore I have to say to you, as sure as you sit in your saddle,
If you go there, you will be killed, if that knight has his way—
Trust me, I'm telling you the truth—even if you had twenty lives
                                        To spend.
             He has lived a long time in this land,
             And stirred up strife no end;
             Against his deadly hand
             There's no way to defend.

"Therefore, good Sir Gawain, please leave the man alone
And ride away by some other road, for God's sake and your own.
Take yourself off to another land, where Christ may give you speed!
And I shall hurry home again; and further, I promise you
That I shall swear on oath, 'By God and all his hallowed saints,
So help me God and the holy relics,' and other oaths enough—

That I shall loyally keep your secret, and never let drop a word
That ever you tried to run away from any man I know of."
"Thank you so much," Gawain replied, though he said it with irritation.
"I should, I suppose, wish you good luck for caring about my welfare,
And you say you will loyally keep my secret, as I believe you would;
But, though you kept it ever so close, if I hurried past this place,
Fleeing away from him out of fear, in the fashion you propose,
I would be called a cowardly knight and could not be excused.
So I will go on to the Green Chapel, to whatever challenge I meet,
And talk there to that knight himself, and tell him whatever I think;
Whether it brings me well or woe, it will only be what Fate
                    Decrees.
            He may be a fearsome knave
            Who could club me to my knees,
            But God shapes things to save
            His servants, should He please."

"By Mary!" said the other man. "Since now you have spelled it out
That you are bringing your own destruction down upon yourself,
And it pleases you to lose your life, I will say nothing against it.
Here, put your helmet on your head, and take your spear in hand,
And ride this rough path downstream by the side of that rock yonder,
Till it brings you to the bottom of the broad and rugged valley.
Then look to the glade not far away, a little off to the left,
And you shall see, set in that dale, the very chapel you're after,
And on its grounds the burly brute who keeps it in his care.
Now farewell, noble Gawain, in God's name, fare thee well!
For all the gold there is in the earth I would not go with you,
Nor travel in your company through this forest one foot farther."
With that, in the middle of the wood, the fellow yanked his bridle,
Kicked his horse's flanks with his heels as hard as he could spur,
Galloped him off across the glade, and left the knight there, all
                    Alone.

"By God's own Self," he said,
"I will not weep or groan.
God's will must be obeyed,
His wishes are my own."

Then he struck his spurs into Gringolet, and followed the stream path down:
He pushed his way on past the rock, at the edge of a small thicket,
And rode along the ragged bank to the bottom of the dale.
Then he looked around on every side, and it seemed a wilderness.
Nowhere could he see a sign of a place where he might shelter,
Only high banks rising steeply, on both halves of the dale,
And rough and knobby rocky knolls, with sharp and craggy outcrops;
It seemed to him that the lowering clouds were grazed by the jutting rocks.
Then he drew his horse to a halt, checked for a little while
As he sat him, turning this way and that, to seek the chapel out.
He saw no such thing on any side—and that seemed strange to him—
Except that a little off to the left in the glade was a sort of mound,
Or a smooth and rounded barrow on a bank-side above the brim
Of the channel of a watercourse that was flowing freely through;
The brook was bubbling within, as if it had come to a boil.
The knight then urged his horse along, bringing him up to the knoll,
Alighted from him gracefully, and at a linden tree
Attached the reins of his noble steed to one of the rough branches.
And then he walked across to the mound and he strode all around it,
Turning over in his mind what this strange thing might be.
It had a hole on one end, and the same on either side,
And it was overgrown with grass in patches everywhere,
And all was hollow on the inside—nothing but an old cave
Or a crevice in an old crag, but which it was he could not
                         Be sure.
            "Ah, Lord!" sighed the noble knight,
            "Can the Green Chapel be here,
            Where the Devil, around midnight,
            Might say his morning prayer?

"Now indeed," said Gawain, "without doubt this is a wasteland;
This chapel is horrifying, overgrown with greenery—
A very fitting place for that man who dresses himself in green
To do his devotions dutifully—in the Devil's fashion.
Now I feel in my five senses that in fact it is the Fiend
Who has imposed this tryst on me, and will destroy me here.
This is a chapel of mischance—may it be checkmated!—
It is the cursedest kind of church that ever I came into!"
With his helmet high up on his head and his lance held in his hand
He climbed up to the top of the roof above the rough abode
Then, farther up on the high hill, he heard, by a hard rock,
Beyond the brook, above the bank, a wondrously loud noise.
What! It clattered against the cliff as if it would cleave it in two,
Like someone at a grindstone who was sharpening a scythe.
What! It whirred and whetted, like water at a mill!
What! It made a rushing, and a ringing, harsh to hear.
Then, "By God!" Sir Gawain said, "that weapon is being prepared
To welcome me as a knight of my rank ought to be greeted, it would
                    Appear.
        God's will be done. To moan
        Will never help me here.
        Though my life may soon be gone,
        A noise won't make me fear."

With that the knight cried boldly out, as loudly as he could,
"Who is the master in this place, who holds this tryst with me?
For right now, good Gawain is walking all around, right here.
If any man wants anything, let him appear at once,
It's now or never, if he intends to get this business done."
"Wait!" shouted somebody on the bank up above his head,
"And you will quickly have it all, that I once promised you."
He kept on making that rushing sound, for a while more rapidly,
As he turned back to finish his whetting before he would come down.
And then he picked his way past a crag and emerged out of a hole,

Whirling from a nook nearby, armed with a dreadful weapon:
A Danish axe that was freshly forged to pay the return blow,
With a mighty blade curving back on itself until it touched the helve;
It had been honed on a whetstone, and it was four feet wide—
No less than that if measured by the brightly shining belt!
And the man came out arrayed in green, as he had been at first,
His face and cheeks, his flowing locks of hair, and his broad beard,
Except that now he went on foot, grandly over the ground,
Setting the haft on the stony earth and stalking along beside it.
When he came to the stream, he wouldn't pause at the water's edge to wade,
But hopped across it on his axe, and hurriedly strode on,
Fiercely grim, on a broad and grassy patch of ground that was cloaked
                    In snow.
        Gawain greeted the seigneur,
        Bowing, but not too low.
        The other said, "Monsieur,
        So—one can trust your vow.

"Gawain," the Green Knight went on, "may God protect you now!
I bid you welcome, sir, to my place, my chapel and domain,
And you have timed your travels well to reach it when you ought;
And you understand the covenant that was agreed between us:
At this time just twelve months ago, you took what was your lot,
And I, at this New Year, should promptly pay you in return.
And here we are in this valley, which is verily ours alone;
Here are no knights to part us; we may dance our dance as we please.
Take your helmet off your head, and receive your payment now.
Do not resist me any more than I resisted you
When you whipped my head off with a single whack of your battleaxe."
"No," said Sir Gawain, "by the God who granted me a soul,
I will not begrudge you a bit for any hurt that happens;
Only hold yourself to a single stroke, and I will stay stock still
And offer no objection at all, whatever you want to do—
                  Not one."

He bent his neck and bowed,
Exposing the bare white skin;
Acting as if uncowed,
Unafraid for him to begin.

Then all in a rush the man in green prepared himself to strike:
He grappled and lifted the grim tool to give Gawain the blow;
With all the force in his massive frame he bore it up aloft
And aimed his swing as mightily as if he meant to destroy him.
If he had driven that stroke down as staunchly as he began,
He would have died from the dreadful blow, the one who was always brave.
But from the corner of his eye Gawain caught a glimpse of the axe
As it came gliding down at him to demolish him in a flash,
And he flinched a little with his shoulders, shrank from the sharp iron.
The other man suddenly checked his swing, held back the shining blade,
And then how he reproved the prince with many disdainful words:
"You are not Gawain," the Green Knight scoffed, "who is held to be so good,
Who never quailed on hill or dale before an enemy horde,
And now you flinch from me for fear before you are even harmed!
I never knew such cowardice on the part of that knight before.
I neither winced nor shied away, friend, when you swung at me,
Nor came up with some caviling argument in King Arthur's court.
My head flew off and fell to my feet, and yet I never fled;
But you, before you take any hurt, are terrified in your heart.
So I deserve, without a doubt, to be called the better man,
                              Therefore."
            Said Gawain, "I flinched once,
            But I will not any more,
            Though if my head falls on the stones,
            It cannot be restored.

"But hurry up, man, by your faith, and come to the point with me—
Deal me the destiny that is mine, and do it out of hand.
For I shall wait to take your stroke and startle at it no more,
Until your axe has hewn into me: you have my plighted oath."

"Have at you then!" the other shouted, heaving it up aloft,
And grimacing as furiously as if he were out of his mind.
Ferociously he swung at him, but did not touch the man,
For in an instant he checked his swing before it might do him harm.
Gawain awaited the blow as he ought, and not a limb of his flinched,
But he stayed as still as any stone, or rather, like a stump
That is anchored into the rocky ground, locked by a hundred roots.
Then once again the man in green harangued him playfully:
"So, now you have your courage back, it's time to strike the blow.
May that high knighthood Arthur dubbed you with preserve you now,
And save your neck from this next stroke, if it can manage to."
Gawain's fury grew more and more, and fiercely he lashed out,
"Why, thrash away, you fearsome fellow, you waste time flinging threats!
I suspect that in your heart of hearts you have terrified yourself."
"Indeed," replied the other knight, "you speak so defiantly,
I will no longer delay about it and hinder you on your mission—
                    Right now."
            He took his stance to strike,
            Puckered both lip and brow.
            Sir Gawain didn't like
            His chance of rescue now.

The knight lifted his weapon up, easily, letting it down,
With the sharp blade of the cutting edge onto the bare neck.
Though he hammered with his full force, it harmed him barely enough
To nick his neck on the one side, severing the skin.
The sharp edge sank into the flesh and through the shining fat
So the bright blood shot over his shoulders and out onto the earth.
And when Gawain glimpsed his own blood there, gleaming on the snow,
He sprang forth more than a spear's length with his feet planted together:
He grasped his helmet hurriedly and clapped it onto his head;
With a shake of his shoulders then he jerked his shield down into place,
And drew his bright sword from his belt and challenged fierily.
Never since he had been a newborn babe in his mother's arms

Had he ever felt himself in this world to be half so happy a man.
"You can put a stop to your bold strokes, sir! Give me no more of them!
For I have taken one blow in this place, without resisting it,
But if you offer me any more, I will pay you back at once,
I will repay you to the full, rely on it—and be
Your foe.

> Only one stroke must fall—
> Thus did we make our vow
> Which we pledged in Arthur's hall—
> And therefore, man, stop now!"

The great lord turned away from him and rested on his axe—
He set the shaft on the riverbank and leaned on the sharp blade
And took a good long look at the knight who had taken a fighting stance,
How that doughty hero stood up to him, so fearless and undaunted,
Fully armed and free of dread: it warmed his heart to watch.
Then he addressed him cheerfully in his resounding voice
And with a ringing resonance he spoke thus to the man:
"Bold knight, don't be so fierce and grim, here on this grassy ground.
Nobody has used you ill, or in unmannerly fashion,
Nor acted against the covenant that we shaped at the King's court.
I pledged you a stroke, and you have it—you may hold yourself well paid;
I release you from the rest of it, from any other claims.
If I had not been nimble, perhaps I'd have dealt you a blow
More out of anger, one that might indeed have provoked your wrath.
The first stroke, though, I threatened you for fun, with only a feint,
Not slicing you open with a slash. In this I gave you justice
According to the agreement we crafted your first night in my castle,
When you faithfully fulfilled our pact and were a man of your word:
All of your winnings you gave to me, as an honest man should do.
The other feint I gave you, sir, because on the following morning
You kissed my lovely wife and gave me back the kisses taken.
For those two days you took from me those merely feigning blows
At your nape.

> If a true man keeps his word,
> Then he meets no mishap.
> You fell short on the third,
> And thus you took that tap.

"For that is my garment you are wearing, that selfsame woven girdle.
It was my own wife gave it to you, I know it very well.
And I know all about your kisses, and all the things you did;
And as for your wooing by my wife, it was I who set it up.
For I sent her to test your worth, and to tell the truth, I think
You are one of the most faultless men who ever went on foot:
As a pearl beside a white pea is so much more to be prized,
So is Sir Gawain, for good faith, beside all other knights.
You were lacking only a little here, and your fidelity failed,
Though not from greed for this craftsmanship, nor for making love,
But only because you loved your life, so I blame you all the less."
The other, valiant as he was, stood silent a long while,
So overcome with mortification he shuddered inside himself;
And all the blood in his breast flushed up and mingled in his face;
So that he winced and shied for shame at what the knight had said.
There at that moment the first words bursting out of him were these:
"A curse upon such cowardice and also covetousness!
In the pair of you are villainy and vice, that destroy virtue."
The good knight then caught hold of the knot, unloosed the fastening,
And roughly flinging the whole belt to the lord who owned it, said,
"Look at it! There the false thing is, may the Fiend take it away!
Because I was anxious about your stroke, cowardice instructed me
To accord myself with covetousness and forsake my character;
The largesse and the loyalty which truly belong to knighthood,
Now I am found faulty in them, and false, who have been afraid
Always of treachery and untruth—both of which lead to sorrow

> And care!
> I confess before you, knight,
> My faults in private here.

Your good will, if I might
Regain, will make me wary."

At that the other lord stood laughing, and answered amiably,
"I hold it to be wholly healed, the injury that I had.
You have confessed yourself so cleanly, acknowledging your faults,
And you had your penance put to you at the sharp edge of my blade,
That I hold you cleansed of that offense, and purified as clean
As if you had never sinned at all since the day that you were born.
And I will give you this girdle, sir, with the gold along its hems;
For it is as green as my gown, Sir Gawain, and wearing it you may
Think back upon this selfsame game, when you are pressing forward
Among other princes of excellence; this will be a noble token
Of the feat you performed at the Green Chapel, when you're among
    chivalrous knights.
And now you shall, in this New Year, come back with me to my house,
And we shall revel away the rest of this glorious festival
                    Most happily."
        He pressed him hard, that lord:
        "I think that with my lady
        We shall bring you to accord—
        Who was your bitter enemy."

"Indeed I cannot," said the knight, and seizing hold of his helmet,
He doffed it out of courtesy, and offered the lord his thanks.
"I have lingered here quite long enough. Good luck to you and yours,
And may He who determines all rewards repay you generously!
Commend me to that courteous lady, your gracious, lovely wife,
Both to her and that other one, my honored noble ladies,
Who so adroitly have beguiled their knight with their trickery.
But it is not an unusual thing for a fool to act foolishly,
Or for a man, through the wiles of women, to be brought down to grief.
For in the same style Adam once was beguiled by one on earth,
And Solomon by many women, and Samson was another—

Delilah dealt him his destiny—and David afterwards
Was blinded by Bathsheba and endured much misery.
Now, since these were ruined by women's wiles, it would be an enormous
    gain
To love them well, but not believe them—if any man could do that!
For these were the favored ones of old whom fortune followed after,
Yet they all went astray, although they were the most excellent men
                    Under heaven!
            All of them had the wool
            Pulled over their eyes by women;
            If I'm an equal fool,
            Might I not be forgiven?

"But as for your girdle," Gawain said, "may God reward you for it!
That I will wear with all good will, though not for gain of gold,
Nor for the cincture, nor the silk, nor for the long pendants,
Nor for its costliness and prestige, nor the wonderful workmanship;
But as a token of my transgression, I shall see it often
When I am riding out to renown, and remember with remorse
The faultiness and the frailty that cling to the obstinate flesh,
How it tends to be easily enticed to the spots and stains of sin.
And thus, when my prowess in battle shall prick me on to pride,
One look at this love-lace will remind me, and humble me in my heart.
But one thing I would like to know, so long as it won't offend you:
Since you are the lord of yonder lands which I have been staying in,
So honorably received by you—may He repay you for it
Who holds the heavens above the earth and sits enthroned on high—
What are you called by your rightful name?—and then I will ask no more!"
"I will tell you that without deceit," the other man replied.
"Bertilak of Hautdesert is how I am known in this land.
Through the mighty force of Morgan le Fay, who is living in my castle,
And her skill in the magical lore and crafts that she once learned so well
Through the masterful arts of Merlin himself, many of which she acquired,
For she had pleasant love-dealings over a long while

With that wise and excellent wizard—as is known to the knights from whence
                    You came.
          Morgan le Fay the goddess
          Therefore is her name.
          Whatever his haughtiness
          There's no man she can't tame.

"She sent me out in this disguise to assail your handsome hall,
To put your vaunted pride to the test, to see if it held true,
The great renown of the Round Table, that is vaunted everywhere.
She sent me out as this marvel you see, to drive you out of your minds,
And to so distress Queen Guinevere that she would be startled to death
From horror at seeing that selfsame knight, that ghastly phantom speaker
Talk from his head that he held in his hand, facing the high table.
She is the one who lives at my home, that ancient, agèd lady;
Even more than that, she is your aunt, half-sister to King Arthur,
She is the Duchess of Tintagel's daughter, whom noble Uther later
Fathered Arthur himself upon, who is now your sovereign King.
Therefore, my lord, I now beseech you, come and visit your aunt,
Make merry once again in my house, where my people love you so,
And I, my fine fellow, bear you as much good will, by my faith, as any
Man living under God on earth, for your great integrity."
Gawain said nothing except that he could not stay, by any means.
The two knights then embraced and kissed, commended one another
To the high Prince of Paradise, and they separated right there
                    In the cold.
          Gawain on his fair steed
          Made haste to the King's stronghold,
          And the knight in brightest green
          Wherever he wanted to go.

Gawain now went riding over many wild ways in the world
On Gringolet, since, through the grace of God, he had gotten away with his
    life.

Often he lodged inside a house, and often out of doors,
And met with many adventures in valleys and won many victories
Which I, at this time, do not intend to tell you all about.
The hurt had healed and was whole again that he'd taken in his neck,
And he wore the gleaming belt about his body all the time,
But slantwise as a baldric that is fastened at the side,
The lace locked under his left arm, and tied there with a knot
As a token of the spot of sin—the fault—he'd been taken in.
And thus that knight, all safe and sound, came to the King's court.
Delight was wakened in that house when the noble folk were told
That good Gawain had come again: they thought it amazing luck.
The King walked out and kissed the knight, and the Queen kissed him too,
And after them many a trusty knight who came to hail him there
Asked him about his travels; he told them fantastic tales,
Describing all the tribulations he'd met with since he left—
His adventure at the Green Chapel, the deportment of its Knight,
The amorous actions of the lady, and then at last, the lace.
He bared the scar of the nick on his neck in order to show them all
What he had taken at that lord's hands for his unfaithfulness,
                                His blame.
            It tormented him to tell;
            He groaned for grief, and pain—
            The blood in his face upwelled
            When he showed the cut, for shame.

"Look at this, lords!" the knight cried out, handling the lace.
"This is the ribbon of the blame that I also bear on my neck.
This is the sign of the injury and damage I have deserved—
From cowardice and covetousness that both caught hold of me.
This is the token of the untruth that I was taken in,
And I must keep on wearing it as long as my life may last,
For though a man may hide his offense, he cannot be rid of it,
For once it is attached to him, it never will come loose."
The King then sought to comfort the knight, as all the court did, too,

Laughing out loud at what he confessed, and they amiably agreed—
The lords who belonged to the Round Table and all their ladies as well—
That each bold knight of that brotherhood should obtain a similar baldric,
A cross-belt slantwise from the shoulder, colored a bright green,
Which for the sake of that good man they would follow suit and wear.
For that was agreed to be the highest glory of the Round Table,
And whoever wore it thus was honored, forever afterwards,
As is recorded, written down in the best book of romance.
Thus it came about in Arthur's day that this adventure happened,
And the books of British history bear witness to it as well,
Ever since Brutus, the bold knight, first landed on these shores,
After the siege and the assault had been exhausted at Troy:

Finis.

Many strange things have been found
In Britain before this:
Now He that once was crowned
With Thorns bring us to bliss.

AMEN

HONI SOIT QUI MAL PENCE

John Ridland, 2010

Old French ▶

RICHARD I *(ca. 1157–99)*

Chanson

Never man caught could muster fit excuse
Lithe to the tongue to parry his distress,
Yet for my comfort I can song devise;
Now giftless hangs of many friends the grace
While I in shame and hopeless of release
Am these two winters held.

Well my knight can recall, and my sworn man,
Englishman, Norman, Gascon, Poitevin,
How I have let no least companion
Lie wasting thus for long his heart in prison.
Pride forbids arguments of worth and ransom,
But still, I am close held.

Ah, I know well enough that in the end,
By death locked up, I shall find parent nor friend
Helpful with gold or capable dear hand.
More than myself I mourn who to me bend
And may, after my death, need, and none lend
While closed I lie, and held.

Count it no marvel that my heart is rent
Now Philip cramps my kingdom in torment,
But were he minded of the covenant
Once we together made by joined consent
I could expect no pain long continent
Nor long in shame lie held.

This though they know, Angevin and Torraine,
Unmarried men whose gold and faith are fine,
Love hides so hampered help cannot be shown,
And past touch of their love fast am I down.

Light from bare swords bent I see flood the plain
Who meantime am close held.

Companions whom old love has held this late,
To you of Caen and Percherain I write,
Long vexed: may song call constancy to sight;
I have dealt no one falsely or in spite
And who shows faithless now is base past hate
For straightly am I held.

Countess and sister, to your fame may the lord
Whose prisoner I stay, to whom is spurred
My prayer, guard you and hold.

To the mother of Louys I send no word
I have here told.

W. S. Merwin, 1949

MIDDLE FRENCH ▶

CHRISTINE DE PISAN *(ca. 1365–1430)*

"Doulce chose est que mariage"

That marriage is a sweet delight
For one whose husband's good and wise,
My married life will demonstrate,
As God has made me realize.
Praise Him who made this man my prize,
His goodness I am swift to tell,
And know of my own expertise,
Surely my sweetheart loves me well.

I learned his goodness on the night
That we were wed and with great ease
Can prove it, for, from dusk to light,
He offered me no injuries;
Before time came for us to rise,
A hundred kisses I recall
He gave, but took no liberties;
Surely my sweetheart loves me well.

His language, courtly and polite,
Assured me: "I was born to please
You, darling—I am yours by right,
To serve you well, as God decrees."
And lest the dream he wove should cease,
He'd tell me this and this retell
All night, unswerving from his course:
Surely my sweetheart loves me well.

Princes, I'm mad with some disease,
For when he says he's mine, I swell
To bursting with Love's ecstacies;
Surely my sweetheart loves me well.

"Seulete suis, et seulete vueil estre"

Alone am I	and wish to be alone,
Alone am I	my love has gone away,
Alone am I	and master have I none,
Alone am I	with none to share my way,
Alone am I	in languor and dismay,
Alone am I	in utter poverty,
Alone am I	*no lover lives with me.*
Alone am I	at door or windowpane,
Alone am I	in corner hideaway,
Alone am I	with tears to feed upon,
Alone am I	in grief or grief at bay,
Alone am I	my pleasure so to stay,
Alone am I	my chamber's company,
Alone am I	*no lover lives with me.*
Alone am I	in every place I've known,
Alone am I	where I abide or stray,
Alone am I	more so than anyone,
Alone am I	to all a castaway,
Alone am I	abased by everyone,
Alone am I	in tears most frequently,
Alone am I	*no lover lives with me.*
O princes	now my sorrow has its sway,
Alone am I	of every grief the prey,
Alone am I	as dark as mulberry,
Alone am I	*no lover lives with me.*

"Sage seroit qui se saroit garder"

Wise would she be, who keeps her own good name
From those deceiving lovers who would wage
War on her reputation as a game:

Groaning, they overdo the amorous rage
That has them pent like finches in a cage,
And go about playacting, wan and pale—
But I endite this plainly on my page:
Who most complain are not those who most ail.

Listen to this one's oaths, to that one's claim
That he's the slave of Love and not his page!
Whoever saw these gawkers without shame
Telling such tales to women as they gauge
Will best deceive them—if that man were sage,
He would correct these lovers without fail.
Confine such overacting to the stage:
Who most complain are not those who most ail.

To mend such lovers surely is God's aim,
For much harm comes from men who will engage
Women with pleas for favors, who defame
Their honesty, who beg them to assuage
Those passions which they feigningly allege;
For my ballade (when asked) will tell this tale:
No matter noble birth or lineage,
Who most complain are not those who most ail.

Charles Martin and Johanna Keller, 1999

FRENCH ▶

FRANÇOIS VILLON *(1431–63)*

From *The Testament*

The Old Woman Regretting the Time of Her Youth, or
Lament of the Beautiful Helmet Maker

I thought I heard an old woman,
The beautiful Helmet Maker,
Grieving for her youth that's gone,
Speaking of it in this manner:
"Ha! Felonious age, destroyer,
Why did you beat me down this way?
Who's to stop me suffering further,
Ending it with a stroke today?

The power I held over men
You took, my beauty at its height.
Clerks, leading merchants, clergymen,
Would have given all for a night
With such beauty, though they might
Regret it later. And would today
If they saw me as I am, a sight
To make a beggar turn away.

Many a man I would refuse—
It wasn't quite so bright of me—
For a smart boy whom I chose,
Fed well, and dressed in finery.
I cheated on him but, believe me,
I loved him, though he drove me mad.
He knocked me around a bit roughly,
And loved me only for what I had.

He could drag me through the mud,
Tread on me . . . I loved him more.
Had he maimed me, I still would.

When he told me to kiss him, the sore
Ribs and curses went out the door.
The glutton, full of wickedness,
Embraced me. And a lot of good
That's done me. Shame and sinfulness.

It's thirty years that he's been dead,
And I remain with my gray hair.
When I think of the times I had,
And what I am now! When I stare
At my naked body, and compare
Its dried up, shriveled ugliness
With what it used to be, I swear
I'm filled with such great bitterness!

Where has the smooth forehead gone,
Blond hair, arched eyebrows, wide-spaced eyes,
The playful look that nets the pigeon
However timorous he is, or wise
He thinks he is? To itemize:
A straight nose, neither big nor small,
The ears too, just the perfect size,
And crimson lips, to cap it all.

Pretty shoulders, long and slender
Arms; beautiful hands and wrists,
That my fate seemed to intend for
Heated tourneys in the lists
Of passion . . . small, tilting breasts,
Rounded thighs, wide loins, and then
The vulva in its little nest
In the middle of the garden.

Wrinkled forehead and gray hair,
Sunken eyebrows, and the eyes

Whose laughter drove men to despair,
Clouding . . . again to itemize.
The nose that was a perfect size,
Hooked. Two hairy ears hang down.
You'd have to look hard to realize
This death's-head is a face you've known.

The end of beauty isn't good:
Shoulders pulled into a hump,
Arms short, fingers stiff as wood.
The breasts? Shrunk, scarcely a bump.
The same goes for the hips and rump.
The vulva? Ugh! The rounded thigh is
A thigh no more, a shriveled stump
Covered with spots, like sausages.

So now here on our heels we squat,
Each miserable poor old fool,
Talking among ourselves of what
We had, when life was wonderful.
Women are like balls of wool
Close to a fire. Soon set aflame,
And soon burned out. All beautiful
Women like us would say the same."

Ballade

The Beautiful Helmet Maker to the Daughters of Joy

"Beautiful Glove Girl, consider.
Blanche the Shoemaker, black or tan,
It's time to think what the future
Holds for both of you. Spare no man!
Grab all the money that you can,
To right and left. Now! Don't wait!

Old women have no more value than
A coin that doesn't circulate.

Sausage Seller, graceful dancer,
And Guillemette for Tapestry,
Don't give your boss a back answer.
Without the shop where'll you be?
With some old priest. All you'll see
For wages—and he'll hate to pay it,
The Lord's work should be done for free—
A coin that doesn't circulate.

You, Bonnet Maker, bonny Jean,
Don't let your boy friend pin you down.
Don't be so choosy, Catherine.
If you want a man all of your own,
Try smiling for a change, don't frown.
A plain girl can always get a date,
But what'll you be when youth has flown?
A coin that doesn't circulate.

Girls, be warned! The reason why
I weep and cry at such a rate,
Is that I'll be like this till I die,
A coin that doesn't circulate."

This was the lesson that she taught
Who once was beautiful and good,
And there it is, well said or not.
I've dictated as well as I could
To Fremin. I hope he understood
And the fool doesn't spoil my work.
He may—his head is made of wood.
People judge the master by the clerk.

Louis Simpson, 1998

Villon's Epitaph

(Ballade of the Hanged Men)

O brother men who after us remain,
Do not look coldly on the scene you view,
For if you pity wretchedness and pain,
God will the more incline to pity you.
You see us hang here, half a dozen who
Indulged the flesh in every liberty
Till it was pecked and rotted, as you see,
And these our bones to dust and ashes fall.
Let no one mock our sorry company,
But pray to God that He forgive us all.

If we have called you brothers, don't disdain
The appellation, though alas it's true
That not all men are equal as to brain,
And that our crimes and blunders were not few.
Commend us, now that we are dead, unto
The Virgin Mary's son, in hopes that He
Will not be sparing of His clemency,
But save our souls, which Satan would enthrall.
We're dead now, brothers; show your charity
And pray to God that He forgive us all.

We have been rinsed and laundered by the rain,
And by the sunlight dried and blackened too.
Magpie and crow have plucked our eyeballs twain
And cropped our eyebrows and the beards we grew.
Nor have we any rest at all, for to
And fro we sway at the wind's fantasy,
Which has no object, yet would have us be
(Pitted like thimbles) at its beck and call.
Do not aspire to our fraternity,
But pray to God that He forgive us all.

Prince Jesus, we implore Your Majesty
To spare us Hell's distress and obloquy;
We want no part of what may there befall.
And, mortal men, let's have no mockery,
But pray to God that He forgive us all.

Richard Wilbur, 2012

JOACHIM DU BELLAY *(ca. 1522–60)*

Les Amours XIII

As often a fire that's laid too close by ferns
Fastens at whim among the fern-bushes,
Or, finding wheatfields where a wind runs loose,
In fury of light limbs hurdles and burns,
As the attendant youngsters of his race
Will filter all the wood in finding out
Where, gnarled in bole or root, the pastor heat
Holds separate from their less canny pace:
So will love tindered in close innocence
Leap often boundless past its own surprise,
And it were wiser my pen here should stop
Than, running, semble a man small of sense
Who in the play and boredom of his house
Spurred off a flame that he could not rein up.

W. S. Merwin, 1949

JEAN-ANTOINE DE BAÏF (1532–89)

Dedication of a Mirror to Venus

I, that for letting a smile's favor
Loose from my youth in a light hour
Would with suitors' press and fervor
Find my doorway darkened over,
Now to Venus, for her to keep,
The promised mirror tender up,
For the shape which of late I wear
Is such as will not bear review
And the face once this surface knew
Stirs no such shadows any more.

W. S. Merwin, 1949

JEAN PASSERAT *(1534–1602)*

Sonnet

Addressed to Henry III on the death of Thulène, the King's fool

Thulène is dead, my lord. I saw his funeral.
But it is in your power to bring him back again.
Appoint some poet to inherit his domain.
Poet and fool are of the same material.
One scorns advancement. One has nowhere to advance.
In both accounts the gain is smaller than the loss.
Both kinds are quick to anger, difficult to cross.
One speaks on impulse, one leaves everything to chance.
One is light-headed, but the other one is seen
wearing a pretty cap and bells, yellow and green.
One sings his rhymes, the other capers to his chimes.
Yet we are different in one important way.
Fortune has always favored fools, or so they say.
She's seldom favored poets in the best of times.

Richmond Lattimore, 1973

PIERRE CORNEILLE (1606–84)

From *Le Cid*

CAST OF CHARACTERS

DON FERNAND, first King of Castile
DOÑA URRAQUE, Infanta of Castile
DON DIÈGUE, Father of Don Rodrigue
DON GOMES, Count of Gormas, father of Chimène
DON RODRIGUE, in love with Chimène; her beloved
DON SANCHE, in love with Chimène
DON ARIAS, Castilian noble
DON ALONSE, Castilian noble
CHIMÈNE, daughter of Don Gomes
LÉONOR, the Infanta's lady in waiting
ELVIRE, Chimène's lady in waiting
A PAGE

ACT II, SCENE 3

INFANTA

> Chimène, my dear, don't grieve and suffer so;
> Don't let yourself be shattered by this blow.
> Calm will return soon, after this little squall;
> A passing cloud has dimmed your bliss, that's all,
> And you'll lose nothing by a brief delay.

CHIMÈNE

> My heart has lost all hope in its dismay.
> The sudden storm that shook my calm has made
> Me certain of our shipwreck, and afraid
> That we shall founder in the port, indeed.
> I loved, was loved, our fathers were agreed,
> And I was giving you that happy word

Just at the moment when their quarrel occurred.—
Which, when the news was brought you, made it plain
That all sweet expectations were in vain.
Cursèd ambition, lunacy which rules
In noblest hearts, and turns men into fools!
Honor, which wrests from me my dearest prize,
What shall you cost me now in tears and sighs!

INFANTA

Their quarrel's nothing to be troubled by:
'Twas a moment's flare-up, and as soon will die.
It's made a stir that quickly will be ended.
The King already bids the breach be mended;
And you well know that I, who feel your grief,
Will spare no pains to bring your heart relief.

CHIMÈNE

Such things won't vanish at the King's behest,
A mortal insult cannot be redressed.
Neither to force nor reason will men yield;
Only in semblance can the wound be healed.
The hatred that men's hearts contrive to hide
Grows hotter still for being kept inside.

INFANTA

Your sacred tie with Don Rodrigue will be
The solvent of your fathers' enmity,
And you will feel your love the stronger for
Its power to make them harbor hate no more.

CHIMÈNE

I wish for that, yet doubt it can be so.
Don Diègue's too proud; my father's mind I know.

I can't hold back these tears of grief I shed.
I mourn the past; the future's full of dread.

INFANTA

Is it a frail old man's revenge you fear?

CHIMÈNE

Rodrigue's courageous.

INFANTA

                    He's too young, my dear.

CHIMÈNE

Brave men, at any age, are always such.

INFANTA

You mustn't fret about Rodrigue too much.
He loves you, and he'll do as you require.
A word from you, and he'll suppress his ire.

CHIMÈNE

How crushed I'd be, if he did not obey!
And if he obeyed me, what would people say?
Would a good son suffer such indignity?
Whether he heeded or resisted me,
I'd either be ashamed of his compliance
Or deeply troubled by his just defiance.

INFANTA

Your soul, Chimène, is noble, and in spite
Of your own interest, sees with honest sight.
But, till the quarrel's settled, what if I were
To make your perfect knight my prisoner,

And stand between his courage and his foe?
Would you be happy if I acted so?

CHIMÈNE

Oh, Madam! I would then be free of fear.

ACT II, SCENE 7

DON ALONSE

Sire, the Count is dead.
Don Diègue has taken vengeance through his son.

DON FERNAND

I feared this outcome when the wrong was done,
And bade the Count make peace then with Don Diègue.

DON ALONSE

Chimène is coming here in tears to beg
For justice, Sire, and clasp your royal knees.

DON FERNAND

Though in her grief she has my sympathies,
What the Count did seems richly to deserve
This just chastisement of his pride and nerve.
And yet, however just his death may be,
I grieve to lose a champion such as he.
After the loyal, long career he led,
And all the blood that for my throne he shed,
Though he was arrogant, his passing yet
Weakens my power and fills me with regret.

ACT III, SCENE 6

DON DIÈGUE

Rodrigue! Thank heaven I've found you, my dear boy!

DON RODRIGUE

Alas!

DON DIÈGUE

    Let's have no sighs to mar my joy.
When I've caught my breath, I'll praise you, for you've shown
A valor that's the equal of my own.
You've learned your trade, and in your derring-do
A race of heroes lives again in you.
Through me, you stem from that intrepid line;
Your first great sword-blow equaled all of mine,
And by your youthful ardor you became
At once the rival of your father's fame.
Prop of my age, fine son of whom I dreamed,
Touch these white hairs whose honor you've redeemed,
And kiss this cheek, the once-insulted place
Whose shame you've had the courage to erase.

DON RODRIGUE

Sir, I could do no less; it was your due
From one who was begot and raised by you;
And I rejoice that he to whom I owe
My life approves my sword's initial blow.
But kindly don't object if I reveal,
Despite your pleasure, what in turn I feel.
Let my despair speak out, which until now
Your joy did not permit me to avow.
I'm happy to have served you, Sir, but I
Am desolate at what I've lost thereby;
Avenging you, this arm deprived me of
My heart's desire, and robbed me of her love.
Pray say no more; my happiness is lost.
I've paid my debt to you at cruel cost.

DON DIÈGUE

Come, be exultant in your victory.
I gave you life; you saved my name for me.
I value honor more than the light of day,
And owe you, therefore, more than I could pay.
For brave hearts, though, amours aren't worth a penny.
We've but one honor; mistresses are many.
Love's a diversion; honor is our career.

DON RODRIGUE

What are you saying?

DON DIÈGUE

                              What you need to hear.

DON RODRIGUE

I'm the chief victim of my vengeance, Sir,
And now you'd have me break my faith to her!
The craven warrior and the perjured swain
Are equally disgraceful, I maintain.
Don't chide my faithfulness, but let me be
A knight who's guiltless of inconstancy.
My bonds to her are far too strong to sever;
Though I've no hope, I shall be hers forever,
And since I cannot leave nor win Chimène,
I seek my death, and shall be peaceful then.

DON DIÈGUE

It's not yet time to seek your death. Tonight
Your King and country call on you to fight.
The ships we feared have come upriver, and
Intend to sack the town and waste the land.
Floodtide and night will bring the Moorish power

Soundlessly to our shore within an hour.
The court's in disarray; the people's fears
Fill all the town with cries and wailing tears.
Amid that panic, there's one cheerful sign;
I found at home five hundred friends of mine
Who, hearing of the insult done me, came
With one accord to vindicate my name.
You have forestalled them, but their valor would
Be better used in spilling Moorish blood.
Go lead them now, as honor bids you do:
Those noble warriors want no chief but you.
Go meet the ancient foe who's drawing nigh,
And die then nobly, if you want to die.
Yes, seize some glorious moment, pay the price,
And win the King's thanks for your sacrifice.
Or better still, return with laurelled brow,
Not just as the avenger you are now,
But with achievements so superlative
That the King will pardon, and Chimène forgive.
If you love her still, the one way you can earn
Her heart's by a victorious return.
But I waste time in telling you these things:
I hold you here, when I would give you wings.
Come, follow me, and show the King that you
Can serve him as the late Count used to do.

ACT IV, SCENE 1

CHIMÈNE

It's not a false report? You're sure, Elvire?

ELVIRE

You'd not believe how all the people cheer
The brave young hero whom they idolize,

Praising his wondrous exploits to the skies.
He put the Moors to rout; if their attack
Was sudden, he more swiftly drove them back.
Three hours of battle saw our men repel
The foe, and seize two kings of theirs as well.
Our leader's valor could not be withstood.

CHIMÈNE

And 'twas Rodrigue who showed such hardihood?

ELVIRE

Both of those kings were captured through his pains;
He bested them, and put them both in chains.

CHIMÈNE

Who gave you this extraordinary news?

ELVIRE

The populace, which shouts his name, and views
Him as its cause and object of delight,
Its guardian angel and its perfect knight.

CHIMÈNE

What does the King say of this brave report?

ELVIRE

Rodrigue does not yet dare appear at court;
Don Diègue, however, has rejoiced to bring
His son's two royal captives to the King,
Entreating him to give, with gracious hand,
An audience to the savior of his land.

CHIMÈNE

Rodrigue's not wounded?

ELVIRE

                            Not to my knowledge, no.
How pale you are! You mustn't worry so.

CHIMÈNE

What I must do is keep my rage awake.
Shall I slight my duty, fretting for his sake?
He's praised, he's lauded, and my heart assents!
My honor falters, and my wrath relents!
Be still, my heart, and don't impede my ire:
Two kings he's captured, but he killed my sire.
These mournful garments, which express my woe,
Are the first results his bravery could show,
And though the world may laud his gallantry,
Here everything bespeaks his crime to me.
You gloomy things which fuel my laments,
Dark veils, dark dress, lugubrious ornaments,
Sad pomp which his first victory requires,
Protect my just resolve from passion's fires;
And, lest my love should gain the upper hand,
Speak to my soul of duty's grave command.
Arm me to face this hero without fear.

ELVIRE

Compose yourself. The Princess, Madam, is here.

ACT IV, SCENE 2

INFANTA

I have not come to bring your woes relief;
My sighs shall mingle with your tears of grief.

CHIMÈNE

My Lady: none but I should grieve today.

The danger that Rodrigue has driven away,
The public weal which through his sword we keep,
Mean that I only have a right to weep.
He's saved the city; he has served his King,
And I alone have grounds for sorrowing.

INFANTA

He has indeed done wondrous things, my dear.

CHIMÈNE

That vexing news has long since reached my ear,
And I am told that he's as famous for
Bad luck in love as for success in war.

INFANTA

Why does it vex you, what the people say?
This young Mars whom they praise was yesterday
Your all in all, your love, and when their voice
Acclaims his valor, they approve your choice.

CHIMÈNE

The people justly praise him, but for me
To hear their praises is an agony.
Those high opinions are for me a cross.
The more his fame, the bitterer my loss.
What pain it is to be enamored of him!
The more I learn his worth, the more I love him:
My duty, nonetheless, is stronger still;
I seek his death with an unshaken will.

INFANTA

Your sense of duty, yesterday, was deemed
Heroic, dear, and all at court esteemed
The self-control with which you rose above

All other claims, and sacrificed your love.
But will you hear a faithful friend's advice?

CHIMÈNE

That gracious gift you need not offer twice.

INFANTA

What made sense then does not make sense today.
Rodrigue is now our one support and stay,
The people's hope and pride and cynosure,
Castile's great prop, the terror of the Moor.
The King himself supports the public view
That in Rodrigue your father lives anew.
What my opinion is, I'll tell you straight:
Seeking his death, you seek to wreck the State.
Come! To avenge a father, is one free
To yield one's homeland to the enemy?
Have you good reason to afflict us thus?
What have we done that you should punish us?
It's not as if you were obliged to wed
The man whose sword-thrust left your father dead.
That's understood. For our sake, dear, deprive
Him of your love, but leave the man alive.

CHIMÈNE

Alas, I cannot do as you advise;
My furious duty will not compromise.
Though I admire this hero, though I love him,
Though King and people are adoring of him,
Though valiant warriors guard him round about,
My cypresses will shade his laurels out.

INFANTA

It's noble if, to avenge a father, we're

Compelled to seek the head of one so dear;
But it is nobler still if we forsake
Our private quarrels for the nation's sake.
Take back your heart from him. If you can snuff
That flame of love, 'twill punish him enough.
For your country's good, then, do that noble thing.
Besides, what can you hope for from the King?

CHIMÈNE

He may refuse me, but my pleas won't cease.

INFANTA

My dear Chimène, I leave you now in peace;
Think deeply, and consult your inmost voice.

CHIMÈNE

After my father's death, I have no choice.

Act IV, Scene 3

DON FERNAND

Brave scion of a family renowned
As bold protectors of their native ground,
A house whose gallant story is well known,
Whose gallantry is matched now by your own:
Your worth is greater than I can repay;
What thanks I'd offer you, your deeds outweigh.
Castile delivered from the savage Moors,
The scepter steadied in my hand by yours,
The enemy defeated long before
I could have roused our citizens for war—
Such exploits leave your King unable to
Imagine any way of thanking you.
But your two captive kings can fill that need.

I heard them both describe you as their *Cid*:
Since, in their language, *Cid*'s the word for "lord,"
I give you that great title as reward.
Henceforward be the *Cid*; may that name make
Granada and Toledo cringe and shake,
And may it show to all my subjects here
That I'm your debtor, and that I hold you dear.

DON RODRIGUE

Your Majesty, don't make too much, I pray,
Of the small service I performed today.
It makes me blush, Sire, that so great a King
Should do me honor for so slight a thing,
I owe to such a monarch, while he reigns,
The air I breathe, the blood that's in my veins,
And if it were my fate to lose them for
His sake, 'twould be my duty and no more.

DON FERNAND

Not all of these who out of duty serve
My throne have shown such valor and such verve;
When courage isn't wed to recklessness,
It can't produce so splendid a success.
Then let yourself be praised; and furnish me
A full account, now, of your victory.

DON RODRIGUE

Sire, when the rumored threat was drawing near
The town, and all the streets were full of fear,
A band of friends at Father's house appealed
To me to lead them, though my head still reeled . . .
Oh, Sire, forgive my rashness if I then,
Without your sanction, chose to lead those men.
Danger approached; resistance must be led;

If I went near the court, I'd risk my head;
If I had to die, 'twas better in my view
To perish fighting for Seville and you.

DON FERNAND

Your rash revenge I pardon and dispense;
The State, defended, speaks in your defense.
Chimène, hereafter, will accuse in vain;
I'll hear her only to console her pain.
Speak on.

DON RODRIGUE

Sire, under me those warriors now
Moved forward, stern resolve on every brow.
We were at first five hundred, but before
We reached the port we'd gained three thousand more,
For, seeing us march by, assured and strong,
The most unnerved took heart and came along.
Once there, I sent two-thirds of them to hide
In vessels anchored at the harborside;
The rest, their number growing constantly
And full of hot impatience, stay with me
And, for some starlit hours, make no sound
But, speechless, lie in wait upon the ground.
The guards, obeying my command to them,
Hide also, to support my stratagem,
I having dared to claim that it was you
On whose behalf I told them what to do.
At last we see, by the stars' glimmering light,
A rising tide bring thirty sails in sight,
And soon the surges of the sea escort
The vessels of the Moors into our port.
We let them pass. To them, all seems serene;
On wall or pier no soldier's to be seen;

Our utter silence renders them unwise;
They're sure that they shall take us by surprise;
They heave to, drop their anchors, wade to land
And blindly run into the trap we'd planned.
We rise then, and a thousand battle cries
Burst from our lips and echo in the skies.
Our comrades in the ships reply, and come
Forth sword in hand; the Moors are stricken dumb;
Half-disembarked, they're seized by deep dismay
And, ere they fight us, feel they've lost the day.
They'd come to pillage; they encountered war.
We rush them in the shallows and on shore,
And ere they can form ranks or strike a blow,
We cause great rivers of their blood to flow.
But soon their princes rally them; they gain
Some courage back; their panic starts to wane;
The shame of being killed without a fight
Restores their weakened spirits and their might.
Now resolute, they draw their scimitars;
Our blood and theirs are sacrificed to Mars;
River and bank and port are soon no more
Than fields of carnage and of mingled gore.
How many feats which history might remark
Went unobserved then in the cloaking dark
Where each, sole witness of the deeds he dared,
Had little sense of how the battle fared!
I moved among our forces as their chief,
Bade some advance, to others gave relief,
Took fresh recruits in hand and urged them on,
And could not guess fate's verdict till the dawn.
Day breaks then, and it's clear we've won the fray;
The Moors look, and their courage drains away;
Seeing new reinforcements at our rear,
Their will to fight gives way to mortal fear.

They fly back to their ships in panic, lift
Hoarse cries to heaven, cut themselves adrift,
And in their wild departure pay no mind
To the two kings whom they have left behind.
Their fear has overcome their loyalty:
The tide, which brought them, takes them back to sea.
Meanwhile their kings fight on, helped by a few
Brave followers, all badly wounded, who
To their last drop of blood dispute the field;
In vain I call upon those kings to yield,
But, scimitars in hand, they won't comply
Till, seeing now that all their soldiers lie
Dead at their feet, they ask for our commander.
I say that I am he, and they surrender.
I send the two of them to you at once,
And the battle ends for want of combatants.
Thus, happily, we overcame the dire . . .

ACT V, SCENE 7

INFANTA

Chimène, your Princess bids you to receive
This hero from my hands, and cease to grieve.

DON RODRIGUE

Forgive me, Sire, if in your court I kneel
To show her the respect and love I feel.
I have not come to claim a prize, Chimène:
I'm here to offer you my head again.
Lady, I shall not cite in this my plea
The laws of combat or the King's decree.
If all I've done has not avenged your sire,
Tell me what satisfactions you require.
Must I confront a thousand rivals more,

Extend my fame to Earth's remotest shore,
Eclipse the fabled heroes of the past,
And with my sword make armies flee aghast?
If through such feats my crime can be forgot,
I'll undertake them and achieve the lot;
But if your fiery honor and your pride
Cannot without my death be satisfied,
Don't send against me any human foes:
Your hands must take my life, for only those
Could hope to vanquish the invincible
And turn this offered head into a skull.
Pray let my death suffice to punish me,
And do not bar me from your memory,
But keep me in your heart, and so requite
A vengeance that will keep your honor bright,
Saying of me at times, with some regret,
"Had he not loved me, he'd be living yet."

CHIMÈNE

Arise, Rodrigue. Sire, I cannot undo
The love I feel, and have confessed to you.
Rodrigue's high virtues I cannot gainsay,
And when a king commands, one should obey.
And yet, whatever you have once decreed,
Can you permit this marriage to proceed?
If I obey your orders, as I must,
Shall that compulsion seem entirely just?
If Rodrigue is now essential to the State,
Must I, for salary, become his mate,
And bear an endless guilt because the stains
Upon my hands are from my father's veins?

DON FERNAND

Often, what seemed at first to be a crime

Has come to be acceptable in time.
Rodrigue has won you; you are his, and though
Upon this day his valor made you so,
I would abuse your honor if I placed
Your hand in his with an unfeeling haste.
We shall defer the marriage. My words still stand,
And you shall wed, in time, by my command.
Take, if you wish, a year to dry your tears.
For you, Rodrigue, another battle nears.
Now that you've thrown the Moors' invasion back,
Foiling their plans and stemming their attack,
Carry the war to them, taking command
Of all my forces, and lay waste their land.
The name of *Cid* will set them quivering;
They've called you *lord*, they'll want you for their king.
But mid these deeds, remain her faithful lover;
Return, if may be, still more worthy of her,
After such splendid exploits that for pride
And honor's sake she'll gladly be your bride.

DON RODRIGUE

To win Chimène, to serve the State and you,
What labors are there that I could not do?
Though to be far from her will mean distress,
That I can hope will be my happiness.

DON FERNAND

Trust in your valor and my promise, then,
And since you're loved already by Chimène,
Hope that this scruple, to which we see her cling,
Will yield to time, to courage, and your King.

Richard Wilbur, 2009

Jean de La Fontaine (1621–95)

The Scythian Philosopher

Once a philosopher famed for austerity,
Left Scythia that he might taste luxury
And sailed to Greece where he met in his wanderings,
A sage like the one Virgil has made memorable—
Who seemed a king or god, remote from mundane things,
Since like the gods he was at peace and all seemed well.
Now a garden enabled his life to expand
And the Scythian found him pruning-hook in hand
Lopping here and there what looked unprofitable.
He sundered and slendered, curtailing this and that,
    Careful that not a dead twig be spared;
Then for care to excess, Nature paid a sure reward.
    "But are you not inconsiderate?"
The Scythian inquired. He said, "Is it good
To denude a tree of twigs and leave it scarcely one?
Lay down your pruning-hook; your onslaught is too rude.
    Permit time to do what needs to be done:
Dead wood will soon be adrift on the Styx' dark flood."
The Sage said,—"Remove sere boughs and when they are gone,
    One has benefitted what remain."
The Scythian returned to his bleak shore,
Seized his own pruning-hook, was at work hour on hour,
Enjoining upon any in the vicinity
    That they work—the whole community.
He sheared off whatever was beautiful,
Indiscriminately trimmed and cut down,
    Persevering in reduction
    Beneath new moons and full
Till none of his trees could bear.
              In this Scythian

We have the injudicious man
   Or so-called Stoic, who would restrain
His best emotions along with the depraved
   And give up every innocent thing he craved.
As for me, such perverted logic is my bane.
Don't smother the fire in my heart which makes life dear;
Do not snuff me out yet. I'm not laid on my bier.

Phoebus and Boreas

The sun and the north wind observed a traveller
   Who was cloaked with particular care
Because fall had returned; for when autumn has come,
What we wear must be warm or we dare not leave home.
Both rain and rainbow as the sun shines fitfully,
   Warn one to dress warily
In these months when we don't know for what to prepare—
An uncertain time in the Roman calendar.
Though our traveller was fortified for a gale,
With interlined cloak which the rain could not penetrate,
The wind said, "This man thinks himself impregnable
And his cloak is well sewn, but my force can prevail
   As he'll find in the blast I create,
That not a button has held. Indeed before I am through,
   I may waft the whole mantle away.
The battle could afford us amusement, I'd say.
Do you fancy a contest?" The sun said, "I do.
   Mere words are unprofitable,
Let us see which can first unfasten the mantle
   Protecting the pedestrian.
Begin: I shall hide; you uncloak him if you can."
Then our blower swelled, swallowed what wind he could,
To form a balloon, and with the wager to win,
   Made demoniacal din,

Puffed, snorted, and sighed till the blast that he brewed
Left ships without a sail and homes without a roof
  Because a mantle proved storm-proof.
It was a triumph for the man to have withstood
  The onslaught of wind that had rushed in,
As he somehow stood firm. The wind roared his chagrin—
A defeated boaster since his gusts had been borne.
Controlling clasp and skirt required dexterity,
  But the wind found nothing torn
  And must stop punctually.
  The cloud had made it cool
Till the sun's genial influence caused the traveller to give way,
  And perspiring because wearing wool,
  He cast off a wrap too warm for the day
Though the sun had not yet shone with maximum force.

  Clemency may be our best resource.

The Schoolboy, the Pedant, and the Man with a Garden

  Here was a youth symbolic of the school—
  Up to his chin in what would mean the cane,
  Fearsomely young and bearing out the rule
  That pedants can impair anybody's brain,
  Stealing fruit from a neighbor, old refrain;
  Deflowering a tree. In the fall every time,
  Pomona's gifts to the neighbor were sublime,
  Superior to whatever others grew
  As seasons led forth their retinue.
  Where in spring find the flowers gardens bore,
  Like Flora's own in bloom at his door?
He saw a boor from the school in the orchard one day,
Who'd got into a fruit-tree and was making it sway—
Wreaking useless damage. Fruit and flowers. What defense?

Injuring buds that might later be sustenance,
The schoolboy maimed the tree, did such harm in the end
　　　　That the fruit-grower, disheartened,
Complained to the school-master of the scapegrace,
Who brought others until the orchard was over-run
　　　　By boys doing what the first had done
Except that they were worse. The pedant—man in its most worthless
　　phase—
　　　　Was adding to all the harm begun,
　　　　Dunces who had been mistaught,
Saying his object was to discipline but one,
The marauder who was originally caught—
All profiting by the demonstration.
Then he droned Virgil and Cicero on and on,
　　　　Each of course with reference.
Meanwhile boys swarmed through the orchard till the miscreants
Did the garden more harm than anybody could mend.

　　　　How I hate far-fetched magniloquence—
Discursive intrusiveness world without end.
　　　　If there are creatures who err
More than boys at play, it is pedants as inane.
I declare, with either near, one or the other,
　　　　God knows which inflicts the more pain.

Marianne Moore, 1954

VICTOR HUGO (1802–85)

So Boaz Slept

Boaz lay down in weariness and pain;
He'd spent long hours laboring on his land
And smoothed his blanket with a dusty hand
To sleep among his heaps of garnered grain.

More fields of wheat stood ready to be mowed;
Though wealthy, he was not an unjust man.
Down his mill-race unclouded waters ran,
And in his forge no hellish irons glowed.

His beard shone silver like a brook in spring.
His sheaves were thick, but bundled without greed,
And when, at harvest, gleaners came in need,
He said, "Leave some ears for their gathering."

On righteous paths his feet were known to dwell,
And goodness cloaked him like a robe of white;
His grain poured forth for all whose hungry plight
Touched him, like water from a public well.

Honest with workers, loyal to his kin,
He honored thrift no less than charity;
The women watched old Boaz wistfully
And saw more in him than in younger men.

An old man sees his source with clearer sight;
Soon passing from this world of troubled days,
He holds eternity within his gaze.
A young man's eyes flash fire; an old man's, light.

———

So Boaz slept beneath the moon's faint glow.
Among the great stones massed outside his mill,

His reapers lay together, dark and still,
In that mild evening age on age ago.

Judges still ruled the tribes of Abram's blood.
The Hebrews, wandering in their land of birth,
Saw footprints left by giants in the earth
Soft and damp from the still-remembered flood.

———

Like Jacob, or like Judith, Boaz too
Lay fast asleep upon his humble bed;
The gates of heaven, far above his head,
Half opened, and a dream came passing through.

And from his loins a great oak, flourishing,
Stirred Boaz in his dream, and, gazing down,
He saw a race ascending it; a king
Sang at the roots; a god died in its crown.

Then Boaz murmured with a heartfelt sigh:
How can it pass that I should bear this tree
When eighty years and more have fled from me?
I have no son, nor wife to get one by.

The woman, Lord, with whom I shared this bed
Has gone forever, sharing one with Thee;
Yet still we two remain together, she
Half-living in my thoughts, and I half-dead.

Shall I conceive a nation sprung from me,
A tree arising from this ancient dust?
Only when I was younger could I trust
That day could wring from night such victory.

For now I tremble like a winter bough;
Alone and widowed, I am dry and old,
And, as night falls, I bend against the cold
As to the trough the plow-ox dips his brow.

Thus Boaz mourned. The cedar does not feel
The rose that clings to it; his dream was sweet
Yet painful to him; and it was so real
He did not sense the woman at his feet.

———————

So Boaz slept, while Ruth, the Moabite,
Laid herself at his feet with naked breast,
Hoping he would not wholly waken, lest
He find her there, unknown in the pale light.

But Boaz did not know that she was there,
Nor did Ruth know what God required of her.
The breath of night caused asphodels to stir,
And all Galgala teemed with perfumed air.

Darkness deepened—nuptial, august, sublime.
Perhaps an angel watched them, hovering
Above them with a barely beating wing;
Blue shadows brushed their eyes from time to time.

The breath of Boaz softened like the tones
Sung by stream water when it flows across
A gentle bed of pebbles thick with moss
While lilies bloom among the hilltop stones.

So Boaz slept, and Ruth awakened first,
To drowsy sheep-bells tinkling in the night;
The false dawn was aglow with kindly light
In that still hour when lions slake their thirst.

The whole world dreamed, from Ur to Jerimadeth;
Stars studded the blue velvet of the air;
The crescent moon hung low; Ruth said her prayer,
Begging the heavens in her softest breath—

Barely moving, with veiled, half-lidded eyes—
To say what god, what summer harvester,
Had come that night to make his peace with her,
Leaving his golden scythe there in the skies.

R. S. Gwynn, 2009

LECONTE DE LISLE *(1818–94)*

Leilah Asleep

No wing-stir, no murmur of springs: all sounds are stayed.
Dust of the sun floats above the blossoming grass,
and the bengalee wren, with furtive beak, taps the rich juice
of mangoes in full bloom and ripe with golden blood.

In the king's orchard, where the mulberries blush red,
beneath a sky that burns limpid and colorless,
Leilah, all rosy in the heat and languorous,
closes her deep-lashed eyes in the dark-branching shade.

Her forehead, circleted in rubies, rests upon
one lovely arm. Her naked foot, with amber tone,
tints the pearled lattice of her slim babouche. Apart

she sleeps; and smiles in dream upon her lover's presence,
like an empurpled fruit, perfumèd and intense,
that makes the mouth's deep thirst a freshness in the heart.

Frederick Morgan, 1953

CHARLES BAUDELAIRE (1821–67)

"Je n'ai pas oublié, voisine de la ville ..."

I remember it well enough, on the edge of town,
That little house, and its quiet, and out in back
The fertile goddesses, naked Venus and so on,
Up to their plaster breasts in wild sumac;
And the sun at evening, flooding the whole place,
Ignited the window with bursting Catherine wheels,
And seemed like a great eye in a prying face,
Watching our mute, interminable meals
And diffusing its votive radiance on all shapes,
On the frowsy tablecloth, the worsted drapes.

The Swan

I

Andromache, I think of you. The little stream,
A yellowing mirror that onetime beheld
The huge solemnity of your widow's grief,
(This deceiving Simois that your tears have swelled)

Suddenly flooded the memory's dark soil
As I was crossing the *Place du Carrousel.*
The old Paris is gone (the face of a town
Is more changeable than the heart of mortal man).

I see what seem the ghosts of these royal barracks,
The rough-hewn capitals, the columns waiting to crack,
Weeds, and the big rocks greened with standing water,
And at the window, Their Majesty's bric-a-brac.

One time a menagerie was on display there,
And there I saw one morning at the hour

Of cold and clarity when Labor rises
And brooms make little cyclones of soot in the air

A swan that had escaped out of his cage,
And there, web-footed on the dry sidewalk,
Dragged his white plumes over the cobblestones,
Lifting his beak at the gutter as if to talk,

And bathing his wings in the sifting city dust,
His heart full of some cool, remembered lake,
Said, "Water, when will you rain? Where is your thunder?"
I can see him now, straining his twitching neck

Skyward again and again, like the man in Ovid,
Toward an ironic heaven as blank as slate,
And trapped in a ruinous myth, he lifts his head
As if God were the object of his hate.

II

Paris changes, but nothing of my melancholy
Gives way. Foundations, scaffoldings, tackle and blocks,
And the old suburbs drift off into allegory,
While my frailest memories take on the weight of rocks.

And so at the Louvre one image weighs me down:
I think of my great swan, the imbecile strain
Of his head, noble and foolish as all the exiled,
Eaten by ceaseless needs—and once again

Of you, Andromache, from a great husband's arms
Fallen to the whip and mounted lust of Pyrrhus,
And slumped in a heap beside an empty tomb,
(Poor widow of Hector, and bride of Helenus)

And think of the consumptive negress, stamping
In mud, emaciate, and trying to see

The vanished coconuts of hidden Africa
Behind the thickening granite of the mist;

Of whoever has lost what cannot be found again,
Ever, ever; of those who lap up the tears
And nurse at the teats of that motherly she-wolf, Sorrow;
Of orphans drying like flowers in empty jars.

So in that forest where my mind is exiled
One memory sounds like brass in the ancient war:
I think of sailors washed up on uncharted islands,
Of prisoners, the conquered, and more, so many more.

Anthony Hecht, 1961

STÉPHANE MALLARMÉ (1842-98)

The Afternoon of a Faun.

Eclogue

The Faun:

These nymphs, I would make them endure.

Their delicate flesh-tint so clear,
it hovers yet upon the air
heavy with foliage of sleep.

Was it a dream I loved? My doubt,
hoarded of old night, culminates
in many a subtle branch, that stayed
the very forest's self and proves
alas! that I alone proposed
the ideal failing of the rose
as triumph of my own.   Think now . . .
and if the women whom you gloze
picture a wish of your fabled senses!
Faun, the illusion takes escape
from blue cold eyes, like a spring in tears,
of the purer one: and would you say
of her, the other, made of sighs,
that she contrasts, like the day breeze
warmly astir now in your fleece!
No! through the moveless, half-alive
languor that suffocates in heat
freshness of morning, if it strive,
no water sounds save what is poured
upon the grove sparged with accords
by this my flute; and the sole wind
prompt from twin pipes to be exhaled

before dispersal of the sound
in arid shower without rain
is—on the unwrinkled, unstirred
horizon—calm and clear to the eye,
the artificial breath of in-
spiration, which regains the sky.

Sicilian shores of a calm marsh,
despoilèd by my vanity
that vies with suns, tacit beneath
the flower-sparkle, now RELATE
how here I cut the hollow reeds
that talent tames; when, on pale gold
of distant greens that dedicate
their vine to fountains, undulates
an animal whiteness in repose:
and how at sound of slow prelude
with which the pipes first come to life
this flight of swans, no! naiads flees
or plunges . . .

          Limp in the tawny hour
all is burning and shows no trace
by what art those too many brides
longed-for by him who seeks the *A*
all at once decamped; then shall I wake
to the primal fire, alone and straight,
beneath an ancient surge of light,
and one of all of you, lilies!
by strength of my simplicity.

Other than the soft nothingness
their lips made rumor of, the kiss,
which gives assurance in low tones
of the two perfidious ones,

my breast, immaculate of proof,
attests an enigmatic bite,
imputed to some august tooth;
leave it! such mystery made choice
of confidant: the vast twinned reed—
beneath blue sky we give it voice:
diverting to itself the cheek's
turmoil, it dreams, in a long sòlo,
that we amused the beauty here—
about by false bewilderments
between it and our naive song;
dreams too that from the usual dream
of back or flawless flank traced by
my shuttered glances, it makes fade,
tempered to love's own pitch, a vain,
monotonous, sonorous line.

Oh instrument of flights, try then,
cunning Syrinx, to bloom again
by lakes where you await me! I,
proud of my murmur, shall discourse
at length of goddesses; and by
idolatries warmly portrayed
remove more cinctures from their shades:
thus, when from grapes their clarity
I suck, to banish a regret
deflected by my strategy,
laughing, I raise the cluster high
and empty to the summer sky,
and breathing into its bright skins,
craving the grace of drunkenness,
I gaze them through till night begins.

Oh nymphs, let us once more expand
various MEMORIES. *My eye,*

piercing the reeds, darted at each
immortal neck-and-shoulders, which
submerged its burning in the wave
with a cry of rage to the forest sky;
and the splendid shower of their hair
in shimmering limpidities,
oh jewels, vanishes! I run;
when, at my feet, all interlaced
(bruised by the languor which they taste
of this sickness of being two),
I come upon them where they sleep
amid their own chance arms alone;
and seizing them, together still
entwined, I fly to this massed bloom—
detested by the frivolous shade—
of roses draining all perfume
in the sun's heat; where our frisk play
may mirror the consumèd day.
I worship you, oh wrath of virgins,
savage joy of the sacred burden
sliding its nakedness to flee
my lips that drink, all fiery,—
like tremor of a lightning-flash!—
the secret terror of the flesh:
from feet of the inhuman one
to her shy sister's heart, who is
forsaken at the instant by
an innocence, moist with wild tears
or humors of a brighter cheer.
My crime is, that in gaiety
of vanquishing these traitor fears
I parted the disheveled tuft
of kisses which the gods had kept
so closely mingled; for I scarce

moved to conceal a burning laugh
beneath glad sinuosities
of one alone (holding the child,
naive and never blushing, by
a single finger, that her white-
swan candor might take tinge of shame
from kindling of her sister's flame:)
when from my arms, that are undone
by obscure passings, this my prey
for ever thankless slips away
unpitying the sob which still
intoxicated me.

                        Ah well!
Others will draw me towards joy,
their tresses knotted to my brow's
twin horns: you know, my passion, how
each pomegranate, purple now
and fully ripened, bursts—and hums
with bees; and our blood, taking fire
from her who will possess it, flows
for the timeless swarm of all desire.
At the hour when this wood is tinged
with ash and gold, a festival
flares up in the extinguished leaves:
Etna! 'tis on your slopes, visited
by Venus setting down her heels
artless upon your lava, when
a solemn slumber thunders, or
the flame expires.   I hold the queen!

Oh certain punishment . . .

                        But no,
the spirit empty of words, and

this weighed-down body late succumb
to the proud silence of mid-day;
no more—lying on the parched sand,
forgetful of the blasphemy,
I must sleep, in my chosen way,
wide-mouthed to the wine-fostering sun!

Couple, farewell; I soon shall see
the shade wherein you merged as one.

Frederick Morgan, 1953

Paul Valéry (1871–1945)

The Birth of Venus

Out of the mothering deep, still cold and sweating,
At the storm-beaten threshold, here the flesh
Vomited to the sunlight by the bitter wash,
Tears itself free from the diamond fretting.

Her smile forms, slips where the white arm lies,
Weeps down a bruised shoulder's rosiness,
Pure treasure of the watery Thetis,
And her hair runs a shiver down her thighs.

The pebbles, spattered, tossed aside—so agile
Her course—crumble a thirsty sound, and fragile
Sands drink as they kiss her childlike bounds;

Vague or perfidious, she has a thousand glances;
Her flashing eye, the lightning's awe compounds
With smiling sea, and the waves' faithless dances.

Bather

Like fruit her naked flesh bathes in a pool
(Blue in the trembling gardens) but over the brim
The gold head shines, detaching the hair's coil,
Strong as a casque, cut off at the throat by a tomb.

Beauty forced open by the rose and the comb!
Born from the mirror itself where her jewels steep—
Bizarre broken fires whose hard cluster bites
Her ear given up to naked words and the soft deep.

A rippling arm drowns in the water's hollow
Because of a flower's shadow plucked in vain,
Ravels, washes, dreams toward delight to follow,

While the other, curved simply under the lovely sky,
Moistening her hair's luxuriant fold,
Catches a drunken insect's flight in gold.

In Sleeping Beauty's Wood

The princess, in a palace of pure rose,
Sleeps under whispers changing shadow brings;
A word on the bright mouth, half-uttered, shows
When the lost birds peck at her golden rings.

She does not hear the raindrops as they fall,
Tinkling a far-off century's lost praise,
Nor hears above the wood a wind's flute call
Tearing across the hunting horn's far phrase.

Let the long echo give back to sleep the waking,
Always, O more resembling the soft vine
That balances and on your sealed eyes beats.

So close to your cheek, and slowly, the blown rose
Will never dissipate those delicate pleats
Secretly sensitive to light's falling rays.

Caesar

Caesar, calm Caesar, standing on all that is,
Fists clenched in his beard, and somber eye informed
By eagles and the sunset's combat stormed,
Your heart swells, and feels itself all-powerful cause.

Vainly the lake quivers and laps its bed of rose;
Vainly the young wheat shines like precious metal;
You harden and knot in the tension of the will
Order, at last forcing your mouth to unclose.

Enormous world, beyond horizon's end,
The Empire waits for lightning, the decree, the brand
Which will change evening to a furious dawn.

Happy on the waters, rocked by chance apart,
A fisherman sings and, indolent, floats on,
Ignorant of the bolt gathering in Caesar's heart.

Louise Bogan and May Sarton, 1959

GUILLAUME APOLLINAIRE *(1880–1918)*

Church Bells

O my dark-headed gypsy boy
You hear how the bells go
We made the two-backed beast of love
Thinking no one would know

But all the bells around the town
Could see our naked fun
And from their perch in steeple-tops
Are telling everyone

Tomorrow Cyprian and Mark
Lawrence upon his grill
The girl who runs the pastry shop
And my own cousin Jill

Will smile whenever I go by
I won't know where to hide
And you'll be gone And I shall cry
And wish that I were dead.

                     Anthony Hecht, 1961

VALERY LARBAUD (1881–1957)

These Sounds and This Movement

Ode

Lend me your great noise, your great smooth speed,
Your nocturnal gliding across lighted Europe,
O train de luxe! and the agonizing music
That hums along your corridors of gilded leather,
While behind lacquered doors with latches of heavy copper
Sleep the millionaires.
I wander through your corridors singing
And I follow your course toward Vienna and Budapest,
Mingling my voice with your hundred thousand voices,
O Harmonica-Zug!

I felt for the first time all the sweetness of life
In a compartment of the North Express between Wirballen and Pskow.
We were gliding by meadows where shepherds
At the foot of groups of great trees like hills
Were clothed in raw and dirty sheepskin . . .
(Eight o'clock on an autumn morning, and the beautiful singer
With violet eyes was singing in the next compartment.)
And you, great squares across which I have seen Siberia as it passed and the
    hills of Samnium,
Harsh, unflowering Castille, and the sea of Marmara under a warm rain!

Lend me, O Orient Express, South-Brenner-Bahn, lend me
Your miraculous deep sounds and
Your vibrant voices like first strings;
Lend me the light and easy breathing
Of tall, slender locomotives with such unconstrained
Movements, the express locomotives
Effortlessly preceding four yellow coaches with gold lettering

In the mountainous solitudes of Serbia,
And, further away, crossing Bulgaria with all its roses . . .

Ah! these sounds and this movement
Must enter my poems and speak
For my life that has no speech, my life
Like a child's that does not want to know anything, only
To hope eternally for vague things.

Images

I

One day at Kharkov, in a densely populated area,
(O that Meridional Russia where all the women
With white shawls on their heads look like Madonnas!),
I saw a young woman coming from the fountain
Carrying, as they do, just as in the time of Ovid,
Two buckets suspended from the ends of a piece of wood
Balanced on her neck and shoulders.
And I saw a child in rags approach and speak to her.
Then, amiably inclining her body to the right,
She let down the bucket of pure water so that it rested on the pavement
Level with the lips of the child that had kneeled to drink.

II

One morning in Rotterdam on the quay of Boompjes
(It was the 18th of September 1900, around eight o'clock),
I observed two young girls going off to their workshops;
And in front of one of the great iron bridges they were saying goodbye,
Their roads not being the same.
They kissed each other tenderly; their trembling hands
Wished and did not wish to separate; their mouths
Drew distant sorrowfully and came together again
While they gazed in each other's eyes . . .

Thus they remained a long moment close to each other
Upright and motionless among the busy passers-by,
While the tugs grumbled on the river
And trains maneuvered whistling on the iron bridges.

III

Between Cordova and Seville
There is a small station where, for no apparent reason,
The South Express always stops.
In vain the traveler searches with his eyes for a village
Beyond that little station asleep beneath the eucalyptus trees.
He sees only the Andalusian countryside, green and golden.
However, on the other side of the track, facing it,
There is a hut of black branches and earth.
And at the sound of the train a swarm of ragged children comes out.
Their older sister precedes them, and approaches on the platform,
And without saying a word, but smiling,
She dances for pennies.
Her feet in the dust appear to be black;
Her swarthy and dirty face is without beauty;
She dances, and through large holes in her skirt the color of ashes
You see, nakedly, the movements of her scrawny thighs
And rolling of her little yellow stomach;
And this is why, every time, some gentlemen laugh
In the odor of cigars in the diner.

Louis Simpson, 1995

La rue Soufflot

Romance

> *For the fan of Madame Marie Laurencin*
> *No, you will never know . . .*
> PARIS.

Our little day will soon be over: the last
Years open before us like these streets;
And the school is there as always and the laid-out
Square, and the old church where we once saw
The dead Verlaine come in. After all, despite the sea
And so many crossings, we have never left
This place, and all our life will have been
A little journey around and zigzag across Paris.
And even afterwards we will still be here,
Invisible, forgotten, but inhabiting as always
The city of childhood and of first love,
With the astonishment of being twelve and of that meeting,
Which still makes us murmur in the crowd:
"*Porque sabes que siempre te he querido . . .*"
And a passer-by, who has heard me, turns to look.

Richard Pevear, 2012

JEAN FOLLAIN (1903–71)

Landscape of a Child on His Way to the Place of the Regents

This great liquid silence
inhabiting the barrels
these tiny insects
trying in vain to devour the skin of virgins
the wheelwrights drinking near the blue thistle
the hornets making their white honey
the bees distilling their blond honey
the flashing cauldrons
that are rubbed with wet ashes
the sounds of the storm's end
the rank smoke
of weeds burning in piles
in box-hedged gardens
and the portrait of a king
on the kitchen wall
and the clay and plaster
in the damp kingdoms:
All of it is the Messenger of an impossible dawn:
there she is already at the top of the hill
the widow
leading by the hand to the distant school
the child with the wild red hair.

Black Meat

Around stones called precious
which only their own
dust can wear down
the eaters of venison
carve in silence
their black meat

the trees on the horizon
imitate in outline
a giant sentence.

The School and Nature

Drawn on the blackboard
in the classroom in a town
a circle remained intact
and the teacher's chair was deserted
and the students had gone
one sailing on the flood
another plowing alone
and the road went winding
a bird letting fall
the dark drops of its blood.

                    W. S. Merwin, 1969

YVES BONNEFOY *(b. 1923)*

To the Voice of Kathleen Ferrier

All gentleness and irony converged
For this farewell of crystal and low clouds,
Thrustings of a sword played upon silence,
Light that glanced obscurely on the blade.

I celebrate the voice blended with gray
That falters in the distances of singing
As if beyond pure form another song's
Vibrato rose, the only absolute.

O light and light's denial, smiling tears
That shine upon both anguish and desire,
True swan, upon the water's dark illusion,
Source, when evening deepens and descends.

You seem to be at home on either shore,
Extremes of happiness, extremes of pain.
And there among the luminous gray reeds
You seem to draw upon eternity.

The Farewell

We came back to our origin,
The place of clarity still, but torn apart.
The windows blended far too many lights,
The stairs climbed over far too many stars
That mean collapsing arches, broken plaster.
The fire seemed to burn in another world.

And now birds fly from room to room,
The shutters have fallen, stones cover the bed,
The hearth is full of sky-debris, just on the edge of dying.
We'd talk there in the evening, almost in whispers

Because of the echoing vaults, and nonetheless
We'd hatch our plans: but a boat
Laden with ruddy stones was pulling away
Irresistibly from a shore, and forgetfulness
Had already placed its ashes on the dreams
We endlessly replayed, peopling with visions
The fire that burned there up to the final day.

Is it true, my friend, my love,
That there is only a single word for naming
The sun of morning and the evening sun
In the language we call poetry,
One word for the cry of joy and the cry of pain,
One word for wildness upstream and the ring of axes,
One word for the unmade bed and the stormy skies,
One word for the newborn, and the stricken god?

Yes, I believe it, I want to believe, but what
Are those shadows about to sweep away the mirror?
And look how brambles root among the stones
On the grassy track, still incompletely cleared,
Our footsteps used to trace towards the young trees.
It seems to me, today and here, that speech
Is that half-broken trough which spills
Its water uselessly, each rainy dawn.

The grass, and water in the grass, that sparkles like a river.
All things of the world remain to be knit up again, united.
Paradise has been dispersed, I know,
The earthly task's to recognize its flowers
Strewn in the humble grass;
But the angel has disappeared, a light
That suddenly was only the setting sun.

And so like Adam and Eve, we'll walk
One last time in the garden.

Like Adam the first regret, like Eve the first
Real courage, we shall wish and shall not wish
To pass beyond the low half-open gate
Down there, at the other end of the narrow fields,
Tinted portentously by a last ray.
Does the future root itself in the origin
The way the sky consents to a curved mirror?
And could we gather from this light,
The miracle of this place, a seed
To hold in our somber hands, for other ponds
Hidden in other meadows "barred with stones"?

Indeed, the place for mastery, for mastering ourselves, is here,
Whence we depart tonight. Here endlessly,
Like water from the trough, slipping away.

Emily Grosholz, 2001

On the Motion and the Immobility of Douve

> Now the life of the spirit does not cringe in front
> of death nor keep itself pure from its ravage. It
> supports death and maintains itself in it.
> —Hegel

Theatre

I

I saw you run on terraces,
I saw you struggle against the wind,
The coldness bled on your lips.

And I have seen you break yourself and be glad of your death,
    O more beautiful
Than lightning, when it stains the white windows of your blood.

II

The dying summer frostbit you with a monotonous pleasure,
we despised the imperfect joy of living.

"Rather the ivy," you said, "the clinging of ivy to the stone of its
night: presence without issue, face without roots.

"Last happy windowpane ripped by the sun's claws, rather in the
mountains this village to die in.

"Rather this wind . . ."

III

It was about a wind stronger than our memories,
Stupor of dresses and cry of rocks—and you passed in front of these flames,
Head graphpapered, hands split open, wholly
Seeking death on the exulting drums of your gestures.

It was day of your breasts
And you were reigning at last absent from my head.

IV

I awake, it rains. The wind pierces you, Douve, resinous heath sleeping
near me. I am on a terrace, in a pit of death. Huge dogs of leafage tremble.

The arm you lift, suddenly, on a door, lights me across the ages.
Village of embers, each instant I see you being born, Douve,

Each instant dying.

V

The arm that is lifted and the arm that is turned
Are of the same instant only for our heavy heads,
But these coverings of verdure and mud thrown back,
All that is left is a fire in death's kingdom.

The dismantled leg pierced by the high wind
Which drives heads of rain before it
Will not light you until the threshold of this kingdom,
Gestures of Douve, gestures already slower, black gestures.

VI

What pallor strikes you, underground river, what artery breaks in you, where the echo of your falling resounds?

This arm you lift suddenly opens, catches fire. Your face draws back. What thickening mist wrenches your gaze from me? Slow cliff of shadows, frontier of death.

Mute arms greet you, trees of another shore.

VII

Wounded one, confounded among the leaves,
But caught by the blood of fading paths,
Accomplice yet of life.

I have seen you, quicksanded at your struggle's end,
Falter at the limits of silence and water,
And, mouth sullied by the last stars,
Break off with a cry the horrible nightwatch.

O raising in air hard suddenly as rock
A beautiful gesture of coal.

VIII

The absurd music begins in the hands, in the knees, then there is the cracking in the head, the music grows loud under the lips, its certainty penetrates the underslope of the face.

Now the woodwork of the face is taken apart. Now begins the tearing out of the sight.

IX

White under a ceiling of insects, poorly lit, in profile,
Your dress stained by the venom of lamps,
I find you stretched out,
Your mouth higher than a river breaking far away on the earth.

Broken being whom the invincible being puts together again,
Presence possessed again in the torch of cold,
O watcher, always I find you dead,
Douve saying Phoenix I wait in this cold.

X

    I see Douve stretched out. At the topmost point of bodily space I hear
her rustling. The black-princes hurry their mandibles across the space where
Douve's hands unfold, their unfleshed bones turning into gray webs which
the massive spider lights.

XI

Covered by the silent humus of the world,
Webbed over by a living spider's rays,
Already undergoing the change into sand,
And cut to pieces, secret knowledge.

Adorned for a festival in the void,
And teeth bared as if for love,

Fountain of my death, with me, unbearable.

XII

    I see Douve stretched out. In the scarlet city of air, where branches
battle across her face, where roots find their way into her body—she radiates
a joy strident with insects, a frightful music.

    To the black tread of the earth, Douve, ravaged and exultant, returns to
the gnarled lamp of the plateaus.

XIII

Your face tonight lighted by the earth,
But I see your eyes' corruption
And the word face makes no sense any more.

The interior sea lighted by turning eagles,
This is an image,
I hold you cold at a depth where images do not take any more.

XIV

I see Douve stretched out. In a white room, eyes dark-circled with plaster, mouth dizzy, and hands condemned to the luxuriant grass invading her on all sides.

The door opens. An orchestra advances. And faceted eyes, woolly thoraxes, cold heads beaked and pincered, flood over her.

XV

O gifted with a profile in which the earth strives
I see you disappearing.

On your lips naked grass and flintsparks
Invent your last smile,

Deep knowledge in which
The old bestiary of the mind burns to ashes.

XVI

Dwelling-place of a dark fire where our slopes converge! Under its vaults I see you glimmer, motionless Douve, caught in the vertical net of death.

Superlative Douve, overthrown: to the march of suns through funeral space, she accedes slowly to the lower levels.

XVII

The ravine enters the mouth now,
The five fingers disperse in casual woods now,

The original head flows among the grasses now,
The breast paints itself with snow and wolves now,
The eyes blow on which of death's passengers and it is we in this
    wind in this water in this cold now.

XVIII

Exact presence whom no flame thereafter could restrain; bearer of secret coldness; living, by that blood that is born again and grows where the poem tears apart.

It was necessary for you to appear, thus, at the deaf limits, and to undergo the ordeal of that land of death where your light increases.

O most beautiful, with death in your laughter! I dare now to meet you, now I can face your gestures' flashing.

XIX

On the first day of cold our head escapes,
Like a prisoner into the higher air,
But, Douve of one instant, that arrow falls
And the palm of its head breaks on the ground.

Thus we had dreamed of reincarnating our gestures
But the head gainsaid we drink a cold water,
And bankrolls of death deck your smiles with flags,
Attempted rift in the thickness of the world.

Galway Kinnell, 1961

PHILIPPE JACCOTTET *(b. 1925)*

"Night is a great sleeping city"

Night is a great sleeping city
where the wind blows. It has come a long way
to the refuge of this bed. It is midnight in June.
You are sleeping, I have been led to the edges of infinity.
The wind shakes the hazel tree. The call comes
that approaches and draws back. One could swear
a light is flying across woods, or surely
shadows turning, they say, in the underworld.
(That call in the summer night, how many things
I could say about it, and your eyes . . .) But it is only
the bird named barn owl calling to us
from suburban woods, and already our smell
is that of corruption. In the morning light
already under our skin that is so warm, bone
pierces, while stars darken at street corners.

Seed Time

I

We would want to be pure
even if evil had more reality.

We would want not to hate
though the storm stuns the seeds.

The one who knows how light seeds are
would hardly be devoted to thunder.

II

I follow the blurred line of trees
where the pigeons flap their wings:

you whom I caress where your hair begins . . .

but under the fingers deceived by distance
the gentle sun is broken like straw.

III

Earth here is threadbare. But let it rain
a single day, you see in its humidity
a mixture from which it returns renewed.
Death, for a moment, has the cool appearance
of the flower snowdrop.

IV

Daylight stamps in me like a bull:
one would like to think that he is strong . . .

If one could tire the bullfighter
and delay a while the death of the bull!

V

Winter, the tree draws into itself.

Then one day laughter is humming
and the murmur of leaves,
ornament of our gardens.

For the one who no longer loves anyone
life is always farther away.

VI

O first days of Spring
playing in the schoolyard
between two classes of wind!

VII

I am impatient and I am anxious;

who knows the wounds and knows the treasures
that another life brings? Spring may
leap toward joy or blow towards death.
—Here's the blackbird. A timid girl
comes out of her house. Dawn is in the wet grass.

VIII

At a very great distance
I see the street with its trees, its houses,
and the unseasonably cool wind
that often changes direction.
A handcart goes by with white furniture
in an undergrowth of shadows.
The days are vanishing before it,
what is left me I count in a short time.

IX

The thousand insects of rain have worked
all night; the trees have blossomed in raindrops,
the downpour sounds like a distant whip.
The sky however is still clear; in gardens
the bell of the tools rings Matins.

X

The air that you do not see
carries a distant bird
and the weightless seeds
that tomorrow will germinate
the edge of the woods.

Oh, how life is running,
mad to be down below!

XI

The Seine, March 14, 1947

The crackled river is muddy. The waters rise
and wash the paving stones on the banks. For wind
like a tall, somber ship has come down
from the ocean, with a cargo of yellow seeds.
It spreads a smell of water, distant and faint. You tremble
only for having surprised opening eyelids.

(There was a mirroring canal that you followed,
the factory canal. You threw a flower
into the spring, to find it again in the town.)
A childhood memory. The one who would take water in his hands . . .

Someone lights a fire of branches on the bank.

XII

All this green stuff does not pile up but trembles and shines,
as when you look at the rustling curtain of a fountain
sensitive to the least current of air; and above the tree
it seems that a swarm of humming bees
has settled; a pleasant landscape
where birds that we never see call to us,
voices uprooted like seeds, and you
with your hair falling over clear eyes.

XIII

A single moment this Sunday brings us together again,
when the winds and our fever have fallen,
and under the street lamps fireflies
light up, then go out. One would say, paper lanterns
far away in a park, perhaps for your feast . . .
I too believed in you, and your light

made me burn, then left me. Their dry shell
cracks as it falls in dust. Others are rising,
others are blazing, and I remain in the shadow.

XIV

Everything gave me a sign: lilacs in a hurry to live
and children losing a ball in the park.
Then the small squares from which one returned,
peeling root upon root, the smell
of a woman in labor . . . The air wove of these nothings
a quivering canvas. And I would tear it apart
by being alone and looking for traces.

XV

The lilacs have opened once more
(but this no longer reassures anyone).
Redstarts flash by, and the servant's voice
is gentler when she talks to the dogs. Bees
are at work in the pear tree. And always
under everything, that vibration of machines . . .

The Ignorant Man

The older I get the more ignorant I am,
the longer I live the less I possess and the less I command.
All I have is a space, by turns covered with snow
or shining, but never inhabited.
Where is the donor, the guide, the guardian?
I keep to my room, and at first I am silent
(silence enters like a servant to impose a little order)
and I wait until, one by one, the lies have gone.
What is left? What is left to this dying man
who is so able to stop dying? What force
makes him speak again to his four walls?

Could I know, I the ignorant, the perplexed?
But I do hear, truly, one who speaks, and his word
comes in with daylight again, though very vague.

"Like fire, love makes itself clear only
by its fall and the beauty of woods in ashes . . ."

Distances

The swifts turn in the heights of air,
yet higher unseen stars are turning.
Let light retire to the ends of earth,
on the dark sand fires will be burning.

So we live in a domain of movements
and distances; so the heart
goes from tree to bird, from bird to distant stars,
from the star to its love. So love
in the closed house increases, turns and labors,
servant of those who care, with a lamp in his hand.

Louis Simpson, 2001

GERMAN ▶

WALTHER VON DER VOGELWEIDE *(ca. 1170–1230)*

"Under the lime-tree,"

Under the lime-tree,
By the heath,
Where with my well-beloved I lay,
You can go and see—
Pleasant both—
Flowers and grass we broke that day.
Where the forest meets the dale:
Tandaradee!
    Sweetly sang the nightingale.

Here we were meeting;
But already
My well-beloved was waiting there.
Such was his greeting,
Gracious Lady,
That ever since I've walked on air.
Did he kiss me? Yes, and well:
Tandaradee!
    Look how red my lips are still.

With the wild flowers
There my love
Made a lavish bed for me;
This bed of ours,
Should you pass above,
Will make you laugh most heartily.
By the roses you can trace—
Tandaradee!
    Where my head lay in that place.

Had anyone seen us
Lying there,

(God grant none did!) I'd be ashamed.
What passed between us
Is our affair,
Never to be known or named
But by us and one small bird—
Tandaradee!
    Which may never breathe a word.

        Michael Hamburger, 1955

Johann Wolfgang von Goethe *(1749–1832)*

To Werther

So once again, poor tear-bedabbled shadow,
You venture in the light of day?
And here, in blossoms of the fresher meadow,
Confront me and not turn away?
Alive as in the early dawn, when tender
Chill of a misty field bestirred the two,
When both were dazzled by the west in splendor
After the drudging summer days were through.
My doom: endure. And yours: depart forlorn.
Is early death, we wonder, much to mourn?

In theory how magnificent, man's fate!
The day agreeable, the night so great.
Yet we, in such a paradise begun,
Enjoy but briefly the amazing sun,
And then the battle's on: vague causes found
To struggle with ourself, the world around.
Neither completes the other as it should:
The skies are gloomy when our humor's good;
The vista glitters and we're glum enough.
Joy near at hand, but we—at blindman's buff.

At times we think it ours: some darling girl!
Borne on a fragrant whirlwind, off we whirl.
The young man, breezy as in boyhood's prime,
Like spring itself goes strutting in springtime.
Astounded, charmed, "Who's doing this, all for me?"
Claims like a cocky heir the land and sea.
Goes footloose anywhere, without a thought;
No wall, no palace holds him, even if caught.
As swallows skim the treetops in a blur,

He hovers round, in rings, that certain her.
Scans, from the height he means to leave at last,
Earth for an answering gaze, that holds him fast.

First warned too soon, and then too late, he'll swear
His feet are bound, traps planted everywhere.
Sweet meetings are a joy, departure's pain.
Meeting again—what hopes we entertain!
Moments with her make good the years away.
Yet there's a treacherous parting, come the day.

You smile, my friend, eyes welling. Still the same!
Yours, what a ghastly avenue of fame.
We dressed in mourning when your luck ran out
And you deserted, leaving ours in doubt.
For us, the road resuming God knows where,
Through labyrinths of passion, heavy air,
Still drew us on, bone-tired, with desperate breath
Up to a final parting. Parting's death!
True: it's affecting when the poets sing
Willow or such, to sweeten suffering.
Some god—though man's half guilty, hurt past cure—
Grant him a tongue to murmur: I endure.

Elegy

Though most men suffer dumbly, yet a god
Gave me a tongue to utter all my pain.

What's to be hoped from seeing her again?
Hoped from the still-shut blossoms of today?
Which opens, heaven or hell, around me? When
I guess, my thoughts go wandering every way.
But steady—there! She's there, at heaven's door;
Her arms enfold and raise me, as before.

So then the heavens are open, take me in
As if deserving life forever blest.
No wish, no longing, and no might-have-been
Stinted: the very goal of all my quest.
Eyes dwell delighted on that loveliest thing,
Their tears subsiding at the passionate spring.

Didn't the day go by on flashing feathers!
Didn't it send the minutes skimming there!
Our sign, the kiss at evening—and what weathers
It promised: fair tonight, tomorrow fair.
Hours were like sisters, lingering as they passed,
Each face alike, each different from the last.

Our final kiss, so shuddering sweet, it tore
The sheerest of all fiber, heart's desire.
My foot, abrupt or dragging, dodged her door
As if an angel waved that sword of fire.
Eyes frozen on the dusky ruts go glum.
Turn, and her door's a darkness, shut and dumb.

My soul's a darkness, shut and dumb—as though
This heart had never opened, never found
Hours of delight beside her, such a glow
As all the stars of heaven let dance around.
Now gloom, remorse, self-mockery—clouds of care
Clutch at it, sluggish, in the sluggish air.

What of the world—it's done for? Cliffs of granite
Crowned shadowy with the sacred grove—they're vapor?
No harvest-moon? Green delta country (can it?)
Turn with its trees to ash, like burning paper?
That grandeur curved above us—all undone?—
Now with its thousand clouds, and now with none.

A form there!—rare and airy, silken, bright,
Floats forth, among the clouds in grave ballet,
An angel in blue noon, or—? No, a white
Slim body—hers!—inclining far away.
You saw her lean so at the gala ball;
Among the loveliest, lovelier far than all.

A ruse for moments only. Don't suppose
The empty air a match for her embraces.
Back to your heart of hearts, that better knows
Her and the changing miracle her face is.
In every guise she's greater. Like a flame,
Forever varying and the very same.

Once by the gate she waited; in she brought me;
Onward from joy to keener joy we passed.
The last last kiss—but how she ran and caught me,
Pressed to my mouth an even laster last.
Still that indelible image of desire
Burns on my heart in script of living fire—

My heart (its battlement a height securing
Her for itself alone, itself for her)
Only for her is happy in enduring;
Knows it has life by stirring if she stir.
Confined in love, is free and on its own;
Praising, with each pulsation, her alone,

Because: when dead to love, and hardly caring
Whether another's love could sink or save it
—She came. And my old verve in dreaming, daring,
Resolving, up-and-doing—this she gave it.
If ever love restored a human soul,
It took my shrunken self and made it whole.

And all through her! In mind and body's gloom

I mooned lugubrious, lurching and agrope.
Look where I would, saw shuddering visions loom
Over the heart's eroded acres. Hope
—Suddenly, out of hopelessness—was there:
A girl with the light of morning on her hair.

To God's own peace, the peace that here below
Passeth all understanding (so the preacher)
I'm minded to compare that heady glow
Of fervor, being near a certain creature.
The heart's at ease; not one distraction blurs
That deepest sense, the sense of *wholly hers*.

In the pure ocean of the soul, a comber
Flings itself, out of thankfulness, self-giving,
Toward something Purer, Higher—Grand Misnomer
However named—to approach the ever-living.
We call it, *being reverent*. And its flight
Sweeps me, when I'm beside her, height to height.

Before her gaze, like sun where winter lingers,
Before her breathing, like the stir of May,
Self-love, that steely ice that digs its fingers
Deep in our rigid psyche, melts away.
No self-concern, no self-importance where
She sets a foot. They squirm away, that pair.

As if I heard her, urgent: "Hour by hour
Life gives itself, exuberant, unbidden.
Yesterday's meaning is a withered flower;
Tomorrow!—who can live there? Where's it hidden?
Today though—if I quailed with sunset near
Never a sun but showed me something dear.

"Then do as I do: Look with knowing pride
Each moment in the face. But no evasion!

Keep every nerve a-tingle! Open-eyed
Rush to it all: day's effort, love's elation.
But where you are, be wholly. Be a child.
You're *all* then. Undefeatable," she smiled.

Easy, I thought, for you to say! Some grace
Shows you forever as the moment's friend.
Anyone near you for a moment's space
Is fortune's favorite—till the moment end.
As end it does! In panic I depart:
You and your pretty wisdom break the heart!

Now miles and miles between us. If I could,
How should I live this minute? Who's to say?
It offers much desirable and good
—All like a shabby pack to shrug away.
Invincible longing dogs me as I go.
Tears are the one philosophy I know.

So let them have their way now, unrepressed.
No chance they'll damp the furnaces within.
Embattled there, all's berserk in my breast
With life and death locked grisly. Which to win?
Herbs dull our suffering when the body's ill,
But if the soul lack nerve, lack even will—?

Or worse, lack understanding? Years without her!
Whose image haunts me in a thousand ways.
Sun on her hair, the falling dusk about her—
The memories lag, or dwindle off in haze.
What good's all this? What comfort? shaken so
By all this coming, going, ebb and flow?

———

Well, leave me here, companions (or I bore you),
Here on the moor alone, with rocks and moss.
You, ever onward, upward! All's before you,

The whole wide earth, the heaven so broad across!
Make your investigations, scour and scout.
Nature has clues to shuffle and sort out.

All's lost to me. Myself lost. Now ignore a
Man the gods coddled with a "lucky star"!
They put me to the proof with that Pandora
So rich in gifts, in havoc richer far.
They pressed me to sweet lips that gave and gave;
Then crushed and flung me headlong. Toward the grave.

Reconciliation

Passion, and then the anguish. And with whom
To soothe you, heavy heart that lost so much?
Love's hour escaped, unstoppered like perfume?
The loveliest—all for nothing—within touch?
Cloudy the mind; mere muddle all it tries.
And the great world adrift before the eyes.

Then music to the fore like angels swarming,
A million tones in galaxy. We surrender
All of our inner fort to forces storming
—Irresistibly overrun with splendor.
The eye goes damp: in longings past tomorrow
We guess at the infinite worth of song and sorrow.

And so the heart, disburdened, in a flash
Knows: I endure, and beat, and pound with pleasure!
Gives itself over utterly, in rash
Thanks for the windfall, life. No common treasure.
Yearns: could it only last!—our feeling of
Fortune on fortune doubled, song and love.

John Frederick Nims, 1969

CHRISTIAN MORGENSTERN *(1871–1914)*

Maids on Saturday

They hang them over the ledge,
The carpets large and small;
In their minds they start to beat
Up masters, one and all.

Wild with satisfaction,
In rage true and berserk,
They cool their souls off for
One week full of hard work.

They beat an infernal rhythm
Until their canes split;
Ears at the front of the house
Take no account of it

But in the back are wailing,
Torn by punch and by thump,
The runners, the Persian pillows,
The eiderdown, German and plump.

  Lore Segal and W. D. Snodgrass, 1961

ERICH KÄSTNER (1899–1974)

Autobiography

For those who weren't born, it's all the same.
They perch above some tree in Space and smile.
Myself, I never thought of it. I came,
A nine-months child.

I spent the best part of my life in school,
Cramming my brain till I forgot each word.
I grew into a highly polished, model fool.
How did it happen? I really never heard.

The war came next (it cut off our vacation).
I trotted with the field artillery now.
We bled the world to ease its circulation.
I kept on living. Please don't ask me how.

Inflation then, and Leipzig, and a whirl
Of Kant and Gothic and Bureaucracy,
Of art and politics and pretty girls,
And Sundays it was raining steadily.

At present I am roughly 31,
And run a little poem factory.
Alas, the greying of my hair's begun,
My friends are growing fat remorselessly.

I plop between two chairs, if that's appealing,
Or else I saw the bough on which we sit.
I wander down the garden-walks of feeling
(When feelings die) and plant them with my wit.

I drag my bags around despite the pain.
The bags expand. My shoulders grow unsure.

In retrospect, permit me to explain:
That I was born. And came. And still endure.

Jerome Rothenberg, 1958

ANCIENT GREEK ▶

HOMER *(ca. Twelfth Century B.C.)*

Helen on the Walls

The Iliad, iii, 121–242

Now to Helen of the white arms came a messenger, Iris,
disguised in the form of her sister by marriage, Laodike,
loveliest of the daughters of Priam, whom Helikaon wed,
the strong son of Antenor. And she found her in her rooms,
weaving with crimson cloth a great web that folded double,
in which she was working the tale of the numberless struggles
between Trojans, tamers of horses, and the bronze-clad Achaians,
all they had suffered for her at the bitter hands of Ares.
And Iris the quick-footed came, and stood beside her, and said:
"Come with me, dear girl, and see the wonder that has happened.
For those who once were at war, each man against the other
struggling in the plain, and whose only lust was for killing,
now sit in a sudden silence, and a lull has come in the war,
and they rest upon their shields and the tall spears are stuck
in the ground beside them. For now in a duel of single spears,
Alexander and brave Menelaos will fight together for you,
and you shall be the wife of the man who wins in the fighting."

So she spoke, and awoke a passion of longing in Helen,
sweet desire for the husband she had before, for her home
and her parents. Over her head she drew a veil of shimmering cloth,
and the tears stood in her eyes as she quickly went from her room;
but not alone, for two serving-girls went with her—
Aithre, daughter of Pittheus, and Klymene with gentle eyes
like the gentle eyes of cattle. And these three went swiftly down
toward the Skaian gates.

Now Priam was already there, and with him
were Panthios and Thmyoites, Lampos and Klytios,
Hiketaion, descended of Ares, Antenor and Oukalegon,
men of perceptive advice and the elders of the people,

whom age had retired from war, but excellent speakers still,
with voices clear and fine, like the voices of cicadas
who sing in the trees of the forest, and its fineness trembles the air
like the whiteness of a lily. Such were they, the leaders of Troy,
who sat upon the tower.

But when they saw Helen ascending,
the old men murmured together and spoke their wingèd words:
"Surely no blame can touch either the men of Troy or Achaia,
because they suffer so long for the sake of a woman like this,
whose face, in its terrible beauty, is like the face of a goddess.
But goddess though she be, let her go away in the ships
and not remain in this land, a curse to us and our children."

So the old men murmured, but Priam called out to Helen:
"Come here, dear child, beside me. Sit here and now look down
on the husband you had before and your former friends and your people.
In my eyes you are blameless; the gods, I say, are guilty
who drove upon me this bitter war with the men of Achaia.
But enough, and now tell me the name of that magnificent man.
Who is that man, so majestic among the Achaians?
He stands shorter by a head than most of the other fighters,
but never before have my eyes seen any man so noble,
so splendid or royal as this. Yes, he stands like a king."

And Helen, the glory of womankind, answered the king:
"Dearest father, never have I failed in the respect and fear
I owe you. But now I wish that I had died by my own hand
on that day when I came with your son across the sea in his ship,
leaving my home behind me, and my growing child, and my friends,
the lovely friends of my girlhood. But it has not happened that way,
and now I am worn with remorse. But this is my answer to you:
that man is the son of Atreus, powerful Agamemnon,
a king but also a fighter, a brave and an able spearsman,
and once my kinsman too—though who could believe that now,
whore that I am?

So she spoke, and the king marvelled at Agamemnon
and exclaimed:
"Happy son of Atreus, favored of fortune,
how many men of Achaia stand mustered beneath your sway!
Long ago I journeyed to Phrygia with its lovely vineyards
and saw the Phrygian people in their wealth of horses assembled,
and all the gathered people of Otreus and Mygdon the godlike
who had pitched his camp beside the riverbanks of Sangarios.
For I too had come as an ally and was mustered among them
on the day when the Amazon women, the peers of men, rode in.
But even they were not so many as all these quick-eyed Achaians."
Then, seeing Odysseus next, the old man questioned Helen:
"But tell me, dear child, who is that man I see there,
shorter by a head than Atreus' son Agamemnon,
but broader still in his build, across the chest and the shoulders?
His weapons lie on the ground, there in the fertile pasture,
but he moves himself like a ram along the lines of his soldiers.
Yes, to some great ram with shaggy fleece would I compare him
as he moves majestic among the ranks of resplendent sheep."
And the lady Helen, descended of Zeus, replied to the king:
"That is the son of Laertes, Odysseus, a shrewd man and cunning,
in Ithaka born and raised, in a poor and a rocky place,
but he is expert in craft and a master of every deception."
But now Antenor, a man of perceptive advice, broke in:
"Lady, what you say is the truth and also shrewdly spoken.
For once before now Odysseus and bold Menelaos
came here to Troy together on an embassy for you,
and I feasted them both in my house and made them welcome as friends,
and learned what each man was like, and shared their intimate thoughts.
Now when the Trojans assembled and these two men were compared,
Menelaos, standing, was the larger man in the shoulders,
but Odysseus the lordlier man when both of them were seated.
But when they rose to weave their words before us in council,

Menelaos spoke little, a few words and rapidly spoken,
but still extremely lucid, for he was sparing of speech
and his tongue never wandered, although he was the younger man.
But when the shrewd, the cunning Odysseus rose to speak,
he stood there stockstill, his eyes staring at his feet,
and made no gestures with his staff, pushing it to and fro,
but held it graceless and rigid, as a clumsy man might do.
You would have said he was stupid or sullen, and an oaf as well,
but when he started to speak, and the great voice swept from his chest
and the words came driving hard and fast like the winter snows,
then no other man on earth could hold his own against him.
And after we heard him speak, his clumsiness seemed to vanish."

But now, seeing Ajax next, the old man Priam asked her:
"Who is that other Achaian, that huge and massive man
looming above them all by the bulk of his head and shoulders?"

And Helen in shimmering robes, the glory of women, replied:
"That is Ajax the great, the bulwark of all the Achaians.
And behind him stands Idomeneus, like a god among the Cretans,
and those are the lords of Crete, the men in a group around him.
Many times, I remember, Menelaos feasted him
at our house in Sparta when he crossed the sea from Crete.
And now I see them all, all the quick-eyed men of Achaia,
the men whom I know so well and whose names I could tell you;
but nowhere do I see those two, the shepherds of the people,
Kastor, tamer of horses, and the boxer, brave Polydeukes—
my own brothers, for we were born of a single mother.
Either they have stayed at home in Lakedaimon the lovely,
or came with their men to Troy across the sea in their ships,
but refuse to enter the fighting along with the other men,
in fear of the shame and the bitter reproaches upon me."

So she spoke, but the fertile earth lay on them already,
there in Lakedaimon, in the beloved land of their fathers.

William Arrowsmith, 1962

From *The Odyssey*

Book 11, lines 1–137

Now when we had gone down again to the sea and our vessel,
first of all we dragged the ship down into the bright water,
and in the black hull set the mast in place, and set sails,
and took the sheep and walked them aboard, and ourselves also
embarked, but sorrowful, and weeping big tears. Circe
of the lovely hair, the dread goddess who talks with mortals,
sent us an excellent companion, a following wind, filling
the sails, to carry from astern the ship with the dark prow.
We ourselves, over all the ship making fast the running gear,
sat still, and let the wind and the steersman hold her steady.
All day long her sails were filled as she went through the water,
and the sun set, and all the journeying-ways were darkened.

She made the limit, which is of the deep-running Ocean.
There lie the community and city of Kimmerian people,
hidden in fog and cloud, nor does Helios, the radiant
sun, ever break through the dark, to illuminate them with his shining,
neither when he climbs up into the starry heaven,
nor when he wheels to return again from heaven to earth,
but always a glum night is spread over wretched mortals.
Making this point, we ran the ship ashore, and took out
the sheep, and ourselves walked along by the stream of the Ocean
until we came to that place of which Circe had spoken.

There Perimedes and Eurylochos held the victims
fast, and I, drawing from beside my thigh my sharp sword,
dug a pit, of about a cubit in each direction,
and poured it full of drink-offerings for all the dead, first
honey mixed with milk, and the second pouring was sweet wine,
and the third, water, and over it all I sprinkled white barley.
I promised many times to the strengthless heads of the perished
dead, that, returning to Ithaka, I would slaughter a barren
cow, my best, in my palace, and pile the pyre with treasures,

and to Teiresias apart would dedicate an all-black
ram, the one conspicuous in all our sheep-flocks.
Now when with sacrifices and prayers I had so entreated
the hordes of the dead, I took the sheep and cut their throats
over the pit, and the dark-clouding blood ran in, and the souls
of the perished dead gathered to the place, up out of Erebos,
brides, and young unmarried men, and long-suffering elders,
virgins, tender and with the sorrows of young hearts upon them,
and many fighting men killed in battle, stabbed with brazen
spears, still carrying their bloody armor upon them.
These came swarming around my pit from every direction
with inhuman clamor, and green fear took hold of me.
Then I encouraged my companions and told them, taking
the sheep, that were lying by, slaughtered with the cruel bronze,
to skin these, and burn them, and pray to the divinities,
to Hades the powerful, and to revered Persephone,
while I myself, drawing from beside my thigh my sharp sword,
crouched there, and would not let the strengthless heads of the perished
dead draw nearer to the blood, until I had questioned Teiresias.

But first there came the soul of my companion, Elpenor,
for he had not yet been buried under earth of the wide ways,
since we had left his body behind in Circe's palace,
unburied and unwept, with this other errand before us.
I broke into tears at the sight of him, and my heart pitied him,
and so I spoke aloud to him and addressed him in winged words:
'Elpenor, how did you come here beneath the fog and the darkness?
You have come faster on foot than I could in my black ship.'

So I spoke, and he groaned aloud and spoke and answered:
'Son of Laertes and seed of Zeus, resourceful Odysseus,
the evil will of the spirit and the wild wine bewildered me.
I lay down on the roof of Circe's palace, and never thought,
when I went down, to go by way of the long ladder,
but blundered straight off the edge of the roof, so that my neck bone
was broken out of its sockets, and my soul went down to Hades.

But now I pray you, by those you have yet to see, who are not here,
by your wife, and by your father, who reared you when you were little,
and by Telemachos whom you left alone in your palace;
for I know that after you leave this place and the house of Hades
you will put back with your well-made ship to the island, Aiaia;
there at that time, my lord, I ask that you remember me
and do not go, and leave me behind, unwept, unburied,
when you leave, for fear I might become the gods' curse upon you,
but burn me there with all my armor that belongs to me
and heap up a grave mound beside the beach of the gray sea,
for an unhappy man, so that those to come will know of me.
Do this for me, and on top of the grave mound plant the oar
with which I rowed when I was alive and among my companions.'

    So he spoke, and I in turn spoke to him in answer:
'All this, my unhappy friend, I will do for you as you ask me.'

    So we two stood there exchanging our sad words, I on
one side holding my sword over the blood, while opposite
me the phantom of my companion talked long with me.

    Next there came to me the soul of my dead mother,
Antikleia, daughter of great-hearted Autolykos,
whom I had left alive when I went to sacred Ilion.
I broke into tears at the sight of her and my heart pitied her,
but even so, for all my thronging sorrow, I would not
let her draw near the blood until I had questioned Teiresias.

    Now came the soul of Teiresias the Theban, holding
a staff of gold, and he knew who I was, and spoke to me:
'Son of Laertes and seed of Zeus, resourceful Odysseus,
how is it then, unhappy man, you have left the sunlight
and come here, to look on dead men, and this place without pleasure?
Now draw back from the pit, and hold your sharp sword away from me,
so that I can drink of the blood and speak the truth to you.'

    So he spoke, and I, holding away the sword with the silver
nails, pushed it back in the sheath, and the flawless prophet,
after he had drunk of the blood began speaking to me:

'Glorious Odysseus, what you are after is a sweet homecoming.
But the god will make it hard for you. I think you will not
escape the shaker of the earth, who holds a grudge against you
in his heart, and because you blinded his dear son, hates you.
But even so and still you might come back, after much suffering,
if you can contain your own desire, and contain your companions',
at that time when you first put in your well-made vessel
at the island Thrinakia, escaping the sea's blue water,
and there discover pasturing the cattle and the fat sheep
of Helios, who sees all things, and listens to all things.
Then, if you keep your mind on homecoming, and leave these unharmed,
you might all make your way to Ithaka, after much suffering;
but if you do harm them, then I testify to the destruction
of your ship and your companions, but if you yourself get clear
you will come home in bad case, with the loss of all your companions,
in someone else's ship, and find troubles in your household,
insolent men, who will be eating away your livelihood
and courting your godlike wife and offering gifts to win her.
You may punish the violences of these men, when you come home.
But after you have killed these suitors in your own palace,
either by treachery, or openly with the sharp bronze,
then you must take up your well-shaped oar and go on a journey
until you come where men are living who know nothing
of the sea, and who eat food that is not mixed with salt, who never
have known ships whose cheeks are painted purple, who never
have known well-shaped oars, which act for ships as wings do.
And I will tell you a very clear proof, and you can not miss it.
When as you walk some other wayfarer happens to meet you
and says you carry a winnowing-fan on your bright shoulder,
then you must plant your well-shaped oar in the ground, and render
ceremonious sacrifice to the lord Poseidon,
one ram and one bull, and a mounter of sows, a boar pig,
and make your way home again and render holy hecatombs
to the immortal gods who hold the wide heaven, all

of them in order. Death will come to you from the sea, in
some altogether unwarlike way, and it will end you
in the ebbing time of a sleek old age. Your people
about you will be prosperous. All this is true that I tell you.'

Richmond Lattimore, 1965

SAPPHO *(ca. 615–550 B.C.)*

1. "Some there are who say that the fairest thing seen"

Some there are who say that the fairest thing seen
on the black earth is an array of horsemen,
some, men marching, some would say ships, but I say
    she whom one loves best

is the loveliest. Light were the work to make this
plain to all. Since she who surpassed in beauty
all mortality beside, Helen, chose that
    man as the noblest

who destroyed the glory of Troy entirely.
Not the thought of child, nor beloved parents,
was remembered, after the Queen of Cyprus
    won her at first sight.

Since young brides have hearts that can be persuaded
lightly, stirred and shaken by their emotions
as am I, remembering Anaktoria
    who has gone from me

and whose lovely walk and the shining pallor
of her face I would rather see before my
eyes than Lydia's chariots in all their glory
    armored for battle.

2. To a Rival

You will die and be still, never shall be memory left of you
after this, nor regret when you are gone. You have not touched the flowers
of the Muses, and thus shadowy still in the domain of Death
you must drift with a ghost's fluttering wings, one of the darkened dead.

3. "When we lived all as one she adored you as"

When we lived all as one she adored you as
symbol of some divinity,
Arignota, delighted in your dancing.

Now she shines among Lydian women as
into dark when the sun has set
the moon pale handed at last appeareth

making dim all the rest of the stars, and light
spreads afar on the deep, salt sea,
spreading likewise across the flowering cornfields;

and the dew rinses glittering from the sky;
roses spread, and the delicate
antherisk, and the lotus spreads her petals.

So she goes to and fro there, remembering
Atthis and her companion, sick
the tender mind, and the heart with grief is eaten.

4. Epitaph

This is the dust of Timas, who died before she was married
    and whom Persephone's dark chamber accepted instead.
After her death the maidens who were her friends, with sharp iron
    cutting their lovely hair, laid it upon her tomb.

Richmond Lattimore, 1952

SOPHOCLES *(ca. 495–406 B.C.)*

From *Antigone*

CHORUS

Eros, invincible in battle,
Eros, consumer of riches,
who slumbers through the night
on a maiden's soft cheeks,
ranges the furthest seas and visits
lonely huts on the high pastures.
No one escapes—neither immortal gods
nor men whose lives are short as those
of mayflies that live for only a day—
the one you touch is driven mad.

Even just men's thoughts you warp to crime,
stirring conflict between kindred—
between father and son.
But triumphant desire
that shines from the eyes
of the newly-married bride
is stronger than the greatest laws.
Unconquerable Aphrodite
sits among the gods
and plays her games of power.

(*Antigone is brought from the Palace through the double doors by guards.*)

And now I too am overcome
and carried beyond the realm of loyalty and law,
no longer able to hold back my tears
when I see Antigone being led towards
the bridal chamber where she will sleep with Death.

ANTIGONE

Behold me, fellow citizens
of my ancestral land,
walking the last mile, the last road,
seeing the sun's light
which I shall never see again
for the last time.
Hades, the god of death,
who puts us all to sleep,
leads me living to the banks of Acheron.
No wedding songs are sung for me
as I become his bride.

CHORUS

What glory and praise you deserve
as you depart for the cavern of death—
not struck by fatal disease nor
slaughtered in war, but still alive
and of your own free will—you alone
of all mortals will enter Hades.

ANTIGONE

Like that story I heard of our Phrygian guest,
the daughter of Tantalus—of how,
on the peak of Sipylus, she was enclosed
and hedged about, as ivy clings to a wall,
by a stony accretion; and how,
they say, the rain and snow that fall
on the mountaintop erode her form,
and the ceaseless tears
that pour from beneath her brows
become streams down the hills. Like her,
in a rocky cave, the gods lull me to sleep.

CHORUS

But she was a goddess, born of gods
and we are mortal, of mortal stock.
Yet it is a great thing to have it said,
when you die, that your destiny
was equal to that of a god.

ANTIGONE

By the gods of my father I ask:
why do you mock me—
not even waiting until I have gone,
but still here before your eyes?
O city! city!—
you propertied men of the city!
But fountains of Dirce,
and holy groves of Thebes with its many chariots,
you at least can testify how no one laments me,
and by what an aberration of justice
I go to the heaped stones of my prison and unnatural tomb.
What a wretched creature I am—
with nowhere to dwell, neither
among mortals nor corpses,
not the living nor the dead.

CHORUS

Boldly you pressed to the furthest limit,
my child, until you stumbled against
the awesome throne of Justice—as if doomed
to pay the price of your father's sins.

ANTIGONE

Ah! now you touch
on the worst thing of all—

that tripled pity, pain and anguish I feel
at the thought of my father,
the dreadful fate
of the noble house of Labdacus,
and the tainted madness of that marriage bed
where my poor accursed mother slept
incestuously with my father, her own son.
Those were my parents—
already at birth I was doomed
to join them, unmarried, in death.
Brother, your ill-fated wedding
killed us both—though I am yet alive.

CHORUS

Your piety is admirable. But
the man who holds the power
must also be acknowledged.
Stubborn wilfulness destroyed you.

ANTIGONE

No funeral hymns, no marriage songs; unloved,
unwept and wretched, I am led along the ordained path.
Never again shall I, miserable one,
raise my eyes towards the sacred eye
and light of the sun—
no dear friend is here to mourn me
nor weep for my harsh fate.

Ruth Fainlight and Robert J. Littman, 2009

A Chorus from *Oedipus Rex*

ἰὼ γενεαὶ βροτῶν . . .

Alas for the seed of men.

What measure shall I give these generations
That breathe on the void and are void
And exist and do not exist?

Who bears more weight of joy
Than mass of sunlight shifting in images,
Or who shall make his thought stay on
That down time drifts away?

Your splendor is all fallen.

O naked brow of wrath and tears,
O change of Oedipus!
I who saw your days call no man blest—
Your great days like ghosts gone.

That mind was a strong bow.

Deep, how deep you drew it then, hard archer,
At a dim fearful range
And brought dear glory down!

You overcame the stranger—
The virgin with her hooking lion claws—
And though death sang, stood like a tower
To make pale Thebes take heart.

Fortress against our sorrow!

Divine king, giver of laws,
Majestic Oedipus!
No prince in Thebes had ever such renown,
No prince won such grace of power.

And now of all men ever known
Most pitiful is this man's story:
His fortunes are most changed, his state

Fallen to a low slave's
Ground under bitter fate.

O Oedipus, most royal one!
The great door that expelled you to the light
Gave at night—ah, gave night to your glory—
As to the father, to the fathering son.

All understood too late.

How could the queen whom Laïos won,
The garden that he harrowed at his height,
Be silent when that act was done?

But all eyes fail before time's eye,
All actions come to justice there.
Though never willed, though far down the deep past,
Your bed, your dread sirings
Are brought to book at last.

Child by Laïos doomed to die—
Then doomed to lose that fortunate small death—
Would God you never took breath in this air
That with my wailing lips I take to cry!
For I weep the world's outcast.

Blind I was, and cannot tell why;
Asleep, for you had given ease of breath;
A fool, while the false years went by.

Dudley Fitts and Robert Fitzgerald, 1949

Women of Trachis

The *Trachiniae* presents the highest peak of Greek sensibility registered in any of the plays that have come down to us, and is, at the same time, nearest the original form of the God-Dance.

A version for KITASONO KATUE, hoping he will use it on my dear old friend Miscio Ito, or take it to the Minoru if they can be persuaded to add to their repertoire.

PERSONAE

The Day's Air, DAIANEIRA, *daughter of Oineus.*
HERAKLES ZEUSON, *the Solar vitality.*
AKHELOÖS, *a river, symbol of the power of damp and darkness, triform as water, cloud and rain.*
HYLLOS, *son of Herakles and Daysair.*
LIKHAS, *a herald.*
A messenger.
A nurse, or housekeeper, old and tottery, physically smaller than Daysair.
IOLE, *Tomorrow, daughter of Eurytus, a King.*
Captive women.
Girls of Trachis.

DAYSAIR: "No man knows his luck 'til he's dead."
    They've been saying that for a long time
    but it's not true in my case. Mine's soggy.
    Don't have to go to hell to find that out.

    I had a worse scare about getting married than any
    girl in Pleuron, my father's place in Aetolia.
    First came a three-twisted river, Akheloös,
    part bullheaded cloud, he looked like,
    part like a slicky snake with scales on it
    shining, then it would look like a bullheaded man
    with water dripping out of his whiskers, black ones.

    Bed with that! I ask you!

    And Herakles Zeuson got me out of it somehow,
    I don't know how he managed with that wet horror,
    you might find out from some impartial witness
    who could watch without being terrorized.

Looks are my trouble. And that
wasn't the end of trouble.

Herakles never gets sight of his children,
like a farmer who sows a crop and doesn't
look at it again till harvest.
Always away on one assignment or another
            one terror after another,
                  always for someone else.

We been outlawed ever since he kill'd Iphitz,
living here in Trachis with a foreigner,
and nobody knows where he is.

Bitter ache of separation brought on me,
ten months then five, and no news,
bitter childbirth in separation
worried for some awful calamity.
Black trouble may be connected with
                  this memo he left me.

I keep praying it doesn't mean something horrible.

NURSE: If a slave be permitted, milady?
    I've heard you worrying time and again about Herakles . . .
    If I'm not speaking out of my turn, ma'am, you got
    a fine lot of sons here, why not Hyllos
            go look for his father?

    He's coming now. There, hurrying!
    If you felt like to tell him,
                  if. . . .

DAY: See here, son, this slave talks sense,
                  more than some free folks.

HYLLOS: What's she say? Lemme hear.

DAY: No credit to you, that you haven't gone to look for your father.

HYL: I've just heard . . . if it's true.

DAY: Heard what? That he's sitting around somewhere or other.

HYL: Farmed out last year to a woman in Lydia.

DAY: He's capable of anything, if . . .

HYL: Oh, I hear he's got out of *that.*

DAY: Do they say he's alive or dead?

HYL: They *say* he's in Euboea, besieging Eurytusville
       or on the way to it.

DAY: You know he left some sort of forecast
       having to do with that country?

HYL: No, I didn't know that.

DAY: That it would be the end of him, or that when he got
    through with the job, he would live happy ever after.
    It's on the turn of the wheel.
    Don't you want to go and work with him?
    If he wins we're saved,
         if he doesn't we're done for.

HYL: Of course I'll go. I'd have been gone before now
       if I had known.
    I've never worried very much about him
    one way or the other. Luck being with him.
    But now I'll go get the facts.

DAY: Well, get going. A bit late, but a good job's worth a bonus.

KHOROS (*accompaniment strings, mainly cellos*):

    PHOEBUS, Phoebus, ere thou slay   (*Str.* 1)
    and lay flaked Night upon her blazing pyre,

Say, ere the last star-shimmer is run:
Where lies Alkmene's son, apart from me?
Aye, thou art keen, as is the lightning blaze,
Land way, sea ways,
    in these some slit hath he
found to escape thy scrutiny?

DAYSAIR is left alone,   (*Ant.* 1)
            so sorry a bird,
For whom, afore, so many suitors tried.
And shall I ask what thing is heart's desire,
Or how love fall to sleep with tearless eye,
So worn by fear away, of dangerous road,
A manless bride to mourn in vacant room,
Expecting ever the worse,
            of dooms to come?

NORTH WIND or South, so bloweth tireless   (*Str.* 2)
wave over wave to flood.
Cretan of Cadmus' blood, Orcus' shafts err not.
What home hast 'ou now,
            an some God stir not?

PARDON if I reprove thee, Lady,   (*Ant.* 2)
To save thee false hopes delayed.
Thinkst thou that man who dies,
Shall from King Chronos take
            unvaried happiness?
Nor yet's all pain.

(*drums, quietly added to music*)

The shifty Night delays not,
Nor fates of men, nor yet rich goods and spoil.
Be swift to enjoy, what thou art swift to lose.
Let not the Queen choose despair.

Hath Zeus no eye (who saith it?)
    watching his progeny?

DAY: You've found out, I suppose, and want to help me stop worrying.
Hope you'll never go through enough to understand how.
One grows up, gets fed. "Don't get sun-burnt."
"Don't get wet in the rain. Keep out of draughts,"
that's a girl's life till she's married.
Gets her assignment at night: something to think about,
that is: worry about her man and the children.
You've seen my load, while it's been going on.
Well, here's another to wail about:
before King Herakles rushed off the last time,
he left an old slab of wood with sign writing on it.
Never could get a word out of him about it before,
for all the rough jobs he went out on,
he just couldn't bear to speak of it,
talked as if he were going to work, not to his funeral.
Now? not a bit of it:
all about my marriage property,
what land each of the children was to get from the entail.
Time to work out in three months,
either he would be dead, or come back and spend
the rest of his life without trouble,
all fixed by the gods, end of Herakles' labours,
as stated
        under an old beech-tree in Dodona
where a pair of doves tell you.
Time up,
       see how much truth was in it.
I started from a sound sleep, shaking,
in terror I should have to live on
robbed of the best man ever born.

KHO: Hush. Here comes a man with a wreath on.
               That means good news

MESSENGER: Queen Daysair,
    let me be the first to calm your anxiety.
    Alkemene's son is alive, and has won,
    and is carrying the spoils to the gods of our country.

DAY: What are you talking about?

MES: You'll soon see him, the man you want,
    crowned with Victory. He's looking splendid.

DAY: You get this from some local bloke, or a foreigner?

MES: There in the summer pastures
    Likhas the herald is telling a whole crowd of people.
    I came on ahead, thought I might get
           a tip for the news.

DAY: Why doesn't he come himself, if there's anything to it?

MES: He can't for the crowd, ma'am.
    They're all jammed round him
           wanting the details.
    He can't move a step. They want it.
    But you'll see him here pretty soon.

DAY: Zeus in the long grass of Oeta,
    joy hast Thou given me with its season.

    Tune up, you there, you women, inside
    and out here.
           I had given up hope.
    Never thought I would see it.
    Let's sing and be happy.

KHOROS: APOLLO
                    and Artemis, analolu
                                        Artemis,
          Analolu,
          Sun-bright Apollo, Saviour Apollo,
                                    analolu,
          Artemis,
          Sylvan Artemis,
          Swift-arrowed Artemis, analolu
          By the hearth-stone
                              brides to be
          Shout in male company:
                              APOLLO EUPHARETRON.
          Sylvan Artemis,
                          torch-lit Artemis
          With thy Ortygian girls,
                              Analolu
          Artemis,
                    Io Zagreus,
          Join now, join with us
                              when the great stag is slain,
          Lord of hearts, Artemis,
          Ivied Zagreus,
                          Analolu,
          Dancing maid and man,
          Lady or Bacchanal
                          dancing toe to toe
          By night,
          By light shall show
                          analolu
                              Paian.

DAY: Yes, my dear girls, I make out the crowd
      and finally and at last and at leisure

the herald, to be received,

                and,

if his news is good,

           welcomed.

LIKHAS: That it is, Milady,

           and worth hearing,

and paying for.

DAY: Is Herakles alive?

LIKH: Sound in wind and limb, mind and body.

DAY: Where? In Greece or in some damn foreign desert?

LIKH: On the cliff of Euboea,
    setting up altars to Zeus Kaenean.

DAY: A vow, or to stave off evil?

LIKH: A vow, made when he went to conquer
        these women's country.

DAY: Good God! What are these poor devils?
        Where do they come from?

LIKH: These are the ones he picked for the gods (and himself)
        when he sacked Eurytus.

DAY: And he's been waiting all this time
        to conquer a city?

LIKH: No, most of the time he was in Lydia,
    that's what he says, sold into bondage,
    and you can't blame it on anyone except Zeus.
    Says he was in servitude to the barbarian Omphale
        (that's what he says).
    So disgusted he swore to get back at the man who'd double-crossed him;
    chuck him and his whole house into slavery,

wife, child and the lot of 'em.
Swore in foreign troops and went to Eurytus' place
               as he blamed it all on Eurytus.
Well, he was drunk, and he killed a man,
threw him off a cliff, and was punished.
Zeus wouldn't stand it,
               and Herakles blamed it on 'Rytus
who had insulted him
               and had him thrown out of the dining hall,
which was how he came to be on the cliff
               up at Tirunth
when Iphytz was there hunting lost horses,
and he killed him, and so on,
and Zeus wouldn't stand it.
So when he'd done his time, he got a gang together
and sacked 'Rytus' city.
               These are the captives.
That's what comes of big talk.
Said Herakles couldn't shoot as well as his kids, 'Rytus's.
Hell's full of big talkers.
He'll be along as soon as he's finished
               the celebration. All very fine—
Sacrifice, captives.
               C'est très beau.

KHO: Yes, isn't it, Your Majesty.
    Everything will now be all right.

DAY: If it lasts, yes. Looks all right, why can't I feel easy about it?
    My luck runs with his. I wonder.
    I'm sorry for these poor girls, in a strange country,
    orphans, slaves,
    I hope no child of mine ever—
               or that I don't live to see it.

(to IOLE)

> You look as if you were taking it worse
> > than any of the others.
> Girl, wife, young; no, you can't have been
> married yet. And good family.
>
> Who is she, Likhas?
> I'm sorrier for her than for the rest of them.
> She seems to feel it.

LIKH: How do I know? She might be top drawer,
> > why ask me?

DAY: Royal? Had Eurytus a daughter?

LIKH: I dunno. I haven't asked her.

DAY: Didn't anyone tell you?

LIKH: I had plenty else to do, without asking that kind of questions.

DAY *(to* IOLE):
> Well then, you tell me.
> What's happened? Who are you?

LIKH: It'll be a change if she does,
> hasn't uttered a pip-squeak
> > since she came down from the windy country.
> Tears, tears, tears,
> > but it's excusable,
> she's had pretty bad luck.

DAY: Let her alone, let her go in,
> I don't want to add to her troubles,
> > she's had enough.
>
> Everybody in!

Have to hurry to get things in order.

[*Exeunt Likhas and captives.*]

MESSENGER: 'Arf a mo' Ma'am! Better find out
  what you're taking in there. I know
        a bit more about that.

DAY: What's this? What are you stopping me for?

MES: Jus' lis'en a bit,
  if what I told you before was worth hearing . . .

DAY: Shall I call 'em back?

MES: We're enough. There's enough of us here.

DAY: They're all gone. Don't talk riddles.

MES: That fellow was lying, one time or the other,
        one heck of a messenger!

DAY: Put it on the line, what do you know?
        Get it out clearly.

MES: All started when he had a letch for the girl, and when her
  pro-eh-Genitor 'Rytus wouldn't let him put her to bed on the Q.T.
  Wasn't about Iphytz or Omphale
  he sacked the town, and killed 'Rytus to get her.
  He's not bringin' her here as a slave. Too het up.
  So I thought I would be telling Your Majesty,
  this is what Likhas was saying,
        and plenty of Trachinians heard him.
  I'm sorry to worry you. But the facts . . .

DAY: What have I done, what have I done!
  Just a nobody, and he took oath that she was.
        What a mess.

MES: She's somebody all right, all right.

Name's Iole, and 'Rytus her father.
And Likhas hadn't found that out
                    'cause he hadn't troubled to ask her.

KHO: To hell with all double-crossers,
                    they are the last of all dirtiness.

DAY: What shall . . . what shall . . . my dear girls,
                    what, what . . . . .

MES: You might start by questioning Likhas,
        scare the lights out of him, and he might tell you.

DAY: I'll do that. You're talking sense.

MES: Want me to go, or . . ?

DAY: You stay here. There he comes, without being asked.

LIKH: What do you want me to tell Herakles, Madam?
                    I'm leaving.

DAY: Not in quite such a hurry. You were
                    in no hurry to get here.
        Let's have a little conversation.

LIKH: Yours to command, Ma'am.

DAY: Have you any respect for the truth?

LIKH: So help me God. Nothing but . . .

DAY: Who was that woman you brought here?

LIKH: I don't know about her family, she comes from Euboea.

MES: Look at here. You know who this is?

LIKH: Who are you?

MES: Don't mind that.
        Answer my question, if you've got sense enough.

LIKH: Her most Gracious Majesty, Queen of Herakles,
    Daughter of Oineus, Daysair.

MES: Right for once! She's your Queen.

LIKH: To whom my most faithful service . . .

MES: Service, duty, yes duty, my dicky-bird
    and if you don't . . .

LIKH: What's this screw-ball?
                                If I don't. . . .

MES: Do your duty, do you get that?
                    It sounds fairly clear.

LIKH: Silly to stop for this nonsense, I'm off.

MES: One little question.

LIKH: Get on with it. Not the quiet type, are you?

MES: That girl, you know which one,
                    you took into the house?

LIKH: What about her?

MES: Don't know her by sight, eh, you don't?
    and you said she was 'Rytus's daughter,
                    the Princess Iole.

LIKH: Nobody ever heard me say anything of the sort.

MES: Oh yes they did. Plenty of us, us Trachinians,
                    a whole agora heard it.

LIKH: Just talk, a mere rumour.

MES: Just an opinion? eh? rumour? eh?
    And you swore pink they were bringing her
                    to be Herakles' wife.

LIKH: Wife? Good God, Your dear Majesty,
       who is this outsider?

MES: Just somebody heard you talking.
     Not the Lydian army, and its queen.
     He sacked a whole town cause he liked the look in her eyes. Took a fancy.

LIKH: Beg to differ, Your Majesty. No use
       bothering with this screw-ball.

DAY: THUNDER of God! By the black vale of Oeta,
     don't weasel to me.
                       And
                             besides
     you're not going to tell it to a bad woman,
     or to one who doesn't know that men
     just naturally don't want the same thing all the time.
     How's any slugger going to stop Love with his hands?
     That's a nice way to think of it?
     He starts off the gods, as he fancies.
     Me, am I going to win at it?
     Be perfectly silly to blame the man while he's crazy,
                       or the girl they're blaming.
     No shame to me .... no harm.
     It's not that at all. BUT ....
                       if he taught you to lie,
     the lesson you learned is
                             not
                                   a nice one.
     And if you taught yourself to lie,
                       thinking some good would come of it,
                       you saw cross-eyed.
     You come out with the truth, the whole
     truth. Now.
     It's no compliment to call a free man a liar,

when a free man is called a liar it's no pretty compliment,
and it'll all come out anyhow,

       how are you going to hide it?
Plenty of people heard you, and will certainly tell me.
And if you think . . . not nice to be in terror of me . . .
not to find out, would pain me, mightn't it?
And what's so awful to know?

       That man Herakles! hasn't he
had plenty of others on me?
Ever driven me to nag him, or blame him?
And if he was overflowing with passion for her,
will I but pity her greatly, and the more.
Her looks have ruin'd her life,

       and ruin'd the land of her fathers,
not knowing, wretched,

       didn't know what it was all about.
All this gone under the wind.
I'm telling you: do dirt to others but . . . .

       Don't weasel to me.

KHO: Better do as she says. She won't blame you, in the long run,
       and I will be grateful.

LIKH: Oh Majesty, Your Dear Majesty, I see you understand
       that human beings are human,
I'll tell the truth, I won't hold back on you.
It's as that chap there says it was.
Herakles was hit by a tremendous passion,
it swept over him,

       and he seized all Oechalia
and gave it over to pillage, her fatherland,
but I'll say this much for him,
he never denied it, or told me to conceal it.
It was me, your Majesty, who was afraid it would pain you,

me who did wrong, eh, if, eh, you
                think it was wrong of me,
and now you know all of it, for his sake
and for your sake, both of your sakes together,
do put up with the girl.
He beat all the champions into subjection
and now Eros throws him down with all his inferiors.

DAY: Yes, We think that's what's to be done
                and just that way.
This imported trouble won't be got rid of
by a losing fight versus the gods.
Let's go in, and I'll get you something for Herakles
and a note to take with it.
Got to send him something suitable, in return.
Wouldn't be right for you to go back
without something, having come with all this.

KHOROS: KUPRIS bears trophies away.   (*Str.*)
        Kronos' Son, Dis and Poseidon,
        There is no one
                shaker unshaken.
        Into dust go they all.
        Neath Her they must
                give way.

        TWO gods fought for a girl,   (*Ant.*)
        Battle and dust!
        Might of a River with horns
                crashing.
        Four bulls together
                Shall no man tether,
        Akheloös neither,
                lashing through Oneudai.

As bow is bent
                    the Theban Cub,
Bacchus' own, spiked is his club,
HE is God's Son.
                    Hurled to one bed,
Might of waters like a charge of bulls crashing.
Get a dowsing rod.
Kupris decides
To whom brides
                    fall.

ROCK and wrack,
Horns into back,
Slug, grunt and groan,
                    Grip through to bone.
Crash and thud
Bows against blood
                    Grip and grind
                    Bull's head and horn.
BUT the wide-eyed girl on the hill,
Out of it all,
                    frail,
Who shall have her?
To stave her and prove her,
Cowless calf lost,
Hurtled away,
                    prized for a day?

[*Music in this Khoros fifes, kettle drums, oboes, etc., with flute solo or clarinet.*]

DAY (*reenters*):   Well, my dears,
    while that outsider is inside
    chatting with the little victims of bow and spear
                    before he pushes off,
    let's figure out how we are to manage this cohabitation with

this virgin who isn't one any longer,
    'cause she's been yoked.
Too much cargo, contraband,
    but keep my mind afloat somehow.
"Double yoke
Under one cloak,"
and I said he was so kind and dependable.
What I get for keeping house
    all this time.
But I can't stay mad at him long,
    I know what's got into him,
And yet . . .
    the two of us,
My husband, her man, the new girl's man,
    and she's young.
And:
    "E'en from fond eyes, olde flowers are cast away."
And
    it's not nice for a woman to be too crotchety,
the ones with nice minds are not peevish.
And
    may be there's a way out.
Nessus, that old ruffian with hair on his chest,
long ago, I was a green girl then,
and he gave me a little present
which I've kept stored away in a brass pot
    all this time.
He was dying from loss of blood
    there at the ferry over Evenus
where it's too deep to ford.
And he had me up on his shoulders
in mid passage
    and got too fresh with his hands.
I let out a shriek, and: WHIZZ ! !

as he turned
Zeuson had an arrow into his lung up to the feathers.
Before he passed out he said:
        "As you're old Oineus' daughter,
I'll give you what I've earned by all this ferrying.
Scrape the drying blood from my wound
where the Hydra's blood tipped that arrow,
        Lernaean Hydra,
and you'll have a love charm so strong
that Herakles will never look at another woman
        or want her more than you."

Well, my dears, I been thinking 'bout that,
I've kept the stuff since his death
        carefully in a cool dark place,
and I've swobbed this jacket with it,
just as the Centaur told me,
        not like a philtre,
I don't believe it's too great a risk.

Deal with that young woman somehow,
        unless you think I am foolish.

KHO: Don't seem a bad idea, if
        you think it will work.

DAY: No absolute guarantee, of course,
        but you'll never tell till you try.

KHO: Nope, no proof without data,
        no proof without experiment.

DAY: There he is. Be gone soon,
  keep quiet about this for a bit,
        what they don't know won't hurt us.
  You can get away with a good deal in the dark.

LIKH: I have considerably overstayed my leave, Madame d'Oineus.
　　Tell me, please, just what I've to do.

DAY: While you've been in there talking to the girls,
　　I've wrapped up this present for Herakles,
　　a jacket I made him myself,
　　nobody else is to put it on first,
　　he's not to leave it in the sun
　　or near the fire inside the holy hedge
　　until he stand before the gods at the altar
　　for killing the bulls.
　　I vowed that if I should ever see him
　　safe home, or hear he had come,
　　I would make him a proper chiton
　　to wear when he sacrificed in the god's presence.
　　The packet is sealed with my signet
　　which he will recognize.
　　　　　　Now you may go, and
　　remember a messenger's first job is
　　to do what he's told, not more, not less,
　　but just what he is told.
　　　　　　Do that, and we'll both be grateful.

LIKH: Properly trained in Hermes' messenger-service, Ma'am,
　　say I'm not, if I slip up on this
　　or don't take him the box, as is,
　　and your message exactly.

DAY: Then go. You know how things are going inside.

LIKH: Yes. I'll say: everything under control.

DAY: And that I'm being nice to the visitor,
　　　　　　you've seen that.

LIKH: And I was most awfully surprised
　　　　　　and cheered by it.

DAY (*reveuse*):   Anything more? No.

    Mustn't say how much I want him
        until I know he's going to want me.

KHOROS: SAFE the port, rocky the narrows,   (*Str.* 1)
    Streams warm to a glaze on Oeta's hill,
    Malis' pool and Dian's beach
    Neath her golden-shafted arrows
        Ye who live here and disdeign
        All greek towns less than the Pelean,

(*fifes, flute & grosse caisse*)
    SOON shall hear the skirl and din   (*Ant.* 1)
    Of flutes' loud cackle shrill return,
    Dear to Holy Muses as
    Phoebus' lyre ever was. From the valours of his wars
    Comes now the God, Alkmene's son
    Bearing battle booty home.

(*clarinette, bassoon*)
    TWELVE moons passing,   (*Str.* 2)
        night long, and day.
    Exile, exile
    Knowing never, to come? to stay?
    Tears, tears, till grief
    Hath wrecked her heart away,
    Ere mad Mars should end him
        his working day.

(*cello, low register*)
    TO PORT, to port.   (*Ant.* 2)
    Boat is still now;
    The many oars move not.
        By island shrine ere he come to the town
    Day long, day long

If the charm of the gown prove not?
'Tis dipped, aye in the unguent
drenched through it, in every fold.
Told, told,
in all as she had been told.

[DAYSAIR *enters now in the tragic mask.*]

DAY: Something's gone wrong, my dears, awfully,
    terribly wrong, and I'm scared.

KHO: Why, Daysair Oineus, what do you mean?

DAY: I don't know, I dunno, I hoped
                    and I don't hope.
    Something awful will come of it.

KHO: You don't mean your present to Herakles?

DAY: Exactly. People oughtn't to rush into
    what they don't understand.

KHO: Tell us what you're afraid of.

DAY: Something too creepy's just happened.
    That thick wad of white sheep's wool
    that I used to daub the jacket, just disappeared.
    Nobody touched it. Seemed to corrode of itself.
    Ate itself up, there on the floor-stones.
    When that brute of a Centaur
    was in agony from the arrow in his lung,
    he told me—and I can remember it
    as if it were engraved on a brass plate—
    and I did just what he told me: kept it cool,
    away from the fire and sunlight, in a cupboard
    until time to use it, which I did inside,
    and nobody saw me take it out of the kettle

with wool I'd pulled out of a fleece from our own sheep
and put it inside the box that you saw.

But just now, something you wouldn't believe,
perfectly inexplicable, I found it all flaming
there in the sunlight. It had got warm
and just crumbled away, like sawdust
where somebody had been sawing a board,
but mixed up with bubbles
like the fat scum that slops over from the wine-press.
I'm out of my mind with worry and misery.
I've done something awful.
Why should that dying brute want to do me a favour?
He was dying on my account.
Wanted to hit back at his killer.
And I've found out what he was up to,
and it's too late.
I'm to murder him, damn it, fate.
I know that arrow hurt even Chiron
                and he was a demigod—
black blood from the death arrow,
                would kill any wild animal.
If he dies, if he's caught,
                I'll die too.
No decent woman would live after that horror.

KHO: Don't give up yet.
    There's danger. But it mayn't necessarily happen.

DAY: There's no hope for those who have done wrong.

KHO: But if you didn't mean it, they won't
    blame you as much as all that.

DAY: Talk that way if you're not involved,
    not if you've got the weight of it on you.

KHO: Better wait to hear what your son's got to say.
      There he is to tell you, himself;
      he went to look for his father.

HYL: Damn you, I wish you were dead,
      or no mother, anyhow, or at any rate not mine.

DAY: What's got into you, son,
                    why do . . .

HYL: You've murdered your man, my father,
                    and you did it today.

DAY: What a thing to say. Oh, oh.

HYL: Well you've done it, and finished it,
      and what's done can't be undone.

DAY: How can you say this! Me! The most loathsome crime known?

HYL: I saw it myself, the way he suffered.
                    This is no idle rumour.

DAY: Where did you find him? You were with him?

HYL: You'll hear it. You've got to hear all of it.
      He sacked Eurytus' city,
                    you've heard of that place,
      and was coming home with the spoils,
      at the top headland of Euboea
      where the sea swashes in on both sides,
      at Kenaion, facing the North.
      He orientated the altars, to the gods,
                    our own.
      Fixed the lay-out, cutting the leaves.
      And I was glad to get the first sight of him
      starting to kill all those bulls.
      Then along comes Likhas the family herald

with that present, that marvelous peplon.
And he put it on, like as you'd said,
and started on the first dozen bulls,
going on to kill the whole hundred, hecatomb.
And the poor devil, at the start,
                  was so cheerful about it,
seemed pleased with his vestments.
Made the prayer, but
                  as the flame went up from the Holy Orgy,
bloody and from the fat oak logs,
sweat broke from his skin,
the shirt stuck to him, like it was glued,
shrinking in on all of his joints
as if made by someone who knew how to do it.
Gnawing into his bones, it seemed to be,
dirty snake poison gave him convulsions,
seemed like it was biting with hate.
And he howled for the miserable Likhas
                  who wasn't guilty. You were.
To know who'd hatched the shirt trick.
And Likhas said he had brought it as it was
                  fixed up and given him.

Then the stuff got another worse grip on him
and he grabbed Likhas by the foot,
                  twisting his ankle,
and threw him out off onto a boulder
                  that stuck up out of the breakers.
Hair! Brains came out of the skull
                  mixed with blood.
The whole crowd groaned:
one dead, another stark raving.
Nobody dared to come near him. There he was
on the ground roaring, or groaning when

he reared part way up, and the rocks echoing
from Locris to Euboea,

        between the crags and the sea-cliffs.
Till he was clean worn out, writhing on the ground,
moaning, and cursing his marriage bed,
cursing you, and that he'd been fool enough

        to get you from Oineus
to ruin his life. The one woman.

Then with his eyes screwed up from the smoke

        that came out of him
and tears running down, he caught sight of me
and called for me:

        "Don't try to keep out of this,
even if you have to die with me.

        Get me out of here
to somewhere, anywhere, where no one can see me.
Get me out of here, quick. I don't want to die here."

        That's what he told me.

So we put him into the hollow of the boat
and brought him to the mainland,
hardly any more noise coming out of him

        but still in convulsions.
You'll see him pretty soon,

        living or dead.

That, my dear mother, is what you have thought up

        to do to my father,
Hell take you, and the Furies, and do you right.
Justice, eh, Justice, if . . .

        lot of justice you had for me!
You spewed it out when you killed

        the best man on earth,
what you see henceforth will be of a different kind.

K H O : Why does she go so quietly?

                Has she no answer?

H Y L : Let her go. And a nice wind take her far enough

            . . . out of sight,

and another label to keep up her maternal swank,

fine mother she is, let her de-part

                in peace . . .

and get some of the pleasure she has given my father.

K H O R O S (*low cello merely sustaining the voice*):

   OYEZ: (*Str.* 1)

   Things foretold and forecast:

   Toil and moil.

   God's Son from turmoil shall

   —when twelve seed-crops be past—

   be loosed with the last,

                his own.

   Twining together, godword found good,

   Spoken of old,

            as the wind blew, truth's in the flood.

   We and his brood see in swift combine,

           here and at last that:

   Amid the dead is no servitude

           nor do they labour.

(*contrabassi & drums muffled*)

   LO, beneath deadly cloud   (*Ant.* 1)

   Fate and the Centaur's curse, black venom spread,

   Dank Hydra's blood

   Boils now through every vein, goad after goad

   from spotted snake to pierce the holy side,

   nor shall he last to see a new day's light,

Black shaggy night descends
                    as Nessus bade.

WHAT MOURNFUL case   (*Str. 2*)
                    who feared great ills to come,
New haste in mating threatening her home,
Who hark'd to reason in a foreign voice
Entangling her in ravage out of choice.
Tears green the cheek with bright dews pouring down;
Who mourns apart, alone
Oncoming swiftness in o'erlowering fate
To show what wreck is nested in deceit.

LET the tears flow.   (*Ant. 2*)
                    Ne'er had bright Herakles in his shining
Need of pity till now
                    whom fell disease burns out.
How swift on Oechal's height
                    to take a bride.
Black pointed shaft that shielded her in flight,
Attest
That
Kupris stood by and never said a word,
Who now flares here the contriver
manifest . . .
and indifferent.

[*The dea ex machina, hidden behind a gray gauze in her niche, is lit up
strongly so that the gauze is transparent. The apparition is fairly sudden,
the fade-out slightly slower: the audience is almost in doubt that she has
appeared.*]

½ KHO: Am I cracked, or did I hear someone weeping?
    In the hall?
                    Did you hear it?

2ND ½ KHO: Not a muttering, but someone in trouble,
                            wailing,
          started again inside there.

[*Enter* NURSE.]

½ KHO: Look,
          look at the old woman's face. Something awful,
          it's all twisted up.

NUR: Children, children,
          no end to the troubles from sending
                            that present to Herakles.

KHO: More, you mean more?

NUR: She's gone . . . . Daysair,
          The last road of all roads
                            . . . without walking.

KHO: What! Dead?

NUR: That's all. You heard me.

KHO: You mean the poor girl is dead?

NUR: Yes, for the second time. Yes.

KHO: Poor thing.   How awful.   But how . . .
          How is she dead?

NUR: In the most violent . . .

KHO: But how, say how, woman.
          How did it happen?

NUR: Did it herself,
          ripped herself open.

KHO: But she crazy? What did she do it with?
          How did she do it all by herself?

Dying one after another.

NUR: Got hold of a sword, a roaring big sword.
    And a sharp one.

KHO: But did you see it, you fool,
    see this outrage?

NUR: Saw it. I wasn't far off.

KHO: What? How? Go on and tell us.

NUR: Did it herself. With her hands.

KHO: But what do you mean?

NUR: Plain fact. What you can see for yourself.

KHO: That new girl's doin' it.
    I'll say she's effective.
    Bride is she, and a fury. Holy Erinyes!

NUR: And then some. You'd feel it more
    if you'd seen it near to.

KHO: But has a woman got the strength in her hands?
    And to stand it?

NUR: Terrible, you can believe me. She came in alone
    and saw the boy in the hall preparing the hearse-litter
    to fetch back his father.
    She hid herself down back of the altar,
    sank down there groaning because her brood had deserted her.

    Then pitifully stroking[1] the things she had used before,

1. Two thousand years later the Minoru had developed a technique which permitted the direct presentation of such shades by symbolic gesture. In Sophokles' time it had to be left to narration.

went wandering through the best rooms—
didn't know I could see her, from a sort of kink in the wall—
drawing her hands over the things she was used to.

Then came on one of the maids whom she liked,
and with the look of doom on her
cried to her daemon, that she was more childless
than any woman. Then stopped. And of a sudden
ran into Herakles' bed room, and threw her cloak
onto Herakles' bed, spread it out like a coverpane,
then threw herself onto it and lay there quiet
for a moment as if asleep.
Choking with tears, then: "Bride's-bed,
good-bye my bride's-bed, never again
folded together!"

And she ripped the dress all off her left side
and the gold clasp with it.

I ran for Hyllos, but she was too quick,
she had jammed a sword side-ways
through her liver into the heart, when we got there,
two-edged.

      The boy screamed
and blamed himself for having driven her to it.
Father, mother, all in one day.
He'd found out that she'd only done what
that animal told her,
          hadn't meant any harm.
Too pitiful he was. Sobbing and holding her in his arms.

You can't count on anything for tomorrow,
got to wait till today is over.

KHOROS (*declaimed*):   (*Str.* 1)

TORN between griefs, which grief shall I lament,
which first? Which last, in heavy argument?
One wretchedness to me in double load.

DEATH'S in the house,   (*Ant.* 1)
                    and death comes by the road.

(*sung*)   (*Str.* 2)

THAT WIND might bear away my grief and me,
Sprung from the hearth-stone, let it bear me away.
God's Son is dead,
                    that was so brave and strong,
And I am craven to behold such death
                    Swift on the eye,
Pain hard to uproot,
                    and this so vast
A splendour of ruin.
                    THAT NOW is here.   (*Ant.* 2)
As Progne shrill upon the weeping air,
'tis no great sound.
                    These strangers lift him home,
with shuffling feet, and love that keeps them still.
The great weight silent
                    for no man can say
If sleep but feign
                    or Death reign instantly.

HERAKLES (*in the mask of divine agony*):
    Holy Kanea, where they build holy altars,
    done yourself proud, you have,
    nice return for a sacrifice:
                    messing me up.
    I could have done without these advantages
    And the spectacle of madness in flower,

incurable, oh yes.
Get some one to make a song for it,
Or some chiropractor to cure it.
A dirty pest,
        take God a'mighty to cure it and
I'd be surprised to see Him
        coming this far . . .

(*to the others*)

Ahj!
Get away,
let me lie quiet, for the last time
aaah. What you doin' trying to turn me over,
let me alone. Blast it.
Bloody crime to start it again,
        sticks to me.
It's coming back.
You greeks are the dirtiest,
        damn you, if you are greeks at all,
where do you come from?
What I've done on sea, and clearing out thickets,
killing wild animals.
And now I'm in torture, no one to finish it off
with fire, or with a knife,
        or do ANYthing useful,
or even let me alone.

If only someone would lop my head off
and get me out of this loathsome existence,
  Aaahj.

OLD MAN: Here, you're his son, and I ain't strong enough
    to lift him.
        Give a hand,
You could do more for him than I can.

HYL: Right, but he's passed out from pain.
    Inside or out here,

                he's dying on me.

    God's will.

HER: Boy, where are you? Hoist me up

                and hang on. What rotten luck!

    It keeps jumping. This beastly pain,

    taken all the fight out of me.

                I can't get at it.

    Pallas Athene! there goes that ache again.

    Oooh boy, have some pity on the father that made you,

    pull out something with an edge on it,

    and get it in here

(with gesture; the exact spot)
(low cellos, contrabassi, muffled drum in gaps between the phrases)

    and get it in here

                under my collar bone.

    Your mother's to blame for this.

    Damn'd atheist, that's what she is.

    And I wish her the same.

(pause, then sotto voce)

    Brother of God, Sweet Hell, be decent.

    Let me lie down and rest.

    Swift-feathered Death, that are the end of shame.

KHO: Scares me to hear him.

                And when you think what he was.

HER: Many and hot, and that's not just talking,

    my own hands, and my own back doing the dirty work.

    But God's bitch never put one like this over on me,

    nor that grump Rustheus either.

And now Miss Oineus
with her pretty little shifty eyes
                    m'la calata,
has done me to beat all the furies,
got me into a snarl, clamped this net onto me
                and she wove it.
It sticks to my sides and
                has gnawed through to my furtherest in'nards.
And now it's stopped the green blood,
got into the lungs and dries up the tubes along with them,
tears up all the rest of me.
Holds me down, like in fetters. I can't explain it.
No gang of plainsmen with spears,
                no army of giants come up out of the earth,
no wild beast was strong enough. Nor Greeks,
nor foreigners whose countries I had cleaned up,
but a pindling female did it,
                not even a man with balls.
Alone and without a sword.

Boy, you start showing whose son you are. I.e. mine,
and as for the highly revered title to motherhood,
you get that producer out of her house
and hand her over to me. We'll see whether
you feel worse watching me rot or
seeing her cut up and brought to justice.

Go, pick up your courage. Get going and
                have mercy on me
or pity, that's it: pity. Me blubbering like a flapper,
no man ever saw me taken like this before
or said I groaned over my troubles,
now I find out I'm a sissy. Come here. Nearer,
see what your father is brought to.

(he throws off the sheet covering him)

Without the wrappings,
look at it, all of you,
ever see a body in this condition?
Gosh!
That's a death-rattle again. Disgraceful.
Got me here on the side again, eating through me.
Can't seem to get rid of it.
Lord of Hell, take me.
Thundering Lord God, if you've got a crash-rattle,
throw it.
God our father of Thunder.
There it is gnawing again,
budding, blossoming.
OH my hand, my hands,
back, chest, my lovely arms,
what you used to be. That lion that was killing off
the Newman cattle-men, the Hydra in Lerna
and those unsociable bardots, half man and half horse,
the whole gang of them all together
arrogant, lawless, surpassing strong,
and the Eurymanthian animal, and that three-headed pup
from Hell down under, the Echidna's nursling
brought up by an out-size viper,
and the dragon-guard of the golden apples
at the end of the world.
And a great lot of other work,
and nobody took any prizes away from me.
No joints, no strength in 'em,
all torn to pieces.
This blind calamity,
and my mother was a notable woman
and my father in heaven, Zeus, mid the stars.

That's what they say.

But I tell you this much. I can't even crawl,
but bring her here and I'll learn her,
I'll make her a lesson: Alive or dead how I
                pay people for dirty work.

KHO: Poor Greece, you can see troubles coming
                if you let such a man down.

HYL: You seem to expect me to answer.
        You're quiet, as if expecting an answer.
        Now if I may ask you for justice,
        and tell you how useless it is to want to break her.

HER: Say what you've got to say, and get it over with.
        I'm too sick to be pestered with double-talk and nuances.

HYL: It's about mother's mistake.
                What's happened. She didn't mean it.

HER: Well of all the dirtiest . . .
        Your bloody murdering mother
        and you dare to mention her
                in my earshot!

HYL: It's about mother's mistake.

HER: No, I dare say past crimes ought to be—

HYL: And you'll mention what's happened today.

HER: Speak up. But be careful,
                it won't show your breeding.

HYL: Well, she's dead. Just been killed.

HER: By whom?
                That's a bad sign.

HYL: She did it.

HER: And cheated me out of the chance.

HYL: If you knew all the facts, you'd quit being angry.

HER: Thazza good tough start. Give.

HYL: She just didn't mean any harm. She meant well.

HER: You louse! Meant well by killing your father?

HYL: An aphrodisiac. Thought it would
     get you back, and went wrong, when she
     saw the new wife in the house.

HER: The Trachinians got witch-doctors that good?

HYL: Nessus told her a long time ago
     that the philtre would start that sort of letch.

HER: Misery. I'm going out
     and my light's gone.
                              The black out!
     I understand perfectly well
     where things have got to . . . Go, son,
     call all my seed and their kindred,
     and Alkmene, ill-starred for the empty name
     of the Godhead, my mother,
     so they can get my last report
     of the oracles, as I know them.

HYL: Your mother is at Tiryns out of reach
     and took some of the children with her.
     Others are in Thebes-burg, I'll round up
     the near ones, if that's O.K.,
     and they'll do what you tell them.

HER: Listen first, and show what you're made of,

my stock. My father told me long ago
that no living man should kill me,
but that someone from hell would, and
that brute of a Centaur has done it.
The dead beast kills the living me.
And that fits another odd forecast
breathed out at the Selloi's oak—
Those fellows rough it,
      sleep on the ground, up in the hills there.
I heard it and wrote it down
      under my Father's tree.
Time lives, and it's going on now.
I am released from trouble.

I thought it meant life in comfort.
It doesn't. It means that I die.
For amid the dead there is no work in service.
Come at it that way, my boy, what
SPLENDOUR,
      IT ALL COHERES.[2]

[*He turns his face from the audience, then sits erect, facing them without the mask of agony; the revealed make-up is that of solar serenity. The hair golden and as electrified as possible.*]

But you must help me
and don't make me lose my temper,
don't dither, and don't ask me why.
This is the great rule: Filial Obedience.

---

2. This is the key phrase, for which the play exists, as in the *Elektra*: "Need we add cowardice to all the rest of these ills?" Or the: "T'as inventé la justice" in Cocteau's *Antigone*. And, later: "Tutto quello che è accaduto, doveva accadere." At least one sensitive hellenist who has shown great care for Sophokles' words has failed to grasp the main form of the play, either here or in the first chorus, and how snugly each segment of the work fits into its box.

HYL: I will obey.

HER (*extending his hand*):   Put her there.

HYL: I'll do it. I don't need to swear.

HER: Put it there.

HYL (*complying*):   What am I swearing to?

HER: Repeat: "By the head of Zeus,"
    you will do what I tell you to.

HYL: I swear, so help me God.

HER: "And God damn all perjurers."

HYL: I'll keep it anyhow.

(*adds after almost imperceptible pause*)

    And God DAMN all perjurers.

HER: You know the highest peak of Zeus' hill in Oeta?

HYL: Sacrificed there quite often.

HER: You must get this carcass up there,
    by hand, with as many friends as you like.
    And cut a lot of wood from deep-rooted oaks
    and from wild olive (male trees)
    lopped off the same way.
    Get it going with the bright flame of a pine torch.
    And put me onto the pyre.
    Don't blubber. Show that you are my son
    or you'll have my ghost heavy on you
    from below there,
                    forever.

HYL: But father . . .
                    have I got all this straight?

HER: Got your orders. Do 'em,
                   or change your name.

HYL: Good lord, you want me to be a murderer
                   and a parricide?

HER: No, a physician,
                   the only one who can heal.

HYL: But how come, if I burn it?

HER: If you are afraid of that,
                   do the rest.

HYL: I don't mind carrying you up there.

HER: And build the pyre? As I tell you to do?

HYL: So long as I don't have to light it
  with my own hands,
                   I'll do my bit.

HER: And another little job
                   that won't take long
  after the big one.

HYL: I don't care what size it is. It'll get done.

HER: You know that kid of Eurytus's?

HYL: Iole? I guess you mean Iole.

HER: Ezakly.
    When I am dead, if you revere your agreement,
    remember it and marry the girl.
    Don't disobey me.
    She has lain beside me. No other man
    but you is to have her.
    You agree to the greater, don't jib at the less.

H Y L: But I'd have to be possessed of a devil to do it.
      Better die with you. She caused mother's death
      and your torture. She's our worst enemy.

H E R: The fellow doesn't seem to want to carry out
      his dad's last request.
      God's worst curse falls on a disobedient son.

H Y L: The delirium's coming back.

H E R: Yes, because you're stirring it up.

H Y L: What *am* I to do, in this mess?

H E R: Start by hearing straight.
      What I'm telling you,
      the dad that made you.

H Y L: Have you got to teach me crime?

H E R: It is no crime to gladden a father's heart.

H Y L: If you order me to, is that legal?
      Perfectly all right?

H E R: I call the gods to witness.

H Y L: Then I'll go ahead. If it's set before the gods
      that way, I can't be blamed for obeying you.

H E R: Fine. At last, and get going.
      Get me onto that fire, before this pain
      starts again. Hey, you there, hoist me up
      for the last trouble.
                    The last rest.

H Y L: Nothing to stop us now. You're the driver.

H E R: Come ere the pain awake,
                    O stubborn mind.

(catches sight of HYLLOS' *face and breaks off with)*

> And put some cement in your face,
> reinforced concrete, make a cheerful finish
> even if you don't want to.

HYL: Hoist him up, fellows.
> And for me a great tolerance,
> matching the gods' great unreason.
> They see the things being done,
> calamities looked at,
> sons to honour their fathers,
> and of what is to come, nothing is seen. Gods!
> Our present miseries, their shame. And of all men
> none has so borne, nor ever shall again.

> And now ladies, let you go home.
> Today we have seen strange deaths,
> wrecks many, such as have not been suffered before.
> And all of this is from Zeus.

[*Exeunt: The girls left,* HYLLOS *and bearers right.*]

A version by Ezra Pound, 1954

GREEK ▶

KOSTIS PALAMAS *(1859–1943)*

The Cypress Tree

I look out the window; the depth
    of sky, all sky and nothing more;
    and within it, utterly sky-swept,
    a slender cypress; nothing more.
Whether sky is starry or dark,
    in happy blue or thunder's roar,
    always the cypress sways, so stark,
    calm, lovely, hopeless; nothing more.

                David Mason, 1997

C. P. CAVAFY *(1863–1933)*

Longings

Like the beautiful bodies of the dead who never aged,
shut away inside a splendid tomb by tearful mourners
with roses at their head and jasmine at their feet—
that's what longings look like when they've passed away
without being fulfilled, before they could be made complete
by just one of pleasure's nights, or one of its shimmering mornings.

Manuel Comnenus

The emperor Lord Manuel Comnenus
one melancholy morning in September
sensed that death was near. The court astrologers
(those who were paid) were nattering on
that he had many years left yet to live.
But while they went on talking, the king
recalls neglected habits of piety,
and from the monastery cells he orders
ecclesiastical vestments to be brought,
and he puts them on, and is delighted
to present the decorous mien of a priest or friar.

Happy are all who believe,
and who, like the emperor Lord Manuel, expire
outfitted most decorously in their faith.

He Asked about the Quality—

From within the office where he'd been taken on
to fill an insignificant, ill-paid position
(eight pounds a month at best: bonuses included)
he emerged, when he'd finished the solitary task

at which he'd been stooped the entire afternoon.
He left at seven, and then strolled slowly along,
and dawdled in the street.—Handsome;
interesting, too: in a way that showed he'd realized
a maximal yield from his senses.
He'd just turned twenty-nine, the month before.

He dawdled in the street, and in the shabby
alleyways that led to where he lived.

As he passed before a little store
where the goods that were for sale were
shoddy, low-priced things for laborers,
he saw a face within, he saw a shape;
they urged him on and he went in, as if keen
on seeing colored handkerchiefs.

He asked about the quality of the handkerchiefs,
and what they cost; in a voice that was choked,
almost stifled by his yearning.
So, too, the answers that came back:
distracted, in a voice kept very low,
secretly concealing consent.

Now and then they'd talk about the merchandise—but
their sole aim: for their hands to touch
atop the handkerchiefs; for their faces to
draw near, and their lips, as if by chance.
Some momentary contact of their limbs.

Quickly and secretly, so the proprietor
wouldn't notice, sitting there in back.

Since Nine—

Half past twelve. The time has quickly passed
since nine o'clock when I first turned up the lamp

and sat down here. I've been sitting without reading,
without speaking. With whom should I speak,
so utterly alone within this house?

The apparition of my youthful body,
since nine o'clock when I first turned up the lamp,
has come and found me and reminded me
of shuttered perfumed rooms
and of pleasure spent—what wanton pleasure!
And it also brought before my eyes
streets made unrecognizable by time,
bustling city centres that are no more
and theatres and cafés that existed long ago.

The apparition of my youthful body
came and also brought me cause for pain:
deaths in the family; separations;
the feelings of my loved ones, the feelings of
those long dead which I so little valued.

Half past twelve. How the time has passed.
Half past twelve. How the years have passed.

Prayer

The sea took into her depths a sailor's life.—
Unaware, his mother goes and lights

a taper before the image of Our Lady
that the weather might be fair, and his return speedy—

while at the wind she always strains her ears.
But as she prays the ikon hears,

solemn and full of mourning,
knowing that the son she awaits won't be returning.

Days of 1908

That year he found himself without a job;
and so he made a living from cards,
from backgammon, and what he borrowed.

A job, at three pounds a month, at a little stationer's,
had been offered to him.
But he turned it down without the slightest hesitation.
It wouldn't do. It wasn't a wage
for him, a young man with some education, twenty-five years of age.

Two or three shillings a day was what he'd get, sometimes not.
What could the boy possibly earn from cards and backgammon
in the coffeehouses of his class, the common ones,
however cleverly he played, however stupid the partners he chose?
And loans—then there were those loans.
It was rare that he'd manage a crown, more often it was half;
sometimes he'd settle for shillings.

Sometimes for a week, occasionally more,
when he was spared the horror of staying up till dawn,
he'd cool off at the baths, with a swim at morning.

His clothes were in a dreadful state.
There was one suit that he would always wear,
a suit of a very faded cinnamon hue.

Oh days of the summer of nineteen-hundred eight,
your vision, quite exquisitely, was spared
that very faded cinnamon-colored suit.

Your vision preserved him
as he was when he undressed, when he flung off
the unworthy clothes, and the mended underwear.
And he'd be left completely nude; flawlessly beautiful; a thing of wonder.

His hair uncombed, springing back;
his limbs a little colored by the sun
from his nakedness in the morning at the baths, and at the seashore.

Voices

Imagined voices, and beloved, too,
of those who died, or of those who are
lost unto us like the dead.

Sometimes in our dreams they speak to us;
sometimes in its thought the mind will hear them.

And with their sound for a moment there return
sounds from the first poetry of our life—
like music, in the night, far off, that fades away.

Daniel Mendelsohn, 1997 (revised)

YANNIS RITSOS (1909–90)

Level Duration

Foundations under foundations. The churches under the houses.
Belfries above the houses. At what depth of rock
does the root of the fig tree grasp? On what branch of the wind
does the gold-winged Archangel grasp? We will ascend above
supported on the shoulders of the dead, with the earth on our chests,
in a procession of ruins, and the prickly pears arranged
along the length of time, mute, unresponsive,
with their broad hands blunting the clang of the buried churchbell.

Announcement

These rocks he carries on his shoulders he carves into his stools and his
    wings.
Here were Stavroula, Nina, Aliki, Thekla, Ourania—
they sang toward the sea from their balconies under an enormous moon,
they took the blue dye for love, plaited songs in their hair.
The rowers took up to the citadel their broken oars. One Sunday morning
before the scorching heat of July set in, a handsome equestrian appeared in
    the doorway
and rode his white horse down into the church. "Stop"—he said—
"I've brought the keys." He dismounted and advanced, pulling his horse by
    the reins,
and placed the black chest with its golden nails in front of the Holy Altar
    Door. The Elkomenos Christ
raised his lowered eyelids. But even now the horseman did not cross himself;
    he jumped
once more on his saddle, mounted up the stone stairs, hoofs pounding, and
    went out. He left behind him
smoke, incense, clouds of dust, speechless archangels, priests, chanters, and
    the entire congregation.

Remembrances

Your boyhood years waited for you in forgotten corners,
in demolished buildings, in Byzantine arcades—
the barber shop was there; there the shoemaker's, over there
must have been the fish store—the low stone wall bears a resemblance. The
   woman
with the very long hair—the mailman had abducted her;
afterward she died. It was raining. The four children
had locked themselves in the other room. They held
the old sea-blue chest. We didn't have more time—
events one on top of the other, wars and wars, expatriations, books,
half-finished recollections, loves, the closed well;
the parish priest omitted names—who remembers them? Later
the same child, during leap years, lugging water in a basket,
and the ordeal of the great desolation on the shattered watch towers.

                                    Kimon Friar and Kostas Myrsiades, 1981

HUNGARIAN ▶

ATTILA JÓZSEF *(1905–37)*

To Sit, to Stand, to Kill, to Die

To give this chair a wicked shove,
to sit in front of a fast train,
cautiously to climb a mountain,
to shake my knapsack down below,
to feed bees to my feeble spider,
to caress someone's old woman,
to sip good tasting bean soup,
there is mud—to walk on tiptoes,
to put my new hat on the tracks,
to skirt the bank of a blue lake,
to squat, clothed, on its bottom,
to sunbathe amid tinkling foam,
to flower with the sunflowers,
or to sigh for something, fine, good,
to simply brush a fly away,
or just wipe off my dusty book,
to spit in my mirror's center,
to embrace my dark enemies,
to kill them all with a long knife,
to study how their blood drips, drips,
or to watch a girl turn, legs, hips,
to make Budapest a bonfire,
to wait for birds to come to crumbs,
to slam my bad bread to the ground,
to force my good lover to cry,
to comfort her little sister,
if I owe accounts to this world,
to leave them, it, unaccounted for—
O binding me, dissolving me,
who now makes me write this poem,

who makes me laugh, who makes me cry,
my life, who makes me choose.

Attila József

He was merry, good, and perhaps stubborn
when they crossed him in his beliefs.
He liked to eat and in one or two things
he bore a striking resemblance to god.
From a jewish doctor he got a coat,
while most of his relatives called him:
Hope-Never-To-See-You-Again.
In the orthodox church he found no rest—
only priests. His decay was like his country's.

Well, that's life, don't anyone cry.

Michael Paul Novak and Bela Kiralyfalvi, 1968

ITALIAN ▶

GIUSEPPE UNGARETTI (1888–1970)

Little Monologue

Under the rinds of trees, as through a vacancy,
Sap is astir already, winding
In a delirium of branches-to-be-budded:
Uneasy in his sleep, winter
Telling February the reason
Why it must stay short; and moody
Though he may be, he is no longer
Secretively cheerless. As if
Over some biblical calamity,
To all appearances, the drop lifts
Along a shore which from that moment
Seeks to repopulate itself:
From time to time, abrupt, re-emerging
Tower follows tower;
In search of Ararat once more
Wanders the ark, afloat through solitudes;
They are climbing up to limewash the dovecotes.
Snow shifts from over the bramble stocks
Across Maremma
And
Near and far, a continuous
Cheeping whispering spreads through the air
Where birds brood;
Speeding from Foggia
To Lucera the car
Disquiets with its headlamps
Foals in their stalls;
In Corsica's mountains, at Vivario,
Men sitting out the night about the fire
Under the room's kerosene light,

With blanched and shaggy beards
Above hands heavy on sticks,
Chewing unhurried pipes, they are listening
To Ors' Antone sing
Accompanied by the murmur of the *rivérgola*
Vibrating between the teeth
Of the boy Ghiuvanni:

Your fate is as glad-
Hearted as mine is sad.

Outside a trampling of feet
Looms louder, mingled with the howls and gurgling
Of swine they bring to be butchered, and butchered
They are, for tomorrow
Carnival begins, and still
Through the windless air it goes on snowing.
Forsaken, behind three
Minute parish churches,
Assembled in ranks across the slope
Roofs red with tiles
The newest houses
And,
Covered in washing
The oldest almost invisible
In the confusion of the dawn,
The fragrant forest
Of Vizzavona is crossed
Without our ever being aware through the windows
Of its larches save for their trunks,
And seen only in scraps,
And
There is the time
We climbed out of the Levant through mountains
And the windings meandered even in the driver's voice:

There was sun here, there shadow, shadow there,

On he follows, repeating it to himself
And whether east or west
Always mountains, and worse—
Where the knot of mountains begins to alternate—
The spread of seclusion:
Is there no term to the tedium of it?
And,
At more than a thousand
Feet the car takes for its track
A road hacked through the chain
Narrow, icy
Leaning over a chasm.
The sky is a sky of sapphire
And wears that clear colour
Which in this month belongs there,
February colour,
Colour of hope.
Down, down until it reaches
To Ajaccio, such a sky
As numbs one but not because it is cold,
Because it is sibylline.
Down, down the unending
Incline until it encompasses
A dark sea in whose
Hidden windings a continual
Roaring is stifled, and the processionals
Of Neptune flow forth.
It sails on into Pernambuco
And,
Alongside rocking skiffs,
And hesitant lighters
Over the lustre and elasticity of the water

Thrusts into the tiny port
The dark and nimble presence of its blade.
Everywhere, up ships' stairs,
Through crammed streets,
On the steps of trams,
One meets with nothing that is not dancing
Whether thing, beast or person,
Day and night, and night
And day, because it is Carnival.
But at night they dance best,
When, hazardous amid the gloom,
Between sky and ground, hail down
From the whirling of fireworks, flowers of fire—
Accomplices of the night,
Multiplying its ambiguities,
Speckling the livid sea.
All are suffocating with heat.
The equator is a couple of steps away.
Hardship harried the man from Europe
Who must accustom himself
To the upside-down seasons,
And by making his blood
More mixed than ever:
Is not February the month for grafting?
And still more did he suffer
When his blood turned mulatto
In that accursed coupling
Of human souls with the labour of slaves;
But, on southern ground,
He found at last that he could oppose
To the glare of those dog days
The stare of his own more unexpected mask.
And now he will never cease to charm
This false February

And,
Putrid with sweat and stench,
Rolling their eyes they dance without pause
Raucously, unendingly singing
With the intent ingenuousness of the place:

O irony, irony
Was all he used to say.

Recollection is the sign of age
And today I have recalled
A few halting places in my long stay
On earth that fell in February,
Because in February, I grow
More watchful than in other months
For what may follow.
I am more bound to it
Than to my own life
By a birth
And by a grief;
But now is not the time to speak of that.
And in this month I too was born.
It was stormy, rain never ceased to fall
That night in Alexandria.
The Shi'ite Moslems were holding their festival
Of moon amulets:
A child on a white horse gallops by
And the people throng around him
Drawn spell-bound into the circle of prophecy.
Like Adam and Eve they seem, stupefied
By the fate which has tied them to the earth:
Ear sharpens now
For divinations,
And a woman out of the mob of Arabs
Rears up, gesticulates where

Lightning on a rock has clawed a form,
And with foaming mouth bears witness:

A prophet, still shapeless in the granite
Is outlining the grasp of his terrible arm;

But my mother, woman
Of Lucca that she is,
Laughs at such tidings
And with a proverb replies:

If in February each pathway's awash, that's sure sign
It is plumping the cobbles with oil and with wine

Poets, poets, we have put on
All the masks; yet one
Is merely one's own self.
With terrible impatience
In that vacancy of nature
Which falls every year in February, we have set
For ourselves a limit on the calendar:
The day of Candlemas
With the re-emergence from shadow
Weak tremor of tiny flames
Where small candles burn
Of unpurified wax,
And the day, after some weeks,
Of *Thou art dust and unto dust thou shalt return;*
In the vacancy, and because of our impatience
To emerge from it,
Each one, and we
Old men too with our regrets,
And none knows
Unless he prove it for himself
How illusion can
Throttle a man

Who lives by regret alone;
Impatient in the vacancy, each one
Raves, futile, wears himself out
To be reborn in some fantasy,
Some vanity,
And terror comes of it,
Time is too swift varying its deceits,
That we should ever take warning from it.
Dreams should be fit
Only for boys: they possess
The grace of candour
That heals after all corruptions, once it renews
Or changes at a breath the voices within.
But why boyhood
And suddenly recollection?
There is nothing, there is nothing else on earth
But a gleam of truth
And the dust's vacuity,
Even if, with incorrigible madness
The living man seems to strain
Toward the lightning flash of mirages
In innermost depth and deed
Again and again.

                    Charles Tomlinson, 1970

LUCIO PICCOLO (1901–69)

Veneris Venefica Agrestis

She springs from the ground-clinging thicket, her face
—gay now, now surly—bound in a black
kerchief, a shrivelled chestnut it seems: no fine fleece
the hair that falls loose, but a lock
of curling goat-hair; when she goes by
(is she standing or bending?) her gnarled and dark
foot is a root that suddenly juts from the earth and walks.

Be watchful she does not offer you her cup of bark,
its water root-flavoured that tastes of the viscid leaf,
either mulberry or sorb-apple, woodland fruit that flatters with lies
the lips but the tongue ties.

She governs it seems
the force of rounding moons
that swells out the rinds of trees
and alternates the invincible ferments,
flow of the sap and of the seas . . .

Pronubial, she, like the birds that bring
seeds from afar: arcane
the breeds that come of her grafting.

And the mud walls of the unstable
cottage where the nettle grows
with gigantic stalk, are her realms of shadows:
she fires the kindlings in the furnaces of fable.

And round the door, from neighbouring orchard ground
the fumes that rise
are the fine, unwinding muslins of her sibyline vespers.

She appears in the guise
of the centipede among the darknesses
by water-wheels that turn
no more in the maidenhair fern.

She is the mask that beckons
and disappears, when the light
of the halfspent wicks
makes voracious the shadows in the room where
they are milling by night, working at the presses,
and odours of crushed olives are in the air,
kindled vapours of grapejuice; and lanterns come
swayed to the steps of hobnailed boots.
     The gestures of those who labour
in the fields, are accomplices
in the plots she weaves:
the stoop of those who gather up dry leaves
and acorns . . . and the shoeless tread and measured bearing
under burdened head, when you cannot see
the brow or the olives of the eyes
but only the lively mouth . . . the dress
swathes tight the flanks, the breasts and has comeliness—
passing the bough she leaves behind
an odour of parching . . .
or the gesture that raises the crock
renewed at the basin of the spring.
     She bends, drawing a circle:
her sign sends forth
the primordial torrent out of the fearful earth;
(and the foot that presses the irrigated furrow
and the hand that lifts
the spade—power of a different desire summons them now)
she draws strength
from the breaths of the enclosures,
the diffused cries, the damp and burning
straw of the litters, the blackened
branches of the vine, and the shadow that gives back
the smell of harnesses of rope and sack,
soaked baskets, where who stands

on the threshold can descry
the stilled millstone, hoes long used to the grip of rural hands:
the rustic shade ferments with ancestral longings.

Rockroses, thistles, pulicaria, calaminths—scents
that seem fresh and aromatic, are
(should your wariness pall) the lures
of a spiral that winds-in all,
(night bites into silver
free of all alloy of sidereal ray) she will
besmirch with dust even the curve of the gentle hill.

Now, she's in day, one hand against an oak,
the other hangs loose—filthy and coaxing,
her dress black as a flue-brush . . .
and the sudden rush of wind
over the headland, sets at large, lets flow
in a flood a divine
tangle of leaves and flourishing bough.

The heat, too, promises, discloses
freshness, vigour of the breath that lets free
peach and the bitter-sweet
odour of the flowering almond tree; under coarse leaf
are fleshy and violent mouths, wild offshoots,
between the ferns' long fans
obscure hints of mushroom growths,
uncertain glances of water glint through the clovers,
and a sense of bare
original clay is there
near where the poplar wakes unslakeable thirst
with its rustling mirages of streams
and makes itself a mirror of each breeze,
where, in the hill's shade,
steep sloping,
the valley grows
narrow and closes

in the mouth of a spring
among delicate mosses.
    If, for a moment,
cloud comes to rest
over the hill-crest or the valley threshold,
in the living shade
the shaft of that plough now shows
which shakes which unflowers unleafs
the bush and the forest rose.

The Night

Sometimes the night turns gentle;
if it can raise from the obscure ring
of mountains a breath of freshness
to bring suffocation to an end, from the walls nearby
it releases a cluster of songs, it rises
with the creepers through the long arches, on the high
terraces, on the great pergolas,
in the openwork of the unstill branches, it reveals
carnations of gold, it gathers
faint secrets from the threads of water on the gravel beds
or moves tired steps
where the dark waves smash against breakwaters of white.

Suddenly on the screen of dreams
it blows into living veins faces already ash, words
that are voiceless . . . sets spinning the girandole of shadows:
on the threshold, above, all around
a vain emptiness, a vast passageway sways into forms,
a moving glance seizes
and a glance that stops cancels them.

Reverberations of echoes, shatterings, insatiate memories,
re-flux of lived-out life that gushes over

from the urn of Time, the hostile waterclock
that breaks into pieces; it is a mouth of air
that furiously feels for a kiss,
a hand of wind that wishes for a caress.

On the stone flights, on the step of slate,
at the door that is splitting with dryness,
the quiet oil is the sole light;
little by little, the rigour of the sung verses
spent, the dark is morè dense—it seems like rest
but it is fever; the shadow hangs from the secret
beating of an immense
Heart
    of
        fire.

Landscape

From Anna Perenna

           Above the roof
ascends, impends all at once
the mountain—to the left, encumbered
with a thorny green on green, with coulters
of a shed leafage, agèd tree-rinds, brush:
and caper, euphorbia hang at the winds'
mercy; where the coastline bends
and summons the shadow in, spreading it across
the scape of wrinklings, at the slope's
summit, folds fall open: valleys
of thicker green, there you can seek
and find puffball, buttercup and wild leek:
on dense leaf, on creeping bronchia
scum, wood spit, dark dew
of the swollen stalk, the thorn, the goitered

and oozing stem, that which remains
clammy with rainbow-coloured stains, which never sees
sunlight (and assiduously the invisible shuttles
weave, mutate, but the cycle will stay
the same forever) fed with an ancient moisture,
a mildew of vegetation . . .
and perhaps an eyeless lizard slides away . . .

Charles Tomlinson, 1967

JAPANESE ▶

KAKINOMOTO NO HITOMARO *(ca. 660–708)*

Ode at the Time of the Temporary Interment of Princess Asuka at Kinoë

They have raised you a bridge of stone
in the upper shoals of Asuka.
The birds glance on the water.
They have built you a bridge of wood
in the lower shoals of Asuka.
And the weeds that spring from the stone
are cut but grow again.
And the grass that grows on the wood
is withered but grows again.
But you, my princess, why have you
gone from the evening palace,
gone from the morning halls
of your lovely lord
on whom you leaned
when you lay together
as the river reed leans on the wave?
Like tall grass I see you standing.
I see you still with the living,
in spring with flowers,
with leaves for fall.
Deep as one looks in a mirror
you looked on your lord,
and were not full, finding him
more and more marvelous
like the fifth-month moon.
You locked your sleeves to his,
and time upon time together
you went with your lord
to the shrine of Kinoë,
bearing in cups the holy wine.

And now Kinoë is your shrine.
I see you still with the living,
and all my words are unwoven.
The duck-wild eyes die away.
Oh, when I see your lord
who goes on loving alone
like a mandarin drake,
who comes and goes
like the bird of morning,
bent down with longing,
as summer grass is bent,
rising here, setting there,
like the evening star,
and his wild heart tossed
like a little shallop,
what could I say,
what should I know?
There is only the sound and the name.
These are endless, like heaven and earth.
We shall go to the stream of Asuka,
the river that runs with your name,
and adore for ten thousand years
     our loveliest princess.

A Naga-uta on the Death of His Wife

There on the road to Karu
(Karu, called for the mallards),
my love, my sister, lived
and I desired to see her.
But too many eyes
and eyes too curious
forbade my coming.
For still our love was secret,

and the ways of love were hidden
like a fountain in the rocks
or a little flame in flint.
And now the flame is out,
for she I loved is gone,
who leaned sleeping against me
as the seaweed leans on the wave,
gone like splendid October,
a ripeness from the days.
This is the news the runner brings,
news like the twang of the yew-wood bow.
I hear the words, but cannot speak,
nor comfort find, nor rest,
nor hope, nor endure such words.

So I go the road to Karu
where she watched for my coming.
I go the road and listen,
straining for a voice,
but hear only the wild geese
screaming over Unebi,
and the people that throng
the spear of the road.
I meet them and scan their faces,
but see no face like hers.
For this is left of love:
to cry her name
to wave my sleeve.

Falling on hillpaths
the red leaves cloud the way.
I seek my love who wanders.
I cannot find the path,
and the mountain is unknown.

Through the ruddy fall,
the red leaves falling on,
I see the runner still.
I see a meeting-day
although we meet no more.

Grief after the Mountain-Crossing of the Prince

The haze rises. The spring evening is woven.
And I am lost. I have no way. I have no words:
ingrown in grief, dumb like the nightjar.
Could I tongue my grief, loosen the sleeves of speech!
O the wind that blew up at the mountain-crossing of our great lord
blows, and blows back, evening and morning, lapping my sleeves!
And I am lost, like a man undone, going a journey
but going in grass, without words, and the way lost,
and a grief in my guts
like the salt-burning of the fisher-girls of Tsumu.

William Arrowsmith, 1955

MOTOMARO SENGE *(1888–1948)*

Tangerines, My Boy, and Me

My boy went and got two tangerines.
He gave one to me
and is peeling the other for himself.
Wordlessly we sit across from each other, hibachi between us.
I look at the tangerine in my hand.
I am startled at its beauty.
A beauty that is uncanny.
Beautiful no matter where I put it.
I put it on the desk and look at it;
I put it in the palm of my hand and look.
I am coupled with the fruit wherever I set it.
It's as beautiful as if plucked this instant from an unseen bough.
Shining and fading into darkness,
the lamplight in the impenetrable night is incomplete,
nothing more than a childish trick.
I furtively steal a glance at my boy.
Head down, he is silently peeling his tangerine,
all thumbs.
I see a tangerine peeping out from inside his kimono.
It's as though I've discovered the secret of a magic trick.
I'll bet he's got a lot of them!

The Soy Mash Vendor

The soy mash vendor,
baby tied to her back,
goes through the predawn city streets
singing like a bird,
marvelously fast of foot,
asking for orders here, then there,
and greets all with good cheer,

wending her way from neighborhood to neighborhood,
cleansing the air as she goes.
Quick as a bird
and as elusive,
she flits along singing;
I love that voice.
I love the sight of her.

Lawrence Rogers, 2009

LATIN ▶

LUCRETIUS *(ca. 99 B.C.–55 B.C.)*

From *The Nature of Things*

From Book 1: Against the evils of religion

One thing I am concerned about: you might, as you commence
Philosophy, decide you see impiety therein,
And that the path you enter is the avenue to sin.
More often, on the contrary, it is *Religion* breeds
Wickedness and that has given rise to wrongful deeds,
As when the leaders of the Greeks, those peerless peers, defiled
The Virgin's altar with the blood of Agamemnon's child,
Iphigenia. As soon as they bound the fillet round her hair
So that its ends streamed down her cheeks, the girl became aware
That waiting at the temple for her there would be no groom—
Instead she saw her father with a countenance of gloom
Attended by the priests who kept the blade well hid. The sight
Of people shedding tears to see her froze her tongue with fright.
She sank to the ground upon her knees. It did not mean a thing
For the princess now, that she had been the first to give the king
The name of *Father*. No, for shaking, the poor girl was carried
By the hands of men up to the altar, not that she be married
With solemn ceremony, to the accompanying strain
Of loud-sung bridal hymns, but as a maiden, pure of stain,
To be impurely slaughtered, at the age when she should wed,
Sorrowful sacrifice slain at her father's hand instead.
All this for fair and favorable winds to sail the fleet along!—
So potent was Religion in persuading to do wrong.

From Book 3: Against the fear of death

You might, from time to time, give yourself this to recite:
"*Even Ancus the Good has looked his last upon the light,*
Who was a better man than *you* by far, you reprobate,
And since his day, the sun of many a king and potentate

Who held sway over mighty peoples has set. Yes, even he[1]
Who for his legions paved a road across the great blue sea
And taught them how to stride the salty main, he who held cheap
The ocean's roar and with his horses trampled on the deep—
Robbed of light, his spirit fled, he too went to the grave.
And Scipio, firebrand of war, the Scourge of Carthage, gave
His bones unto the earth like any slave of humble duty.
Add to these the pioneers of Wisdom and of Beauty,
Add the companions of the Muses, poets of renown.
Even Homer, the one and only who deserves the crown,
Even he now sleeps one sleep with all the rest. The sage
Democritus, when he was warned by his advanced old age
That the motions of his mind—his very memory—were fading,
He *himself* gave his own head to Death, unhesitating!
Even great Epicurus, once the light of life had run
Its course, perished, the very man whose brilliance outshone
The human race, eclipsing all, just as the burning sun,
Risen, snuffs out all the stars. So who are *you* to balk
And whine at death? You're almost dead in *life*, although you walk
And breathe. You fritter away most of your time asleep. You snore
With your eyes open; you never leave off dreaming, and a score
Of empty nightmares fills your mind and shakes it to the core.
Often, addled and dizzy, you don't even know what's wrong—
You find yourself besieged at every turn by a whole throng
Of cares, and drift on shifting currents of uncertainty."

Men feel a heaviness upon their minds, it's plain to see,
That weighs them down. If they could grasp the cause of this ennui,
This heap of misery and care that hunkers on the heart,
They would not lead the lives we see they *do* for the most part,

---

1. Xerxes, king of Persia, who built a pontoon bridge over the Hellespont in 480 B.C., on his way to invade Greece.

None knowing what he wants, each ever seeking a change of place—
As if he could lay his burden down by traveling through space.
Often a man who's sick and tired of his own hearth will roam
From his roomy mansion, only in a trice to come back home
Because he feels no better when he's somewhere else. He heads
For his country villa, driving his imported thoroughbreds
Hell-for-leather, as though to save a house on fire. And yet
The fellow starts to yawn the very moment he has set
Foot in the door, or falls in a heavy sleep, seeking to drown
In oblivion. Or even wants to hotfoot back to town!

Thus in this way each man is running from himself, yet still
Because he clings to that same self, although against his will,
And clearly can't escape from it, he loathes it; for he's ill
But doesn't grasp the cause of his disease. Could he but see
This clear enough, a man would drop everything else, and study
First to understand the Nature of Things, for his own sake:
It's his condition for *all time*—not for one hour—at stake,
The state in which all mortals should expect themselves to be
After death, for the remainder of eternity.

For what's this great and wicked lust for living all about,
If it just drives us to distraction, amidst danger and doubt?
The life of mortals has a limit set to it, my friend.
Death has no loopholes. All of us must meet it in the end.
We go through the same motions in the same old place. No measure
Of added life will ever coin for us a novel pleasure.
True, while we lack that which we long for, it is an obsession,
But we will just crave something *else* once it's in our possession;
We are forever panting with an unquenched thirst for life.
No one knows what the years to come will bring—what joy or strife
May lie in store for us, what outcome's looming in our lot.
But by adding on to life, we don't diminish by one jot
The length of death, nor are we able to subtract instead
Anything to abbreviate the time that we are dead.

Though you outlive as many generations as you will,
Nevertheless, Eternal Death is waiting for you still.
It is no shorter, that eternity that lies in store
For the man who with the setting sun *today* will rise no more,
Than for the man whose sun has set months, even years, before.

From Book 4: Against passion

Add this—lovers fritter away their strength, worn out in thrall.
This also—one lives ever at the other's beck and call.
They grow slack in their duties. Good name stumbles and malingers.
Wealth, turned to Babylonian perfumes, slips through the fingers.
But you can bet that *she's* well heeled, in shoes from Sicyon,
And those are genuine emeralds, the rocks that she's got on.
The wine-dark sheets, from rough and constant use upon the bed
And drinking up the sweat of Venus, are worn down to the thread.
The father's hard-earned fortune turns to tiaras for her hair,
Alindan silks, diaphanous gowns from Cos for her to wear.
He shells out for fantastic feasts with all the trimmings—fine
Linens, music, perfume, garlands, wreaths, free-flowing wine—
But in vain—since in the very fountain of delights, there rises
Something of bitterness that chokes even among the roses.
Perhaps it's that remorse, gnawing at the conscience, taunts
The lover he's thrown his life away in sloth, among low haunts;
Or else his darling wings a two-edged word at him, a dart
That smolders like a fire, and rankles in the love-struck heart;
Or else he thinks her roving eye too freely wanders after
Another, and imagines in her face a trace of laughter.

And these are just the problems of a love that's going *well*!
Imagine a love that's crossed and doesn't have a chance in hell—
Even with your eyes shut, you can grasp that the amount
Of troubles in unhappy love are more than you could count.
Best to keep eyes open, as I've said—don't take the bait.
It's easier to avoid the toils of love than extricate

Yourself once you are caught fast in the nets and to break free
From the strong knots of Venus. Yet you're still able to flee
The danger, even if you're tangled up, snared in the gin,
So long as you don't stand in your own way, and don't begin
To overlook all shortcomings in body and in mind
Of the woman you lust after. For desire makes men blind—
And generally they overlook their girlfriends' faults, and bless
These women with fine qualities they don't in fact possess.
That's how it comes that we see girls—malformed in many ways,
And hideous—are petted darlings, objects of high praise.
Indeed, one lover often urges another he would mock:
"Venus has it out for you—your love's a laughingstock."
(Poor fool—that *his* delusion's worse would come as quite a shock!)

The black girl is *brown sugar*. A slob that doesn't bathe or clean
Is a *Natural Beauty*; *Athena* if her eyes are grayish-green.
A stringy beanpole's a *gazelle*. A midget is a *sprite*,
Cute as a button. She's a *knockout* if she's giant's height.
The speech-impaired has a *charming lithp*; if she can't talk at all
She's *shy*. The sharp-tongued shrew is *spunky*, a little *fireball*.
If she's too skin-and-bones to live, she's a *slip of a girl*, if she
Is sickly, she's just *delicate*, though half dead from TB.
Obese, with massive breasts?—a *goddess* of fertility!
Snub nosed is *pert*, fat lips are *pouts* begging to be kissed—
And other delusions of this kind too numerous to list.
Yet even if her face has every beauty you could name,
And she pours out the power of Venus from her entire frame,
The truth is, there are other fish in the sea. The truth is, too,
We've lived without her up to now. She does—we know it's true—
Exactly the same things as all the ugly women do,
And fumigates herself, poor girl, to cover the stench after,
While her maids steer clear of her and try to hide their laughter.
But the lover, locked out, weeps, and strews the stoop with wreaths in bloom,
And anoints the haughty doorposts with sweet-marjoram perfume,

And presses his lips to the door, the fool—when if he were let in,
One whiff and he would seek a good excuse to leave again!
His long-rehearsed heartfelt lament would then come crashing down,
Right then and there he'd curse himself for being such a clown,
And for granting her perfection that no mere mortal attains.
Our Venuses are on to this—that's why they take great pains
To hide the backstage business of life, keeping unaware
Those whom they wish to hold bound fast, caught in desire's snare.
But all in vain, because your mind can drag everything out
Into the light, and find what all the tittering is about—
Yet if she is good-natured, never spiteful, it's only fair
To make allowances for foibles that all humans share.

From Book 5: On the development of civilization

The race of mankind then was far more hardy, as befit
The very hardness of the earth that had engendered it,
And they were built on scaffolding of bigger, denser bone,
Fixed with brawny sinews throughout the flesh, and weren't as prone
To being overwhelmed by heat or cold, could stomach all
Kinds of changes in their diet, and they did not fall
Ill from any sickness. For many a cycle of the blaze
Of the sun rolling through the heavens, they dragged out their days
Like the far-roaming wild brutes, nomadic in their ways.
Back then there was no sturdy ploughman to guide the curving plough,
No one knew how to work the land with iron tools, or how
To plant young slips in soil, or cut the barren branches down
From the tall trees with pruning hooks. Whatever sun and rain
Provided them, whatever the earth, unasked for, would impart,
They found these things were boon enough to satisfy the heart.

Mostly they would take a mess of acorns for their meat
Amongst the groves of oaks, or from arbutus they would eat
The berries—which you see are just now in the wintertime
Ripening to scarlet. But when the Earth was in her prime,

She bore more generously, and larger things besides. Back then,
When the Earth was in her first bloom, she provided wretched men
With many foods, more than enough to eat, though rustic fare.
And springs and rivers beckoned them to slake their dry throats there,
As now tall waterfalls cascading down the mountainside
Thunderously call the thirsty creatures far and wide.
Then men took up the wooded haunts of nymphs, places they'd found
During their wanderings, where they knew water to abound,
Trickling from a spring and slipping over stones, across
The slippery damp stones, and dripping on the verdant moss,
Welling up here and there, and on the broad plain widening out.
They did not know how to treat things with fire, or know about
The use of hides, or how to dress in skins despoiled from kills.
They dwelt in glades and forests and in caverns in the hills.
When lashing wind and rain made them seek shelter from the sky,
They hid their dirt-caked bodies under thickets to keep dry.
They could not look out for the common weal. There were not then
Laws or customs governing the ways men dealt with men;
But each man seized what plunder Chance put in his way. To thrive,
Each learned to watch out for himself, his own will to survive.
Then Venus wedded the bodies of lovers in a sylvan bower.
Man won his mate by shared desire, or he would overpower
Her with his violent strength and lust—or wooed her with a treat
Of acorns and arbutus fruits, or fine ripe pears to eat.

And relying on the wondrous abilities of hands and feet,
They chased their quarry of forest animals, and felled their prey
With stones or cudgels. Many they slew—from some, they ran away
By fleeing into their lairs. And like the wild and bristly boar,
When night caught up with them, they lay down on the forest floor
Rolling their naked, woodland-dwelling limbs up in a nest
Of foliage and the boughs of trees. They did *not* go in quest
Of the vanished sun when day was done, shivering with fright,
Roaming the fields with loud lament through shadows of the night;

But quiet, tombed in sleep, they waited for the sun to rise
Again and with his rosy torch illuminate the skies.
For since they had been used to seeing the alternating change
Of light and dark since childhood, it could never have seemed strange,
Nor could it make them fear that on the earth, eternal night
Held sway, and that the sun would never come back with his light.
What worried wretched man instead was, when asleep, he lay
At the mercy of the tribes of wild animals, easy prey.
At times he fled, evicted from his rocky dwelling, when
A wild boar frothing at the mouth or powerful lion burst in,
And in the dead of night, roused terror-stricken from his rest,
He yielded up his leafy pallet to the savage guest.

Back then the fate of an untimely death was no more rife
Than now, when men with moaning leave the sweet light of this life.
To be sure, each was more likely to be caught by some wild beast,
Gulped down in toothy jaws, supplying it a living feast,
Filling the groves, the hills and woods with moans, because he was
Buried alive, he found, inside a live sarcophagus.
And those who managed to escape, but with their bodies mauled,
Later placed shaking hands on suppurating sores and called
On Orcus with hair-raising cries, until the pains that racked
Their flesh released them from their lives, and all because they lacked
Aid and the know-how to dress a wound. But no one day would yield
At that time myriads of men reaped on the battlefield;
Neither in those days did tossing surges of the main
Shiver ships and sailors on the rocks. Blindly, in vain,
To no purpose, often the sea would rage with rising tide,
Then fickle as you please, would toss her empty threats aside.
Nor then could the bewitching laughter of the sparkling waves
And peaceful-seeming sea beguile men to watery graves;
The perverse science of navigation still lay hid in gloom.
Back then a dearth of food sent swooning bodies to the tomb;
Now men are sunk beneath excess, and eat more than their fill.

Then, men unwittingly ingested poison that would kill;
But now men poison others, being expert in that skill.

Then after acquiring shelter, hides, and fire, man and wife
Were joined, and lived beneath one roof, and learned to share a life,
And realized it was their union that produced a child.
That was when the race of man first started to grow mild.
Then fire saw to it that their shivering bodies could no more
Endure the cold beneath the vault of heaven as before,
And Venus drained their powers, and the little ones, with ease,
Broke down the stubborn pride of parents with their coaxing pleas.
Then neighbors began to form the bonds of friendship, with a will
Neither to be harmed themselves, nor do another ill,
The safety of babes and womenfolk in one another's trust,
And indicated by gesturing and grunting it was just
For everyone to have mercy on the weak. Without a doubt
Occasional infractions of the peace would come about,
But the vast majority of people faithfully adhered
To the pact, or else man would already have wholly disappeared;
Instead, the human race has propagated to this day.

A. E. Stallings, 2007

CATULLUS *(ca. 84 B.C.–54 B.C.)*

CI

By strangers' coasts and waters, many days at sea,
  I came here for the rites of your unworlding,
Bringing for you, the dead, these last gifts of the living
  And my words—vain sounds for the man of dust.
    Alas, my brother,
You have been taken from me. You have been taken from me,
  By cold Chance turned a shadow, and my pain.
Here are the foods of the old ceremony, appointed
  Long ago for the starvelings under earth:
Take them; your brother's tears have made them wet; and take
  Into eternity my hail and my farewell.

Robert Fitzgerald, 1952

HORACE *(65 B.C.–8 B.C.)*

I, 25

The young men come less often—isn't it so?—
To rap at midnight on your fastened window;
Much less often. How do you sleep these days?

There was a time your door gave with proficiency
On easy hinges; now it seems apter at being shut.
I do not think you hear many lovers moaning

"Lydia, how can you sleep?
"Lydia, the night is so long!
"Oh, Lydia, I'm dying for you!"

No. The time is coming when *you* will moan
And cry to scornful men from an alley corner
In the dark of the moon when the wind's in a passion

With lust that would drive a mare wild
Raging in your ulcerous old viscera.
You'll be alone and burning then

To think how happy boys take their delight
In the new tender buds, the blush of myrtle,
Consigning dry leaves to the winter sea.

Robert Fitzgerald, 1952

Prayer to Venus

iii.26

Not long ago I was alive with passion,
and not without my glory in your wars.
But now these fabled weapons, like my words,
are blunted, worthless. I give them up for good.

I hang them here in meager supplication
to you, Goddess of love, born of the sea.
Here, my crowbar, my brilliant torch, my bow—
what use are they? She has shut her doors forever.

But I ask you this, o Goddess, only this,
Queen of Cyprus, far from Thracian snows:
Please let her feel just once what I have felt.
Raise the lash high above her arrogant head.

Craig Watson, 1999

MACEDONIAN ▶

BOGOMIL GJUZEL *(b. 1939)*

How the Eagle Sees It

For me, the Caucasus is just a prison, too.
Though I'm unbound. No rock, after
all's said and done, holds him.
I tear at his liver every day. By night,
obviously, I'm exhausted.

So then the damn thing grows back again.
And he recovers. I dream of that infinite space
I lived in, thermalling on unfettered air,
before the gods handed me this horrid work.

They themselves have no idea what it is they want.
They'll tell me: *Consume his innards, make him suffer,*
but don't let him croak! Taunt him every now
and then just to let him know we care . . .

Our languages, of course, are different—can't understand
a thing he tells me. How could I, how could anyone
understand the voice of such exquisite pain,
the voice inside his singing blood?

They may be gods, but they're all doomed by ignorance.
While I ravage this titan, who screams and thrashes,
does he know I'll never really damage him
enough? Rats gather at his feet
and slaughter one another for the pickings.

Mankind will bring him offerings, autumn
harvests and winter grains. I, meanwhile, remain
so stuffed I cannot fly. (A diet of liver,
forever!) Those fools, they think
Prometheus is just his liver.

P. H. Liotta, 1998

PERSIAN ▶

FAKHR ADDIN GORGANI *(ca. Eleventh Century)*

From *Vis and Ramin*

Now when the nurse saw Vis's furious face
And heard her talk of heaven and God's grace
She searched within her scheming heart to find
Some means to soothe her charge's troubled mind:
Her demon did not rest, but wondered how
Vis and Ramin could be united now,
And how like fat and sugar they could be
Blended entirely, and inseparably.

Then one by one the sly nurse recollected
All the old tricks and spells that she'd collected,
And when she spoke her voice was lovelier than
The frescoes at Nushad. The nurse began:
"You're dearer to me than my soul, more blessed
And virtuous even than I'd ever guessed;
May you seek justice always, may you stay
Truthful and honored, wise in every way.
Why should I need or want, dear Vis, to grieve you?
What fear or greed could drive me to deceive you?
Ramin is not my brother or my son;
And can you tell me what it is he's done
To make me favor him, so that I'd be
His faithful friend and your sworn enemy?
I only want one thing from life, that you
Find happiness in everything you do,
And that your reputation stay intact.
But I must tell you an undoubted fact:
You are a woman, not a demon, not
A fairy, houri, or I don't know what.
Viru has gone, and as for Mobad, well
He's been disposed of by a clever spell:

No one's enjoyed your body, no one can,
You've never truly slept with any man.
You've had no joy of men, you've never known
A man whom you could really call your own.
You've married twice, but each time you've moved on;
Both husbands crossed the river, and they're gone!
But if you want a man, I've never seen
A finer specimen than this Ramin:
What use is beauty if it doesn't bless
Your life with pleasure and love's happiness?
You're innocent, you're in the dark about it,
You don't know how forlorn life is without it.
Women were made for men, dear Vis, and you
Are not exempt, whatever you might do.
The well-born women of the world delight
In marrying a courtier or a knight,
And some, who have a husband, also see
A special friend who's sworn to secrecy;
She loves her husband, she embraces him,
And then her happy friend replaces him.
You can have royal riches beyond measure,
Brocades, and jewels, and every kind of treasure,
But joy is something that you won't discover
Until you have a husband or a lover.
If you need riches it's to make you more
Attractive to him than you were before;
What use are all your red and yellow dresses
Unless they lead to kisses and caresses?
If you can see this, it was wrong of you
To slander me when all I said is true;
I spoke maternally, and as your nurse,
I'm trying to make things better now, not worse.
Ramin is worthy of you, and I've seen
That you, dear Vis, are worthy of Ramin:

You are the sun and he's the moon; if he
Is like an elegant, tall cypress tree,
You are a bough of blossoms in the spring;
If you are milk, he's wine. In everything
You're worthy of each other's love, and I
Will never grieve again until I die
If I can see love mutually requited
When you and he are happily united."

And as the nurse spoke, at her voice's sound,
A horde of devil's demons crowded round,
And set a thousand traps, a thousand snares
Before her feet, to catch Vis unawares.
The nurse went on: "A noble woman spends
Her life in pleasure, with her special friends
Or with her husband; you sit here and sigh,
And weep your heart away, and moan and cry.
Your youth will soon be gone, and you'll have had
No time at all when you were young and glad;
How long will you stay grieving and alone?
You're not composed of brass, my dear, or stone."

And gradually the heart of Vis was stirred
And softened by the arguments she heard:
She felt herself assent, but did not let
Her tongue bear witness to her heart as yet.

———

Vis and Ramin then swore no force could sever
The love that bound the two of them forever.
Ramin spoke first: "I swear by God, and by
His sovereignty that rules the earth and sky,
I swear now by the sun, and by the light
The shining moon bestows on us at night,
I swear by Venus and by noble Jupiter,
I swear by bread and salt and flickering fire,

I swear by faith and God's omnipotence,
And by the soul and all its eloquence,
That while winds scour the wastelands and the mountains,
While waters flow in rivers and in fountains,
While night has darkness, and while streams have fishes,
While stars have courses, and while souls have wishes,
Ramin will not regret his love, or break
The binding oath that he and Vis now make,
He'll never take another love, or cease
To give his heart exclusively to Vis."

Vis promised love when Prince Ramin had spoken
And swore her promises would not be broken.
She gave him violets then and murmured, "Take
This pretty posy, keep it for my sake,
Keep it forever, so that when you see
Fresh violets blooming you'll remember me.
May any one who breaks our promise bow
And wither as these purple flowers do now,
And when I see the spring's new flowers appear
I will recall the oaths we swore to here;
May any soul that breaks this oath decay
And shrivel as fresh flowers do—in a day."

And once these promises of love were given,
And they had called to witness God and heaven,
They lay beside each other telling tales
Of all their former sorrows and travails.
Vis lay beside her prince now, face to face,
The full moon lay in Prince Ramin's embrace,
And when Ramin affectionately placed
His gentle arm about her yielding waist
It was as if a golden torque should grasp
A silver cypress in its circling clasp,
And then Rezvan himself could not declare

Which was the lovelier of this noble pair.
Their pillow smelt of musk, and jeweled bed-covers
Bestrewed with roses lay upon the lovers.
Now lip to lip and cheek to cheek they lay
And struck the ball of pleasure into play;
So close together were their bodies pressed
That rain could not have reached to either's breast,
And Vis's heart was now a balm that cured
The agonies Ramin's heart had endured,
For every wound she'd dealt his heart before
He kissed her face a thousand times and more.
Now happiness emboldened him, and he
Placed in the lock of pleasure longing's key,
And felt his joy and eagerness increase
As he discerned the virgin seal of Vis;
Ramin pressed on and pierced this precious pearl,
And Vis was now a woman, not a girl.
When he withdrew the arrow, blood was seen
On wounded Vis, and on her prince, Ramin,
But though Ramin had wounded her she knew
A heartfelt pleasure and contentment too;
And now that their desire was satisfied
Their love grew deeper and intensified.
So for two months of luxury and leisure
They gave themselves to happiness and pleasure.

Dick Davis, 2007

POLISH ▶

ZBIGNIEW HERBERT *(1924–98)*

Arion

This is he—Arion—
the Grecian Caruso
concertmaster of the ancient world
expensive as a necklace
or rather as a constellation
singing
to the ocean billows and the traders in silks
to the tyrants and mule herders
The crowns blacken on the tyrants' heads
and the sellers of onion cakes
for the first time err in their figures to their own disadvantage

What Arion is singing about
nobody here could say exactly
the essential thing is that he restores world harmony
the sea gently rocks the land
fire gossips with water without hatred
in the course of one hexameter lie down
wolves and roedeer merlins and doves
and the child goes to sleep in the lion's mane
as in a cradle
Look how the animals are smiling
People are living on white flowers
and everything is just as good
as it was in the beginning

This is he—Arion
expensive and multiple
the author of giddiness
standing in a blizzard of pictures
he has eight fingers like an octave
and he sings

Until from the blue in the west
the luminous threads of saffron unravel themselves
which indicate that night is coming close
Arion with a friendly shake of his head
says good-bye to
the mule herders and tyrants
the shopkeepers and philosophers
and takes his seat upon the back
of his tame dolphin

—I'll be seeing you—

How handsome Arion is
—say all the girls—
when he floats out to sea
alone
with a garland of horizons on his head

To Marcus Aurelius

For Prof. Henryk Eizenberg

Good night Marcus put out the light
and shut the book For overhead
is raised a gold alarm of stars
while heaven talks some foreign speech
this the barbarian cry of fear
your Latin cannot understand
Terror continuous dark terror
against the fragile human land

begins to beat It's winning Hear
its roar The unrelenting stream
of elements will drown your prose
until the world's four walls go down
As for us?—to tremble in the air

blow in the ashes stir the ether
gnaw our fingers seek vain words
and drag the fallen shades behind us

Well Marcus better hang up your peace
give me your hand across the dark
Let it tremble when the blind world beats
on senses five like a failing lyre
Traitors—universe and astronomy
reckoning of stars wisdom of grass
and your greatness too immense
and Marcus my defenseless tears

Maturity

It's good what happened
it's good what's going to happen
even what's happening right now
it's o.k.

> In a nest pleated from the flesh
> there lived a bird
> its wings beat about the heart
> we mostly called it: unrest
> and sometimes: love
>
> evenings
> we went along the rushing sorrow river
> in the river one could see oneself
> from head to toe
>
> now
> the bird has fallen to the bottom of the clouds
> the river has sunk into the sand
>
> helpless as children
> and practised as old men

we are—simply—free
that is—ready to withdraw

In the night a nice old man arrives
and coaxes us with a deprecating shrug
—who are you?—we ask alarmedly

—Seneca—say the ones who finished grammar school
and those who aren't familiar with Latin
just call me: the deceased

The Wringer

The inquisitors are in our midst. They live in vast subterranean houses and only the shop-sign WRINGER HERE betrays their presence.

Tables with flexed bronze muscles, powerful rollers, crushing slowly but with precision, a driving-wheel, which knows no mercy—are waiting for us.

The sheets, which they carry out of the wringer-shop, are like empty bodies of magicians and heretics.

Episode in a Library

A blonde girl is bent over a poem. With a stiletto-sharp pencil she transfers the words to a sheet of paper and changes them into stresses, accents, caesuras. The lament of a fallen poet now looks like a salamander eaten away by ants.

When we carried him away under machine-gun fire, I believed that his still warm body would find its resurrection in his words. Now, as I watch the death of the words, I know there is no limit to decay. All that will be left after us in the black earth will be the dissipated sounds. The accents over nothingness and dust.

Peter Dale Scott, 1963

PORTUGUESE ▶

PERO MEOGO *(Thirteenth Century)*

"He goes, my lover,"

He goes, my lover,
With the love I have given,
Like a wounded deer
Before the king's huntsman.

He goes, my lover,
With my love, mother,
Like a wounded deer
Before the tall hunter.

Down to the sea he will go
And die of his wound;
That way will my lover go
If I let him leave my mind.

—Have a care, daughter;
There was one such, lately,
Who showed great desire
For the favor of me.

And have a care, daughter;
I knew such another
Once, who showed great desire
Only for my favor.

W. S. Merwin, 1952

JOAN DE GUILHADE *(Thirteenth Century)*

"Friends, I cannot deny"

Friends, I cannot deny
Love wears me grievously,
For I walk sorrowfully
And sorrowfully I say:
    Those green eyes I have seen
    Changed me in this fashion.

He that lends ear may learn
Whose eyes draw my lament;
And he may make complaint;
This, live I or die, is mine:
    Those green eyes I have seen
    Changed me in this fashion.

But no man should betray
His senses' weakening
By sorrow in his speaking,
And I say sorrowfully:
    Those green eyes I have seen
    Changed me in this fashion.

              W. S. Merwin, 1952

NUNO FERNANDES TORNEOL *(Thirteenth Century)*

"Waken, my love, who sleep in the cold morning,"

ALBA

Waken, my love, who sleep in the cold morning,
—all the birds in the world, of love were speaking.
Merrily walk I.

Waken, my love, in the cold morning sleeping,
—all the birds in the world, of love were singing.
Merrily walk I.

All the birds in the world, of love were speaking,
Thinking upon our love, on our love thinking.
Merrily walk I.

All the birds in the world, of love were singing,
Remembering our love, remembering.
Merrily walk I.

Thinking upon our love, on our love thinking.
But you have hushed the boughs where they were swinging.
Merrily walk I.

Remembering our love, remembering.
But you have hushed the boughs where they were sitting.
Merrily walk I.

But you have hushed the boughs where they were swinging
And you have dried the springs where they were drinking.
Merrily walk I.

But you have hushed the boughs where they were sitting
And you have dried the springs where they were bathing.
Merrily walk I.

W. S. Merwin, 1952

Francisco de Sá de Miranda *(1481–1558)*

"At the voice of the enchanter"

At the voice of the enchanter
Even the serpent shuts his ear:
Lo, I who listened would that sense
Deranged with grief might disappear.
Those most chary of the sea
Flee the singing of the siren;
Not strength restrained nor policy
When your voice invading me
Struck soul and senses alien.

W. S. Merwin, 1952

PROVENÇAL ▶

GUILLEM COMTE DE PEITAU *(1071–1127)*

"That the fevered breath attain relief"

VERS

That the fevered breath attain relief
I shape a song upon my grief
Who will to love no more hold fief
Here in Poitou or Limousin,

Who in terror turn and peril
A stranger, and commence my exile,
And where neighbors work his evil
In time of war forsake my son.

Ah lords and counties of Poitou,
In this forsaking is my sorrow!
I beseech Foucon d'Angou
To guard this country and his kin.

If not his hand avails us, nor
That king in whom I rest my honor,
How great the pack eyeing the plunder:
Gascon thieves and Angevin.

Lords, if valor and wit be small
These when I leave will seize the wall
And quickly shake it, and it fall
Where little I left it, young and thin.

May he nearest who follows me
If ever I wronged him pardon me;
To Jesus on his throne I pray
This in my own tongue and in Latin,

Who have been kin to strength and mirth
And know this parting from them both

Toward that demesne whose king and faith
Wall them with peace even who sin.

I have been gay but this my laughter
The lord forgets from his desire;
I can no burden longer bear,
So near I come to the last pain.

From all I love I turn aside,
I leave my knighthood and my pride;
May all reach welcome under God
And pray him that he take me in.

May those my friends after I die
Form in honor about my body
Who have been guest to mirth and joy
Far and near and in my mansion,

And thus depart mirth and joy,
The colored robes and sable skin.

W. S. Merwin, 1950

"Friend, I would make verses . . . that's understood,"

VERS

Friend, I would make verses . . . that's understood,
But I witless, and they most mad and all
Mixed up, *mesclatz*, jumbled from youth and love and joy—

And if the vulgar do not listen to them?
Learn 'em by heart? He takes a hard
Parting from men's love who composes to his own liking.

Two horses have I to my saddle, sleek,
Game: but husband both for battle? I have
Not the skill, for neither will allow the other.

But could I fasten them both to serve my rein
   I would not change cavalage with any other,
For then would I be better mounted than any man living.

   The first is of mountain stock, the swifter running;
   Sure-footed, well-composed she treads, but wild,
Shy, fierce, so savage she forbids currying. The other

   Was nourished up and bred past Cofolens
   And I have seen none more beautiful to my knowing,
No, nor would exchange her, not for gold or silver.

   I gave her to her lord a grazing colt,
   Yet, by the saints, so well have I retained her
At a sign her bridle would she rive asunder to come to me.

   Lord, in this difficulty counsel me!
   Never was I more harassed in a choice.
Agnes or Arsen! Madness or death will take me first.

   At Gimel have I a castle under domain,
   At Nieul have I pride before men; for both
These *nonpareils* are sworn to me, and pledged by oath.

                              Paul Blackburn, 1952

GIRAUT DE BORNELH *(Twelfth Century)*

"Glorious Lord, fountain of clarity,"

ALBA

Glorious Lord, fountain of clarity,
God of all power, if it please Thee,
Be by my friend unslumbering vigil
Whom I no longer see, for the night fell,
    Until arrives the dawn.

Friend, whether dreaming or half-roused you stay,
Slumber no longer, but renew the eye
Where in the east I see the light rise
That salutes day, and the star recognize
    That trembles upon dawn.

Friend, I smooth the entreaty into song:
Slumber no more, for I hear the bird sing
That goes inquiring day among the trees,
And tremble lest one jealously surprise
    You as now the dawn.

Friend, but approach and by the window stay
And see the stars diminish from the sky;
Judge if the word is amiable I send you
That you neglect, and yours will be the sorrow
    When the time fades to dawn.

Friend, friend, since you departed me,
I have not slept nor straightened from the knee
Petitioning the holy Virgin's son
That he to me render my companion,
    And soon arrives the dawn.

Friend, on these garden and indifferent stones

I prayed that no sleep touch my orisons
Till all dark vanishing rewarded day,
But comes no answer when I sing or pray,
    And early comes the dawn.

        W. S. Merwin, 1950

RAIMBAUT DE VAQUEIRAS *(ca. 1155–1205)*

"Guard us well, my sentry,"

ALBA

Guard us well, my sentry,
Cold the pike and heavy
While your radiant mistress, she
Most superb, most lovely,
I have to lie thus close to me 'til dawn.
Command the night stand to,
Bid or forbid as I will, day
Puts out my joy
                    l'albe, oc l'albe.

'Til the auzel wakens,
Watchman guard this richness;
'Til the morningstar rises
Eastward, I am wantless.
Enemy am I of that gravesman, dawn:
But a long day forces
All candor from our eyes,
Wholly destroys us
                    l'albe, oc l'albe.

Cry the hour from the keep, friend;
Keep us here below you from
Your ill-favoured master, warm,
Snug, snoring, cozened, Christ!
Flat on his back, symmetrical, 'til dawn.
Be warder on his treasure
That I may count her over
And only fear
                    l'albe, oc l'albe.

Love, adieu, adieu!
Longer I could not stay
Beyond our kinsman night, who flies
Before the sun's uprising.
How soggy red these fields lie in the dawn.
And changing his routine watch, unbuckling
Massive keys, my sentry
Cries from the tower
—l'albe, oc l'albe!—

Paul Blackburn, 1952

"High waves that shift and gather from the sea"

PLANH

High waves that shift and gather from the sea
With any wind or fancy, from my lady
What do you, syllable or sighing, carry,
Or casual song, who comes not back to me?
      And ah, Deus d'Amor,
Grant in its hour joy as grief in its hour.

Such sweetness folds him who returns from where
My lady holds her sojourn and glad slumber
As seems reprieve and liquid offered where
These lips wait parted, agèd with desire;
      And ah, Deus d'Amor,
Grant in its hour joy as grief in its hour.

Poor is the love one sends from alien fires
When all his hopes must make content with tears.
Now from her dreams the shape of me retires
As promises forgetfulness requires.

Ah, Deus d'Amor,
Grant in its hour joy as grief in its hour.

W. S. Merwin, 1950

PEIRE VIDAL *(ca. 1175–1205)*

From the *Vida*

CANSO

I suck deep in air come from Provence to here:
All things from there so please me, when I hear
In dockside taverns traveler's gossip told,
                  I listen smiling,
And for each word ask a hundred smiling words—
                  all news is good

For no man knows so sweet a country as
                from the Rhône down to Vence.
If only I were locked between
                Durance and the sea:
Such pure joy shines with the sun there.
I left my heart-for-rejoicing
                there among noble people,
And with her who bids my sadness dance.

No man can ever pass a day in boredom
                who has remembrance of her,
For in her is the beginning and birth of all joy.
                And he who would praise her,
No matter how well he speak of her, he lies;
For the world shall not look on one
                better or fairer.

And if there is aught I know to say or do,
                I merit no praise from it,
For in her is all Good; and through
Her have I wit and knowledge of fulfilment;
Hence I am both a poet and happy,
And all I make which has in it any fineness

I have from the rich delight of her fine body
Even as my heart longs for her in straightness.

Paul Blackburn, 1952

QUECHUA ▶

Anonymous Poets

(ca. Late Eighteenth Century, Early Nineteenth Century)

Prayer

O you

from whom it came
    comes
    you
lord of what is

whether you're
    a man
whether you're
    a woman
    lord
of what's born

whatever you are
lord of the sight beyond

where are you

you above at this moment
you below at this moment

presence
throne sceptre
    shining around them

hear
me

maybe the sky is your floor
maybe the sea is your roof
    maker of above and below

as we are you made us
lord above lords

my eyes are weak
with longing to see you
    only with longing
to know you

make it be
    that I see you
make it be
    that I know you
make it be
    that I hold you in my thought
make it be
    that you are clear in my mind

look at me
for you know me

sun and moon
day and night
spring and winter
you set them in order
    you

    from whom it came
    comes
all of them run
    the course you marked out for them
all of them reach
    the goal you set for them
wherever you wanted it

you bearing
the king's scepter

hear me
choose me

do not let me grow tired
do not let me die

Prayer

You

from whom the universe came
from whom the universe came

you
who made it everything

burn alone
alone only you
in the night that is my heart

when dawn comes let it show me
the joy of your eyes

when the wind
comes let it warm me with
your breath

let your hand that gives
be held out forever

and what you want forever
be the only
flower

Prayer

Come closer truth from above us
truth from below us

who made the form of the world

    you
    who let it all exist

    who alone made man

ten times with eyes full of darkness
    I must worship you

    saying Brightness

    stretched out before you

look at me
    lord
    notice me

    and your rivers your waterfalls
    your birds

    give me your
    life
    all you can

    help me to call
    with your voices

even now we taste
    the joy of your will
    and we remember it all
    we are happy

even so we are filled
    as we go away
    as we go

Herder's Song

I wish for a llama

with a gold coat
like the sun's

strong as love
soft as the cloud dissolving
at daybreak

from its hair I'd make
a knotted cord

the knots counting
the moons going
the flowers dying

"Joy in your mouth"

Joy in your mouth
joy on your tongue
all day
and tonight

you will fast
and later you will sing like a lark

then it may be that in our joy
in the smiling upon us

from some place in the world
the one who made us

the lord of the powers
will hear you

Ho

he will say to you

and wherever you are
you will live

forever

with no other lord

you will be

"I'm bringing up a fly"

I'm bringing up a fly
   with golden wings
   bringing up a fly
   with eyes burning

it carries death
   in its eyes of fire
carries death
   in its golden hair
   in its gorgeous wings

in a green bottle
   I'm bringing it up

     nobody knows
     if it drinks

     nobody knows
     if it eats

at night it goes wandering
   like a star

     wounding to death
     with red rays
     from its eyes of fire

it carries love
   in its eyes of fire
   flashes in the night
   its blood

the love it bears in its breast

insect of night
fly bearing death

in a green bottle
I'm bringing it up

    I love it
    that much

but nobody
    no
nobody knows

if I give it to drink
nobody knows if I feed it

"My mother brought me to life"

My mother brought me to life
    ay
in a rain cloud
    ay
like rain to weep
    ay
like rain to go around
    ay
passing from door to door
    ay
like a feather in the air
    ay

"When you find you're alone on the island in the river"

When you find you're alone on the island in the river
your father won't be there

to call you
        aloo
        my daughter

your mother won't be able
to reach you
        aloo
        my daughter

only the royal duck will stay near you
with the rain in its eyes
with tears of blood
        with the rain in its eyes
        tears of blood

and even the royal duck will leave you
when the waves of the river
        boil
when the waves
        race on the river

but then I'll go and stay near you
singing
        I'll steal her young heart
        on the island

        her young heart
        in the storm

                    W. S. Merwin, 1971

ROMANESCO ▶

G. G. BELLI *(1791–1863)*

The Creation of the World

The year that Jesus baked the world, he found
The dough was there already that he kneaded;
Wanting to make it big and green and round,
He traced a watermelon and proceeded.

He made a sun, a moon, a globe—just one of each,
Though he made a pile of stars out of the dough:
He set birds over beasts, beasts above fish:
He planted the plants, then said, "That's it—I'm through."

Forgot to tell you that he made a person,
A man—and then a woman, Eve and Adam,
And this apple that he put some sort of curse on.

And he yelled, by God, as loud as he knew how,
Soon as he saw that they had disobeyed him,
"Folks of the future, you are fucked up now!"

The Life of Man

Nine months in the stench: and then in swaddling bound,
Among the kisses, the milksops, and the bawling;
Then strapped into a basket, hauled around
With a stiff neck brace to keep the head from falling.

Then there begin the torments of the school,
The ABCs, the cold, the cane's hard knocks,
Measles, the potty seat, the squeezed-out stool,
A touch of scarlet fever, chickenpox.

Then hunger comes, and weariness, a trade,
The rent, the jailhouse, and the government,
The hospitals, the debts, the getting laid;

The scorching summer and the winter's snow . . .
Then, blessèd be God's name, when life is spent,
Comes death to finish it with hell below.

The Worldwide Flood

God says to Noah, "Listen, Patriarch,
You and your sons fetch hatchets, I'll provide
The blueprints and you build for me an ark
To my design: this high, this long, this wide.

"Then make a roof for it [So says the Lord],
"Just like the boat at Porto de Ripetta;
And when you've got her yare as you can get 'er,
Take beasts from everywhere and get on board!

"The worldwide flood that's coming, kid you not,
Will make those fountains out at Tivoli
Look like an overflowing chamber pot.

"You'll know that it's the right time to abandon
Ship, when you see a rainbow in the sky;
Just screw the mud and sow the site you land on!"

Free Trade

Well? I'm a whore! Behind my little gate
I show myself, I do, and sell my hide.
I take it in the narrow and the wide.
Cat got your tongue? Isn't my life great?

Once, Mister Dickbrain, I was pure, a maiden
Like other maidens, just as chaste as any;
Now anyone can have me who has money,
Here on a bed that everyone's got laid in.

You know what riles me? Not that I'm a whore,
That's well and good, and when the bed is shakin',
No job in this whole world could please me more.

It's high-class ladies who pretend to be
So virtuous, but, seeing what I rake in
By whoring, steal my customers from me!

A Dog's Life

You call this *idleness*, you idiots?
You say the Pope does *nothing*? *Nothing*, eh?
May you be damned for belittling the way
He labors through the grueling days and nights.

Who speaks to God Almighty in his chapel?
Who pardons whoreson rogues for their offenses?
Who sends out barrels of indulgences?
Who blesses, from his coach-and-four, the people?

Who counts the little coins up of his pelf?
Who helps him with the cardinals he invests?
Who else may levy taxes but himself?

And what of the fatigue that must set in
From tearing up petitions and requests
And tossing all the scraps into the bin?

The Popess Joan

A woman right enough, who first of all
Exchanged her apron for a soldier's billet,
And then became a priest and then a prelate,
A bishop then, at last a cardinal.

And when the ruling pope, a manly one,
Took ill (from poisoning, some say) and died,

She was made pope herself and given a ride
To Saint John Lateran on the papal throne.

　To make our little comedy complete,
She unexpectedly goes into labor
And drops a baby boy right on the seat.

　Since then they've used a seat with a hole to assess
The goods from underneath, and thus discover
If the Pontiff is a Pope or a Pop*ess*.

The Sovereigns of the Old World

　A King there was, who once upon a time,
Sent forth this edict to his huddled masses:
"I am I, and you are no more than slime,
You lying scoundrels, so just shut your faces.

　"I make straight the twisted, and I twist the straight;
You are what *I* could sell off by the lot,
And if I were to hang you all—so what?
You rent your lives and stuff from Me, the State.

　"If you don't have a title to your name,
If you're not Pope or King or Emperor,
You haven't got the cards to play the game."

　With this decree there came a hangman who
Asked all, Did they—or did they not—concur?
And all as one replied, "It's true, it's true!"

The Spaniard

　A Spaniard claimed that everything in Rome—
Its churches, castles, its antiquities,
Its fountains, columns, palaces—all these
Were equaled or improved upon at home:

To put him down and keep myself amused,
I one day went and bought at the bazaar
Inside the Pantheon a hefty pair
Of testicles a sheep had lately used.

I boxed them up quite nicely and I had him
Take a good look. I said: "These very ballocks
Are the same two that once belonged to Adam."

At first I thought him well and truly gaffed,
Until he said: "These *are* impressive relics,
But in *my* country, we've got Adam's shaft."

The Good Soldiers

As soon as any earthly sovereign
Receives a slight in his own estimation,
"You are the enemy—" he tells his nation,
"—Of this or that king! Go and do him in!"

His people, eager to avoid the pen
Or some such pleasantry I will not mention,
Hoist muskets and ship out with the intention
Of making war on French or Englishmen.

So, for some martinet's fantastic whims,
The sheep come stumbling back into the stall
With broken skulls and mutilated limbs.

They toss their lives as children toss a ball,
As if that old whore, Death, who lops and trims
The human race, comes only when we call.

The Coffee-House Philosopher

Men are the same, on our little sphere,
As coffee beans poured in the coffee mill;

One leads, one follows, one brings up the rear,
But a single fate is waiting for them all.

Often they change their places in the parade,
The greater beans displace the weak and small,
And all press toward the exit with its blade,
Through which, ground into powder, they must spill.

The hand of Fortune stirs them all together,
And that is how men live here with their fellows
Going around in circles with each other,

Lost in the depths, or struggling in the shallows,
Not comprehending what or why or whether,
Until Death lifts his little cup and swallows.

The Day of Judgment

Four angels, all with upraised trumpets fixed
Against their lips, each from his corner plays;
And then, in a thunderous voice, each angel brays,
"Come out if it's your turn, whoever's next!"

Then from the earth will come what once were men,
A row of skeletons crawling from the grave,
Each one resuming the shape he used to have,
As baby chicks surround a brooding hen.

The hen here will be God, who'll separate
The dead into two groups, one white, one black,
And the cellar or the roof will be their fate.

A vast array of angels all in flight
And looking like they're headed for the sack
Will put the lights out, and that's all: *Good night!*

Charles Martin, 2009

RUSSIAN ►

FYODOR TYUTCHEV *(1803–73)*

At the Imperial Village

Autumn advancing to the close,
That garden draws me: stilled
In its neither sleep nor waking,
The apparitional twilit white
As swanshapes, never breaking
The lake's dull calm,
Loom on its glass
In a delight of dumbness.

Shade settles there
On palace porphyry,
In the October early evening
Climbs Catherine's stair;
And, as the garden darkens like a wood,
Star-lit against its deepened ground
The past's gold image
Reflects from a still-emerging cupola.
. . . .
Above, the dissolving clouds
Lucent in heat. Glints
From its steel and steady mirror
Run with the river. Heat
Densened each hour, shade
Fled to the wood-cool under oaks,
And from the fields
White in their flowered and sunlit acres
The breath of honey.

Order perpetual
Governs this passing,
This changeless change

In fieldfare by riverflow.
. . . .
Neither thought nor threat,
But a limp and sullen sleep
This night-sky gloom
Clouded from every quarter.
Only the intermittent flare as
Lightnings, deaf-mute demons
Converse with one another.

And now hangs lit
As by a preappointed sign
The whole stretch of sky,
Fields in the flash, far woods
Breaking from dark. They remerge
And the dark once more
Hushed, listens about them
As if it were aware
Of a decision taken
In the secret convocation
At the central height.

The Past

Tsarskoe selo—site of the imperial palace

Place has its undertone. Not all
Is sun and surface.
There, where across the calm
Gold roofs stream in,
The lake detains the image:
Presence of past,
Breath of the celebrated dead.

Beneath the sun-gold
Lake currents glint . . . .

Past power, dreaming this trance of consummation,
Its sleep unbroken by
Voices of swans in passing agitation.

Charles Tomlinson, 1959

ANNA AKHMATOVA (1889-1966)

Under the Icon

Under the icon, a threadbare rug,
It's dark in the chilly room.
The wide window is overgrown
With ivy, thick, dark-green.

A sweet scent streams from the roses;
The icon lamp creaks, barely aglow.
Here are the chests, gaily painted
By the craftsman's loving hand.

Near the window, the white lace frame . . .
Your profile is delicate, severe.
Under your shawl you conceal, ashamed,
The fingers he has kissed.

Your heart began to beat so wildly;
It's full of anguish now . . .
And in your dishevelled braids
Lurks a trace of tobacco smell.

Kiev,

The ancient city, as though deserted . . .
My arrival is strange.
Over its river Vladimir raised
A black cross.

Dark are the rustling lime trees,
And the elms along the gardens,
And the diamond needles of the stars
Are lifted out toward God.

Here I will finish my journey,
My path of sacrifice and glory,
And with me only you,
My equal, my love.

For Us to Lose Freshness

For us to lose freshness of words and simplicity of feeling,
Isn't it the same as for a painter to lose his sight?
Or an actor, his voice and the use of his body?
Or a beautiful woman, her beauty?

But it's useless to try to save
This heaven-sent gift for yourself.
We are condemned—and we know this ourselves—
Not to hoard it, but to give it away.

Walk alone and heal the blind,
That you may know in the heavy hour of doubt,
The gloating mockery of your disciples,
The indifference of the crowd.

Ah! You've Come Back

Ah! You've come back. You've come into this house
And the look you give me is not the look
Of an enamoured youth, but of a man,
A daring, stern, inflexible man.
My soul is frightened by the lull before the storm.
You ask me what I've done with you,
Forever entrusted to me by love and by fate.
I have betrayed you. And to have to repeat—
Oh, if only you'd get tired!
This is how a dead man speaks,
Disturbing the sleep of his murderer.

This is how the Angel of Death waits by the bed.
Forgive me now. The Lord has taught us to forgive.
My flesh is tormented by sorrow and pain
And my spirit, freed, already sleeps, serene.
I remember only the garden,
Tender, autumnal, so easy to walk through,
The black of the fields, the cry of the cranes . . .
Oh, how sweet was the earth for me with you!

The Twenty-First

The twenty-first. Night. Monday.
The outlines of the capital are dim.
Some idler invented the idea
That there's something in the world called love.

And from laziness or boredom
Everyone believed it and began to live
As if it were so: they wait for meetings,
Fear partings and sing the songs of love.

But the secret, revealed, will be different,
And a hush will fall on them all . . .
I stumbled on this by accident
And since then have been somehow unwell.

Judith Hemschemeyer, 1982

From *Rosary*

1913

We will not drink out of one single cup,
Neither water nor a sweet champagne,
Nor kiss by morning as the sun comes up,
Nor look by evening through one windowpane.

I breathe by moonlight, you breathe by the sun,
But we are living only to love one.

My fond, true friend is with me every day,
And with you always is your merry friend.
But clear to me is fear in eyes of gray,
And you are the culprit in my discontent.
Our brief encounters we do not repeat,
Thus it is judged for us to rest in peace.

In your voice only are my verses read,
And in your poetry, my own voice lingers.
O, there is the fire against which neither dread
Nor oblivion dares to lift a finger,
And if you only knew how I love now
The rosiness and dryness of your mouth!

As One Falls Ill

Spring 1922

As one falls ill, delirious and burning
With fever, I again meet everyone
Walking through the wide *allée*, and turning
Through seaside gardens filled with wind and sun.

These days, I welcome in my home the exiled,
Agreeable would be a very corpse.
Hand in hand, bring to me the child
Whom, long ago, I found to be a bore.

Watching while the waterfall cascades
To wet, gray beds of rock, with frosty wine
For drinking, I will dine upon blue grapes,
And be with those beloved who are mine.

Epigram

Summer 1957
Komarov

Could Beatrice like Dante have conceived,
Or Petrarch's Laura glorified love's heat?
I have instructed womankind to speak . . .
But, God, now how to make them hold their peace!

Jennifer Reeser, 2012

OSIP MANDELSTAM *(1891–1938)*

"Insomnia. Homer. Taut sails."

Insomnia. Homer. Taut sails.
I've read down the ships to the middle of the list:
the strung-out flock, the stream of cranes
that once rose above Hellas.

Flight of cranes crossing strange borders,
leaders drenched with the foam of the gods,
where are you sailing? What would Troy be to you,
men of Achaea, without Helen?

The sea—Homer—it's all moved by love. But to whom
shall I listen? No sound now from Homer,
and the black sea roars like a speech
and thunders up the bed.

Tristia

I have studied the science of good-byes,
the bare-headed laments of night.
The waiting lengthens as the oxen chew.
In the town the last hour of the watch.
And I have bowed to the knell of night in the rooster's throat
when eyes red with crying picked up their burden
of sorrow and looked into the distance
and the crying of women and the Muses' song became one.

Who can tell from the sound of the word "parting"
what kind of bereavements await us,
what the rooster promises with his loud surprise
when a light shows in the acropolis,
dawn of a new life
the ox still swinging his jaw in the outer passage,

or why the rooster, announcing the new life,
flaps his wings on the ramparts?

A thing I love is the action of spinning:
the shuttle fluttering back and forth, the hum of the spindle,
and look, like swan's down floating toward us,
Delia, the barefoot shepherdess, flying—
o indigence at the root of our lives,
how poor is the language of happiness!
Everything's happened before and will happen again,
but still the moment of each meeting is sweet.

Amen. The little transparent figure
lies on the clean earthen plate
like a squirrel skin being stretched.
A girl bends to study the wax.
Who are we to guess at the hell of the Greeks?
Wax for women, bronze for men:
our lot falls to us in the field, fighting,
but to them death comes as they tell fortunes.

"We shall meet again, in Petersburg,"

We shall meet again, in Petersburg,
as though we had buried the sun there,
and then we shall pronounce for the first time
the blessed word with no meaning.
In the Soviet night, in the velvet dark,
in the black velvet Void the loved eyes
of blessed women are still singing,
flowers are blooming that will never die.

The capital hunches like a wild cat,
a patrol is stationed on the bridge,
a single car rushes past in the dark,

snarling, hooting like a cuckoo.
For this night I need no pass.
I'm not afraid of the sentries.
I will pray in the Soviet night
for the blessed word with no meaning.

A rustling, as in a theater,
and a girl suddenly crying out,
and the arms of Cypris are weighed down
with roses that will never fall.
For something to do we warm ourselves at a bonfire,
maybe the ages will die away
and the loved hands of blessed women
will brush the light ashes together.

Somewhere audiences of red flowers exist,
and the fat sofas of the loges,
and a clockwork officer
looking down on the world.
Never mind if our candles go out
in the velvet, in the black Void. The bowed shoulders
of the blessed women are still singing.
You'll never notice the night's sun.

"Armed with the sight of the fine wasps"

Armed with the sight of the fine wasps
sucking at the earth's axis, the earth's axis,
I recall each thing that I've had to meet,
I remember it by heart, and in vain.

I do not draw or sing
or ply the dark-voiced bow.
I make a little hole in life. How I envy
the strength and cunning of the wasps!

Oh if only once the sting of the air and the heat
of summer could make me hear
beyond sleep and death
the earth's axis, the earth's axis.

W. S. Merwin and Clarence Brown, 1972

MARINA TSVETAEVA *(1892–1941)*

Poem of the End

> *Prague, February 1—Illovishchi, June 8, 1924*

1

In the sky, rustier than tin,
A finger, a pole.
Risen in our appointed place,
Like fate.

—Quarter to. Right?
—Death wouldn't have waited.
Smooth. Exaggerated.
He tosses his hat.

In every eyelash—challenge.
His mouth—clenched.
Low. Exaggerated.
He bows to me.

—Quarter to. Sharp?
His voice rings false.
My heart sinks: what's wrong?
Brain speaks: watch out!

———

Sky of ugly portents:
Rust and tin.
He's waited at our usual place.
It's six.

Our kiss is soundless:
Stuporous lips.
As one might kiss the hand
Of a queen or corpse . . .

Some hurrying idiot
Shoves an elbow—into my side.
Boring. Exaggerated.
Some siren begins to wail.

And wails,—like a howling dog,
Long-drawn, raging.
(The exaggeration of life
At the point of death.)

What yesterday rose to my waist
Is risen—beyond the stars.
(Is exaggerated, that is:
At flood-stage.)

To myself: darling, darling.
—*What time is it? Past six.*
To the cinema, or? . . . —
His explosion: *Home!*

2

Wandering tribe,—
See where this brought us!
Thunder over our heads,
A drawn sword,

All the ghastly
Words, lying in ambush,
Like a house collapsing—
One word: *Home.*

———

Wail of a lost, spoilt
Child: *home!*
A one-year-old's grunting:
Give me and *mine!*

My friend in dissipation,
My chill and fever,
Much as others long to stray,
You want to go there!

———————

Like a horse, jerking its tether—
Up!—so the rope breaks.
—There's no house, is there?!
—There is,—ten steps more:

A house on the hill.—Any higher?
—A house on top of the hill.
A window set under the eaves.
—"Lit, and not by a single morning's

Sun?" Then, back to life, again?
—That would be the simplicity of poetry!
House, that means: *out-of-the-house*
Into the night.
              (O, to whom shall I breathe

My sorrow, my misfortune,
My terror, greener than ice? . . .)
—You've thought too much.—
A thoughtful reply:—*Yes.*

3

Then—the embankment. I follow
The water's edge, as if it were solid and thick.
Semiramis' hanging gardens—
So this—is where you are!

The water's—a steely strip,
The color of a corpse—
Which I follow, as a singer
Follows her sheet music, as one blind

Follows the edge of a wall—*Come back!?*
No? If I crouch—will you listen?
To the quencher of all thirsts
I cling, like a lunatic

To a gutter . . .
                    And I'm not shivering
From the river—for I was born Naiad!
To follow the river, as if it were your hand,
Of a lover, walking beside me—

And faithful . . .
                    The dead are faithful.
Yes, but not everyone dies in a squalid room . . .
Death to the left, and to the right—
You. My right side numb, as if it were dead.

Shaft of stunning light.
Laugh, like a cheap tambourine.
—You and I need to . . .
                    (Shivering.)
—Will we have the courage?

4

A wave of fair-haired
Mist—a flounce of gauze.
Much too stale, much too smoky,
And, above all, too much talk!
What does it reek of? Extreme haste,
Indulgence and peccadillo:
Inside information
And ballroom powder.

Men with children, acting single,
Wearing their rings, venerable youths . . .
Too many jokes, too much laughter,

And above all, too much calculation!
Prominent and petty, alike,
Top to bottom
. . . Inside trading
And ballroom powder.

(Half turned away: *is this—*
Our house?—No, I won't be your hostess!)
One—bending over his checkbook,
Another—over a tiny kidskin glove,
And another—over a little patent leather pump
Works unobtrusively.
. . . Advantageous marriages
And ballroom powder.

Silver notches at the window—
Like a Star of Malta!
Too much caressing, too much petting,
And above all, too much pawing!
Too much pinching . . . (*Yesterday's*
Leftovers—don't be so picky: they are ripe!)
. . . Commercial intrigues
And ballroom powder.

Do you think this chain's too short?
But then it's not just plated; it's platinum!
With their triple chins
Trembling, they chew their veal
Like calves. Over each sweet neck
A devil—a gas burner.
. . . Business failures
And some brand of gunpowder—
Bertold Schwartz's . . .
                              He was so—
Gifted—such a philanthropist.

—We need to talk.
Will we have the courage?

5

I detect movement in his lips.
But know—he won't speak first.
—You don't love me?—No, I love you.
—You don't love me!—But I'm tormented,

And wasted, and worn out.
(Like an eagle surveying the terrain):
—You call this—a home?
—Home is—in my heart.—How very literary!

Love is flesh and blood.
A flower—watered with blood.
Do you think love is—
Idle chat across a table?

An hour—and then we both just go home?
Like these ladies and gentlemen?
Love is . . .
                    —An altar?
Sweetheart, to that altar bring scar

Upon scar!—Under the eyes of waiters
And revelers? (I think:
"Love is—a bow drawn
Taut: a bow: separation.")

—Love is—a connection. When
Everything we have is separate: our mouths, our lives.
(I did ask you: not to speak of it!
Our hour that was secret, close,

That hour on top of the hill,

That hour of passion. *Momento*—like smoke:
Love is—all one's gifts
Into the fire, —and always—for nothing!)

The shell-like slit of your mouth
Goes white. No smile—an inventory.
—*First on the list, one*
Bed.
        —*You may as well have said*

One wide gulf? —The drum-wail
Of your fingers. —*I'm not asking you to move mountains!*
Love means . . .
                —*You are mine.*
I understand you. So?

————————

The drum-wail of your fingers
Grows louder. (Scaffold and square.)
—*Let's go away.—And I: Let's die,*
I was hoping. It would be simpler!

Enough of this squalor:
Rhymes, rails, rooms, stations . . .
—*Love is: a life.*
—*No, it was something else*

To the ancients . . .
                —*So what?*—
                        The shreds
Of a handkerchief in my fist, like a fish.
—*So, should we go?—And what would we take?*
Prison, the rails, a bullet—you choose!

Death—and none of these arrangements!
—*A life!* —Like a Roman tribune

Surveying the remnants of his force,
Like an eagle.
                    —*Then, we should say goodbye.*

6

—*I didn't want that.*
Not that. (I'm thinking: listen!
Desire is the traffic of bodies,
While we should be souls—to each other
Hereafter . . .) —And *he* didn't say it.
(Right, when the time comes for the train to pull out,
You let pass to your women, as it were some
Goblet, the sad honor of

Parting . . .) —*Perhaps it's my delirium?*
Did I hear you right? (You, polite liar,
Letting pass to your lover, as it were some
Bouquet, the bloodstained honor of this

Rupture . . .) —Clearly: syllable
After syllable, *so—should say goodbye,*
That's what you said? (As it were some handkerchief
Let drop at a point of sweet

Excess . . .) —*In this battle*
You—are Caesar. (What an impudent thrust!
To let pass to your adversary the sword
You surrender, as if it were a

Trophy!) —He goes on: (some ringing
In my ears . . .) —I double over:
The first time I am spoken of personally
In this breakup. —*Do you say this to every woman?*

Don't deny it! A vengeance
Worthy of Lovelace.

A gesture, doing you honor,
And stripping the meat from my

Bones.—A chuckle. Above the laughter—
Death. A gesture. (Without desire.
Desire is the traffic—*of others*
While we shall be shades—to each other

Hereafter . . .) A last nail
Driven home. A screw, if the coffin is lead.
—*A last, very last request.*
—Yes. —*Not a word, ever,*

About us . . . to any . . . well . . .
Men after me. (From their stretchers
The wounded—do yearn for spring!)
—*And I would ask the same of you.*

Should I give you a ring, a keepsake?
—No. —Your wide-open eyes are
Unreadable. (Like a seal
Set upon your heart, a signet ring

On your finger . . . No scenes!
I swallow.) More ingratiatingly, quieter:
—*A book then?—What, like you give to everyone?*
No, don't even write them, those

Books . . .

———

This means, I mustn't.
This means, I mustn't.
Mustn't cry.

In our wandering
Fishermen's tribe we
Dance—and don't cry.

Drink—and don't cry.
Pay with our hot
Blood—and don't cry.

Pearls in a glass
Melt—and rule
The world—and don't cry.

—*So it's me who's leaving?*—I see
Right through you, Harlequin, for her fidelity,
You fling your own Pierrette—a bone,
That most contemptible

Prize: the honor of ending it,
Of ringing down the curtain. The last
Word. An inch of lead
In my breast: would be better, hotter

And—cleaner . . .
                              My teeth
Press into my lips.
I will not cry.

All my strength—to press into
My softest flesh.
And not cry.

In our wandering tribe
We die, and don't cry,
Burn, and don't cry.

In ashes, in songs,
We do bury the dead
In our wandering tribe.

—*So am I first? Mine the first move?*
As in chess then? And
You see, even mounting a scaffold

Men ask we go first . . .
                    —*And quickly.*

Then please, don't look! —*One glance,*—
(Any moment mine will come thick and fast!
And then how will I drive them back
Into my eyes?!) —*I tell you, you mustn't*

Look!!!

Clearly and abruptly,
Looking up:
—*Darling, let's go,*
Or I'm going to cry!

———

I forgot! Among all the breathing
Money-boxes (and commodities!)
The blonde back of *her* head flashed:
Wheat, corn, rye!

All the commandments of Sinai
Washed away—Maenads' pelts!—
In a pile to rival Golkonda,
That storehouse of pleasure—

(For everyone!) Nature doesn't amass
Riches in vain, is not completely niggard!
From these blonde tropics, my
Hunter,—how will you find your way

Back? With her rude nakedness,
Teasing and dazzling to tears—
Adultery, like solid gold,
Pours out. Laughing.

—*Isn't it true?* —A clinging, pushy
Look. In every eyelash—an urge.

—And above all—at her core!
—A gesture that twists into a braid.

O, gesture that is already tearing off—
Its clothing! Easier than eating or drinking—
A smile! (For you, there's some hope,
Alas, of salvation!)

From—that nurse or your fraternal order?
From an ally: from our alliance!
—Buried as I am—to be able to laugh!
(And unburied—I laugh.)

7

Then—the embankment. A last.
That's all. Apart, not holding hands,
Like neighbors avoiding each other,
We wander on. Away from the riverside—

Weeping. Salty, falling
Quicksilver I lick away, not caring:
Whether Heaven sent Great Solomon's
Moon to meet my tears.

A pole. Why not bang my forehead against it
Until it bleeds? Until it shatters, not just until it bleeds!
Like two criminal accomplices, fearful,
We wander on. (What was murdered—is Love.)

Wait! Are these really two lovers? Walking
Into the night? Separately? To sleep with others?
—You understand, the future
Lies there? —I lift my head up and back.

—To sleep! —Like newlyweds, on a floor . . .
—To sleep! —When we can't even manage to fall

In step. In time. Plaintively: —*Take my arm!*
We're not criminals, that we have to walk like this! . . .

Electric. (As if it were his *soul*—has
Come to lie on my hand.) A current
Strikes through feverish leads and
Excites,—his hand comes to lie on my soul!

And clings. Everything is iridescent! What could be
More iridescent than tears? Like curtains, a rain
Of many beads. —*I don't know of any banks like this*
That really come to an end. —*There's a bridge, and:*

                              —*What then?*

Here? (A hearse draws up.)
Calm eyes
Fly up.—*May I take you home?*
A la—st time!

8

A la—st bridge.
(I won't let go, won't pull away!)
A last bridge.
A last toll.

Wa—ter and dry land.
I lay out my coins.
Mo—ney for death,
Charon's token to cross Lethe.

A sha—dow of a coin
Into the hands of a shade. This money
Is sou—ndless.
So, into the hands of a shade—

A sha—dow of a coin.
Without glint, without tinkle.

My coins go—into his.
The dead have their poppies.

A bridge.

————

Ha—ppy destination
Of lovers without hope:
Bridge—you are passion:
A convention: an unbroken between.

I nestle: it's warm,
I'm your rib—so I cling.
Neither *ahead of*, nor *behind* you:
At some interval of insight!

Without hands, or feet.
With all my bones and forces:
Only my side is alive, O
Which I press to you, next to me.

The whole of my life—in that side!
Which is my ear—and my echo.
As the yolk to the white
I cling, like a Samoyed to his fur,

I press myself, I cling,
I nestle. Siamese twins,
What are you—to our conjunction?
The woman—you remember: the one you called

Mama? Forgetting everything and even
Herself, in the motionless triumph
Of ca—rrying you,
She held you no closer than I do.

See! We li—ke this!
It's true! On your chest you cradled me!

I won't jump do—wn!
To dive—I would have to let go of—

Your hand. I press close,
Press closer . . . And I can't be torn away,
Bridge, you are a bad husband:
A lover—slipping away!

Bridge, you have taken our side!
We feed your river with bodies!
I have fa—stened on you like ivy,
Like a tick: so tear me out by my roots!

Like ivy! Like a tick!
Godless! Inhuman!
To ca—st me aside, like a thing,
Me, who never cared for

A single thing in this
Inflated, material world!
Tell me it's unreal!
That night follows night—some

Morning, an Ex—press to Rome!
Grenada? Even I don't know,
Throwing back the featherbeds
Of Mont Blancs and Himalayas.

The de—ep valley of the bed:
I warm it with the last of my blood.
Lis—ten to my side!
After all, it's much finer

Than po—etry . . . It's good and warm
Still? Who will you sleep with tomorrow?
Te—ll me it's my imagination!
That there's not, never will be any end

To this bri—dge . . .
                    —As it ends.

———————

—*Here?*—With a child's, or a god's
Gesture.—*We—ll?* I cling.
—*Ju—st once more:*
A last time!

9

Walking the factory blocks, loud
And resonant to our call . . .
A concealed, sublingual
Secret of wives from husbands, of widows

From their friends—to you, I impart the whole secret
Eve took from the tree—here:
I am no more than an animal,
Wounded in the belly by someone.

I burn . . . as if it were my soul peeled away with my
Skin! Steam disappeared down a hole,
That notorious and foolish heresy,
We call the soul.

Pallid green Christian sickness!
Steam! You don't treat a soul with poultices!
When it never existed!
There was only a body, who wanted to live,

That now does not want to live.

———————

Forgive me! I didn't mean it!
Just a wail out of my gut!
As the condemned await execution
After three in the morning

Over their chessboard . . . Grinning
To mock their warder's eye.
After all, we're just pawns!
And someone plays with all of us.

Who? The kind gods? Or the evil?
In the eye of the peephole—
An eye. Clanging down the red
Corridor. A latch thrown up.

A drag on cheap tobacco.
Spit, we've lived our lives, you know, spit.
  . . . These checkered pavements are
A direct route: to the ditch

And to blood. The secret eye:
The moon's hearing eye . . .

. . . .
And casting one sidelong glance:
—*How far away you already lie!*

10

One mutual
Wince—Our café!

Our island, our chapel,
Where in the mornings we—

Lowlives! Transitory couple!—
Celebrated our matins.

Smell of the market, of something gone sour,
Of drowsiness, of spring . . .
Here the coffee was vile,—
Like burnt oats!

(The spirit of good horses
Is broken with oats!)
Not a bit Arabian—
That coffee stank of

Arcadia . . .

But how she smiled on us,
Sitting us down beside her,
Worldly and compassionate,—
As a grey-haired mistress

With her doting smile:
Carpe diem! Carpe . . . Smiling
On our madness, our poverty,
Our yawning and love,—

And, above all, upon—our youth!
Our giggling—without provocation,
Our laughter—without malice,
Our faces—without lines,—

O, above all, upon—our youth!
Our passions unfit for this climate!
Blown in from somewhere,
Surged in from somewhere

Into this lackluster café:
—Burnous and Tunis!—
On our hopes and our muscles,
Under our threadbare robes . . .

(My dear, I'm not complaining:
Scar upon scar!)
O, how she saw us off, our
Proprietress in her stiff cap

Of Dutch linen . . .

———

Not quite remembering, not quite understanding,
As if led away from a festival . . .
—*Our street!—No longer ours . . . —*
—*How many times we walked it . . . —but no longer we . . . —*

—*Tomorrow let the sun rise in the West!*
—*David break with Jehovah!*
—*What are we doing?—Separating.*
—A word that has no meaning to me,

A supremely senseless word:
—*Sep—arating.—Am I just one of a hundred?*
Just some word of four syllables,
Beyond which emptiness lies.

Stop! In Serbian, in Croatian,
Really, is it just the Bohemian cropping up in us?
Sep—arating. To separate . . .
A supremely supernatural Babel!

A sound to burst the eardrums,
To test the limits of anguish . . .
Separation—is not a Russian word!
Or a woman's! Or a man's!

Or a god's word! What are we—sheep,
To gape as we eat?
Separation—what language is that?
There's no meaning in it,

No sound of it! Well, maybe an empty
Noise—a saw perhaps, through drowsiness.
Separation—is just Khlebnikov's school
Of nightingales groaning,

Of swans . . .
                How did it come to this?

A dammed-up lake gone dry—
Air! The sound of hand clapping hand.
Separation—it's thunder

Over my head . . . An ocean flooding our cabin!
Off our most distant promontory, off our farthest cape!
These streets—are too steep:
To separate—after all, means to descend,

Down the hill . . . Two leaden feet,
A sigh . . . A palm, finally, and a nail!
An overwhelming argument:
To separate—is to go separately,

We—who have grown together . . .

11

To lose everything at a stroke—
Nothing is cleaner!
Beyond town, the outskirts:
An end to our days.

To our legs (read—to stones),
To our days, our homes, and to us.

Abandoned summer homes! Like mothers
Grown old—just so, do I revere them.
It is, after all, something—to stand vacant:
Nothing hollow can stand vacant.

(Summer homes, standing half vacant,
Better you were to burn down!)

Just don't cringe,
Re-opening the wound.
Beyond town, beyond town,
Breaking the sutures!

For—with no superfluous words,
No magnificent word—love is a line of sutures.

Sutures, and not a sling, sutures—and not a shield.
—*O, don't beg me for protection!*—
Sutures, with which the dead are sewn in for burial,
With which I am sewn to you.

(Time will tell how strong a seam:
Single or triple stitched!)

One way or another, my friend,—our seams
Would go! To shreds and tatters!
Our only glory is the seam burst open:
By itself, didn't just unravel!

Under the basting—living tissue,
Red, and not rotted!

O, he loses nothing—
Who bursts a seam!
Beyond town, the outskirts:
Our foreheads separate.

On the outskirts they are executing people
Today—wind blowing through brain matter!

O, he loses nothing who departs
At an hour when dawn catches fire—
I've sewn a whole life for you through the night,
A fair copy, with no loose ends.

So don't upbraid me now, if it's crooked.
The outskirts: stitches ripped out.

Untidy souls—
Marked by scars! . . .

Beyond town, the outskirts . . .
The ravine with its descending sweep

Of outskirts. With the boot of fate,
Hear it? —across the watery clay?
. . . Consider my quick hand,
My friend, and the living thread,

The live, clinging thread—no matter how you pick at it!
The la—st lamppost!

———————

Here? A conspiratorial—
Look. The lowest form of human—
Look. —*Shall we go back up the hill?*
A la—st time!

12

Like a heavy mane
Across our eyes: rain.—Hills.
We've passed the outskirts.
We are beyond town.

This place doesn't belong to us!
Any more than a stepmother is mother!
No further. Here
We will lie down and die.

A field. A fence.
As brother and sister.
A life—in the outskirts.—
Build here, beyond town!

Ahh, it's a played-out
Business—gentlemen!
Everywhere—outskirts!
Where are the villages?!

Let the rain tear and rage.
We stand and part,
These three months,
First time we are two!

Did God seek a loan
Of Job, as well?
This isn't working out.
We're beyond town now!

———————

Beyond town! Do you get it? Out of it!
Outside! We've crossed a divide!
Life is a place no one can live:
A Jew—ish ghetto— . . .

Wouldn't it be a hundred times more
Worthy to be a Wandering Jew?
Since for anyone who is not vile,
Life is a Jew—ish pogrom,—

Life. Only converts survive!
Judases of every faith!
On to the leper colonies!
On to hell!—beyond the Pale!—not back into

Life,—where only converts survive, only
Sheep—go to slaughter!
Underfoot, I trample
My perm—it to live here!

Into the ground! As my revenge, on David's
Shield!—Joining the heaps of bodies!
Isn't it fascinating the Jew
Had no wish—to live?!

Ghetto of God's chosen! A divide
And a ditch: Ex—pect no mercy!

In this most Christian of worlds
All poets—are Jews!

13

Knives sharpened on stone,
Sawdust swept
With a broom. Under my hands
It is furry and wet.

Where are you, twin male
Virtues: hardness and dryness?
Under my palm—
Tears, and not rain!

What greater temptation—is there?
Than to make land—turn to water!
When your hard and glittering eyes
Stream under my palm,—

There's no greater loss
For me. An end to the end!
I stroke—I stroke—
I stroke your face.

Such is the arrogance of Marinas,
Like me,—of we Polishwomen.
After your eagle eyes
Stream under my palm . . .

You're crying? My friend!
Now I have it all! Forgive me!
O, how big and salty
In my cupped hand!

A man's tears are brutal:
Like an ax striking a forehead!

Cry, with someone later you will
Make up for the shame lost on me.

Out of—the same sea—
We are fish! A flourish:
    ... Like an empty shell
Lips upon lips.

———————

In your tears
I taste—
Wormwood.
—*And tomorrow,*
When
I wake up?

14

Down our steep path—
Downhill. The noises of town.
We meet three streetwalkers.
Laughing. At your tears,

Laughing—high and
Low—both—billowing!
Laughing!
            —at your inappropriate,
Shameful, male

Tears, visible
Through the rain—like two scars!
Like a pearl—shameful
On the bronze of a warrior.

Your first tears, and
Your last—O, let them fall!—
Your tears—are pearls
In my crown!

I don't avert my eyes,
I stare—through the downpour.
Go on, you toys of Venus,
Stare! This union of ours

Is more than your attraction,
Your going to bed.
The very Song of Solomon
Gives way to us,

Infamous birds that we are,
Solomon yields to us,
—Crying together is better
Than fooling ourselves!

———

So, into the hollow waves
Of darkness—stooping and equal,—
Traceless—and speechless—we go
Down, like a sinking ship.

Mary Jane White, 2009

SERGEI ESSENIN *(1895–1925)*

"I am the last poet of the villages"

I am the last poet of the villages
the plank bridge lifts a plain song
I stand at a farewell service
birches swinging leaves like censers

The golden flame will burn down
in the candle of waxen flesh
and the moon a wooden clock
will caw caw my midnight

On the track in the blue field
soon the iron guest will appear
his black hand will seize
oats that the dawn sowed

In a lifeless and alien grip
my poems will die too
only nodding oats
will mourn for their old master

The wind will take up their neighing
they will all dance in the morning
soon the moon a wooden clock
will caw caw my midnight

"Wind whistles through the steep fence"

Wind whistles through the steep fence
    hides in the grass
a drunk and a thief
    I'll end my days
the light sinking in red hills
    shows me the path

I'm not the only one on it
    not the only one
plowed Russia stretches away
    grass and then snow
no matter what part I'd come from
    our cross is the same
I believe in my secret hour
    as in ikons not painted by hands
like a tramp who sleeps back of a fence
    it will rise my inviolate savior
but through the blue tattered fogs
    of unconfessed rivers
I may pass with a drunken smile
    never knowing him
no tear lighting up on my lashes
    to break my dream
joy like a blue dove
    dropping into the dark
sadness resuming
    its vindictive song
but may the wind on my grave
    dance like a peasant in spring.

"It's done. I've left the home fields."

It's done. I've left the home fields.
    There'll be no going back.
The green wings all over the poplars
    will never ring again.

Without me the hunched house sinks lower.
    My old dog died long ago.
I know God means I'm to die
    among the bent streets of Moscow.

I like the city, in its old script,
    though it's grown fat with age.
The gold somnolence of Asia
    dozes on the cupolas.

But at night when the moon shines, shines,
    shines, the devil knows how,
I take a side street, head down,
    into the same tavern.

A lair full of din and roaring,
    but all night till daylight
I read out poems to whores
    and drink with cut-throats.

My heart beats faster and faster,
    I pick the wrong moments
to say, "I'm like you, I'm lost,
    I can never go back."

Without me the hunched house sinks lower.
    My old dog died long ago.
I know God means I'm to die
    among the bent streets of Moscow.

      W. S. Merwin and Olga Carlisle, 1968

Olga Sedakova (b. 1949)

Portrait of the Artist as a Middle-Aged Man

When, why, who
with what housepainter's brush
covered these features over,
which were once meaningless as the sky,
without purpose, end, or name—
pounding storms, squadrons of aircraft, a child's jackstraws—
the sky stirring the trees
without wind, yet stronger than wind:
so that they get up and walk
away from their roots,
away from their earth,
away from their kith and kin:
o, there, where we do not know ourselves *at all*!
into the meaningless never-darkening sky.

With what lime-plaster, what clay
what meaning,
profit, fear and success
have they been sealed tight, dead—
slots, oriel windows,
loopholes in never-whitewashed stone,
through which, remember, you looked and could never get your fill?

Ach, du liebe Augustin,
dear Augustine, it's all over,
all over, all ended.
Ended in the usual way.

The Angel of Rheims

For François Fédier

Are you ready?
This angel smiles—
I ask, although I know
That you are doubtless ready:
For I am not speaking to just anyone,
But to you,
One whose heart will not survive the betrayal
Of your earthly king,
Who was crowned here before all the people,
Or of your other Lord,
The King of Heaven, our Lamb,
Who dies in the hope
That you will hear me again;
Again and again,
As every evening
My name is rung out by the bells
Here, in the country of excellent wheat
And bright grapes,
And tassel and cluster
Trembling respond—

But all the same,
Set in this pink crumbling stone,
I raise my hand,
Broken off in the World War.
All the same, let me remind you:
Are you ready?
For plague, famine, earthquake, fire,
Foreign invasions, wrath visited upon us?
All this is doubtless important.
But it is not what I mean.

It is not what I was sent for.

I say:

Are you

Ready

For unbelievable joy?

Music

For Alexandre Vustich

By the gates of air, as they say now,

before the celestial steppes,

where half-incorporeal salt marshes prepare to float away,

alone, as usual, straying across the splendor

of the oecumene,

distorting various languages,

expecting who knows what: not happiness, not suffering,

not the sudden transparency of nontransparent existence,

listening intently, like a watchdog, I distinguish sounds—

sounds not sounds:

a prelude to music which no one calls "mine."

For it is more than no one's:

music that has no tune or tone,

no stock or root, nor bar line,

nor the five lines invented by d'Arezzo,

only shiftings of the unattainable, of height.

Music, sky of Mars, star of archaic battle,

where we are at once and irrevocably defeated

by the approach of armed detachments of distance,

by the beating of breakers,

by the first touch of a wavelet.

I pleaded for you on the hill of Zion, forgetting

friend and foe, everyone, everything—

for the sake of unsounding sound,
of unrung ringing,
of your almightiness,
your all-suffering.

This is a city in central Europe
                    its gates of air:
perhaps Budapest, I think,
but that magnificent display
of embankments and towers I will not see, don't even wish to,
I'm not sorry at all. In transit.
Music is in transit.

The bubbling of lava in a volcano's crater,
the chirping of a cricket on a village hearth,
the heart of the ocean, pounding in the ocean's breast,
as long as it beats, music, we are alive,
                              as long as no least patch

of land belongs to you,
no glory, no assurance, no success,
as long as you lie, like Lazarus, at another's gate,
the heart can still look into the heart, like echo into echo,
into the immortal,
into the downpour that, like love, will never cease.

                Emily Grosholz and Larissa Volokhonsky, 2009

DIMITRI V. PSURTSEV (b. 1960)

Third Rome Man

I like the wintertime feeling of "Big" and warm,
Done up in mittens and boots, long johns and pants,
In a short coat of fur even though it's not really real,
Shaggy earflaps tied tight to keep out the cold and the wind—
The wind's fierce—how handy my eyes are Polovtsian slits
And the terrible cold can't get under my high Tartar cheekbones;
My moustache does get frosted and my blood's like chilled vodka:
But here I am, happy-go-lucky, at home in the last, the Third Rome,
A barbarian scion, a forefather maybe someday,
My breathing engraved on its quick, immortal air.

F. D. Reeve, 2009

Two Monasteries

In the cloister where day tourists scurry
Back and forth like phantoms,
And the President in a photograph
In the vestibule is like a choir director
Among full-bearded archbishops,
 There's no peace and quiet.

In the old monastery there's no
Place to worship, only a brick
Ruin like the skeletal frame of a stove
With a houseless chimney. The solitary
Green-eyed, white-chested, chestnut-faced
Lady cat Masha lives here without grieving,
And like a Holy Roller having scraped on rusty iron
Over the porch of the wing, now rubs herself
 Against a standing seam on the roof.
In this monastery now owned by the city

Where the studios of artists who come and go
Are also part of Masha's world,
Where varnishing day has nearly come round
For the city jubilee, and there's
An exhibit of the best works to benefit
The regional children's hospital—
Here there's peace and quiet,
And like cupolas the clouds float overhead
    Eternally golden.

F. D. Reeve, 2011

SPANISH ▶

LOPE DE VEGA *(1562–1635)*

"Dawns hung with flowers"

Dawns hung with flowers
In the cold winter,
Be mindful of my child
Who sleeps upon the ice.
Joyful mornings
In cold December,
Though the sky sow you
With flowers and roses,
Yet are you severe
And God is tender;
Be mindful of my child
Upon the ice who sleeps.

"In Santiago the Green"

In Santiago the Green
Jealousy seized me,
Night sits in the day,
I think to avenge myself.

Poplars of the thicket,
Where is my love?
If with another
Then should I die.

Clear Manzanares,
O little river,
For lack of water
Run full with fire.

Harvest Song

From The Grand Duke of Muscovy

White I was
When I came to the harvest
Now I am brown where the sun touched me.
White once on a time I was
Before I came to the harvesting
But the sun would not allow
Whiteness to the fire I wield.
My youth at break of day
Was a lustrous lily;
Now I am brown where the sun touched me.

W. S. Merwin, 1957

RUBÉN DARÍO (1867–1916)

Urna Votiva

I'd carve this for the ashes of years:
a garland of immortelle to adorn
the Grecian fret on a votive urn;
a chalice to hold heaven's tears;

now a lark surprised on the wing;
and an olive branch where she'll
sing; and, wrapped in a Muse's veil,
Diana's statue near a forest spring.

My work, if I could work the stone,
releasing the marble's cold fire,
I'd crown with a rose and a lyre.

My dream, as day turns back night?
To see in the face of a weeping girl
one tear full of love and of light . . .

Lorna Knowles Blake, 2011

ANTONIO MACHADO (1875–1939)

Waters

I

Sun in the ram. My window
stands open to cold air.
Evening wakens the river—
hark! the rumour of the water there.

II

Gregarious sound begins to wane
within the ancient hamlet, storks
crowning its ample turrets. In the plain
the water speaks from solitude and rocks.

III

As before, my thought
is water's captive;
but of water in the live
rock that is my heart.

IV

Can you tell the water's sound?
Whether of summit or of valley,
plaza, garden, orchard ground?

From "Galerías"

Blue mountains, river, the erect
and coppery wands
of poplars in their delicacy,
and on the hill, the almonds white—
oh, snow in flower, butterfly in tree!

A bean-scent on its breath,
the wind goes by
runs in the plain whose solitude is gay.

Guadalquivír

Oh, Guadalquivír!
in Cazorla I saw you a spring;
today, dying in Sanlúcar.

A gushing of clear water
under a green pine
you were: how keen your chime!

Like myself, close to the sea,
river of brackish mud, do you
dream of your source's clarity?

                    Charles Tomlinson, 1962

Gabriela Mistral (1889–1957)

The Death Sonnets

I

From the cold niche where they laid you down to rest,
to the sunny, humble earth I'll let you go.
I too must sleep there, though they have not guessed
we'll dream on the same pillow down below.

I'll lower you into the sun-warmed ground
as a mother gently lays a child to sleep,
and the earth, become a cradle soft as down,
shall wrap your hurt child's body safe and deep.

Then I shall sprinkle earth, and dust of roses,
and in the moonlight's floating azure mist
the slight remains of you will lie alone.

I'll boast, victorious, as one who now supposes
in such a secret depth no other fist
will wrestle with me for a single bone!

II

This long fatigue will grow until one day
soul tells the body that it can no more
bear its great weight along the flowery way
where men pursue the life they settle for . . .

You'll sense they're digging near you, with great strength:
a new sleeper for your quiet neighborhood.
I'll wait until they've covered all my length . . .
and then take up our talk again, for good!

You'll know, then, why your flesh cannot mature
toward the deep boneyard that awaits it yet;

you had to go, unwearied, there to lie.

New light will show, where fate resides obscure,
how, to unite us two, the stars were met,
then, when our great pact failed, you had to die . . .

III

Evil hands seized his life the very hour
when, drawn by stars, he left behind his source,
snowy with lilies. In joy he came to flower.
Evil hands ruined and entered him by force . . .

And I said to the Lord, "To deadly lands
ignorant guides have borne my dearest shade!
Wrest him away, Lord, from those fatal hands,
or he sinks to the deep sleep that you have made!

I cannot call, or follow where he goes!
His ship obeys dark storm winds from above.
Back to my arms, or you take him in full bloom."

His life's vessel detained, fresh as a rose . . .
You say I have no pity, feel no love?
You know it, Lord, who will pronounce my doom!

Close to Me

Little fiber from my body
that I spun so tenderly,
little fiber cold and trembling,
fall asleep here, close to me!

In the clover sleeps the partridge,
hears it stirring in the breeze:
let my breathing not disturb you,
fall asleep here, close to me!

Tender shoot still all aquiver
and amazed simply to be,
do not leave my breast that holds you:
fall asleep here, close to me!

I who've lost my every treasure
tremble now before I sleep.
Do not slip from my embracing:
fall asleep here, close to me!

Rhina P. Espaillat, 2011

JORGE GUILLÉN *(1893–1984)*

The Nymphs

They seek, high and alone,
that brilliance of a sun
which would prefer them pure.

And, glory, the level garden
will elevate the new
perfection of its morning.

Now the heights are heavens,
populous with light,
without edge or penumbra.

The splendor springs again
as though a form akin
to its own hope in-dwelling.

Further: the flesh, in greater
reality, ascends
thus naked, unto fortune.

Time unto Time, or The Garden

All the garden is offered to the glance.
A casual lord who reigns, who so admires,
I stare, and from the palace I prevail.

If gifts from the largess of nature flow,
Only the slope of this ravine defies,
Changeless, such austerity of beauty.

By certain boxwood trees that tempt the touch,
Two fountains as a pair of myths direct
The garden and my soul, who know each other.

And there, among their lean extremities,
Sight dwindles through those grovèd poplar trees
Amenable to rustle and to thought.

Below, always the water of the pool
Saves us a few skies that approximate
Their adventures in that interior.

Murmurs that from the leaves approach, murmurs
Make passage by me like the lights of seasons
Receding for the moment—where I abide.

It is the garden lifts and honors me
Above his height, above the tangible
Centuries here saved contemporary.

Between the flower, exact in its return,
And the flat turf continually growing,
Now more a friend, what has been is gathered in.

Here beside this infancy of a stream
The perpetual succession of the instant
Gathers and merges, presides over me.

Here the years compass time; the fountain is
Divinity: this water has no end.
Through the grove shivers a profounder sun.

W. S. Merwin, 1954

VICENTE HUIDOBRO *(1893–1948)*

Ars Poetica

Let the line be like a key
that opens a thousand doors.
A leaf falls; something flies by;

Whatever the eyes see, let it be created,
and let the soul of the hearer tremble.

Invent many worlds and look to your word;
the adjective, when it does not vivify, kills.

We are in the age of nerves.
The muscle hangs loose,
like a memory, in museums;
but we are not the weaker for that:
true power
resides in the head.

Why do you sing of the rose, you poets!
Make it flower in the poem;

Only for us
do all things live under the sun.

The poet is a small god.

Rhina P. Espaillat, 2011

JORGE LUIS BORGES (1899–1986)

Rose

From Fervor de Buenos Aires

O rose,
Imperishable rose I do not sing,
All density and fragrance,
Rose of the black garden in deepest midnight,
Or any garden on any given evening,
Rose that is resurrected from delicate ashes
By the art of alchemy,
Rose of the Persians, Ariosto's rose,
Rose that is always one, alone,
Always the rose of roses,
The ageless Platonic flower,
Ardent and blind, o rose I do not sing,
Rose, unattainable.

Buenos Aires

From El otro, el mismo

And now the city is like an unfolded plan
of all my failures and humiliations;
before this door I watched the sun go down
so often, and waited in vain before this statue.
Here the uncertain past and exacting present
offered my thoughts the common circumstances
of every kind of person, here my footsteps
traced out a labyrinth, unforeseeable.
Here the ashen evening waits and hopes for
the outcome owed or promised by tomorrow;
here my shadow in the no less hopeless
evening shadows loses itself, but lightly.

If love binds us at all, it is by terror;
and that is the explanation of desire.

> Emily Grosholz, 2011

Poem of the Gifts

Let no one see self-pity or rebuke
In this avowal of the mastery
Of God, Who has, with consummate irony,
Given me books and darkness at one stroke.

Over this city of books He has, it seems,
Given dominion to sightless eyes, that can
Read only in the libraries of dreams
The senseless paragraphs that every dawn

Yields to their yearning. All in vain the day
Lavishes on them its infinities
Of books as rigorous as the codices
That went up in smoke at Alexandria.

From thirst and hunger (we learn from a Greek story)
A king dies amid garden plots and fountains;
I weaken aimlessly in the blind confines
Of this profound and lofty library.

The high stacks proffer in their vast detail
Encyclopedias, atlases, dynasties
Of East and West, symbols, cosmogonies,
Eras and eons,—but to no avail.

Haltingly, slowly in the vacant gloom,
I explore these shadows with a cane for eyes,
I, who always imagined Paradise
Under the aspect of a reading-room.

Something that certainly cannot be conveyed
By the word *hazard* governs all these things;

Another man in other murky evenings
Received the myriad volumes, and the shade.

Pacing along the unhurried corridors
I often feel with a kind of sacred dread
That I am that other person who, now dead,
Paced the same paces in the selfsame hours.

Which of us two is writing out this verse
Of a single shadow and a plural I?
What matter my surname if it signify
A singular and indivisible curse?

Groussac or Borges, I contemplate this cherished
World as it blazes up and changes shape
And flickers out into a vague white ash
That looks much like oblivion, or sleep.

My Books

My books (which do not know that I exist)
Are as much a part of me as this visage
With its grey hair at the temples and grey eyes
That I look for vainly in glass surfaces
And wonderingly run my curved hand over.
And not without some logical bitterness
It occurs to me that the essential words
That most express me are not in my own writings
But in those books that don't know who I am.
Better that way. The voices of the dead
Will utter me forever.

Simón Carbajal

Antelo's fields, 1890 or so,
My father had charge of him. Perhaps they exchanged

A few sparing and long forgotten words.
He remembered nothing of the man but this:
The back of his dark-skinned left hand crisscrossed
With scratches,—claw marks. Back then, on the ranch,
Everyone worked out his own destiny:
This one broke horses, that one was a wrangler,
Another man could rope like nobody else—
Simón Carbajal was the jaguar man.
Whenever a jaguar preyed upon the sheepfold
Or someone heard her growling in the darkness,
Carbajal would track her into the mountains.
He took a knife with him, and a few dogs.
And when at last he closed with her in a thicket
He would set the dogs on her. The tawny beast
As like as not sprang suddenly on the man
Shaking a poncho draped over his left arm,
Both shield and a muleta. The white belly
Was unprotected and the animal
Felt the knife as it entered her and felt
The steel burning inside her as she died.
The duel was fatal, and it was infinite.
He went on killing always the same jaguar
Which was immortal. Don't let this surprise you
Too much. His destiny is yours, and mine,
Except for the fact that our jaguar takes forms
That change continuously. Call it Hatred,
Or Love, or Hazard, call it Every Moment.

The Temptation

Here goes General Quiroga to his funeral,
Invited by the venal Santos Pérez,
And above Santos Pérez there is Rosas,
The deeply hidden spider of Palermo.

As a devout coward, Rosas knows
That of all men there isn't anyone
More vulnerable and fragile than the brave man.
Juan Facundo Quiroga is audacious
To the point of lunacy. This fact may be
Worth the consideration of one who hates him.
Who has resolved to kill him. Vacillates,
But at last finds the weapon he was seeking:
What else but the dark hunger and thirst for danger?
Quiroga leaves for the north. This same Rosas
Tips him off, almost at the foot of the carriage,
That rumor has it that that bastard López
Premeditates his murder. He suggests
That he not undertake so bold a journey
Without escort. He himself offers one.
Facundo has been smiling. He does not
Need help. He can rely on himself. The creaking
Carriage leaves the settlements behind.
Miles of heavy rain mire it down,
Mud and swirling mist and the rising water.
At last they make out Córdoba. The Córdobans,
Having already given them up for dead,
Look at them as if they were their ghosts.
Last night all Córdoba watched as Santos Pérez
Handed out the swords. The hunting party
Consists of thirty riders from the sierra.
Never before, Sarmiento will write,
Has a crime been set afoot so brazenly.
Juan Facundo Quiroga seems untroubled.
He moves on. In Santiago del Estero
He gives himself to the sweet risk of cards;
Between sundown and dawn he wins or loses
Hundreds and hundreds of gold doubloons. By dawn
Danger signals have multiplied. Abruptly

He decides to turn back and gives the order.
Over those mountains, through that open country
They retrace their steps along the dangerous roads.
In a nondescript place called Ojo de Agua
The posthouse keeper tells him that the party
Dispatched to murder him has passed that way
And lies in wait for them in a place he names.
No one is to be spared. Those are the orders.
Or so he has been told by Santos Pérez,
Their captain. But Facundo doesn't frighten—
The man who has the nerve to kill Quiroga
Hasn't been born yet, is his cool rejoinder.
The other men are ashen and say nothing.
Night falls, and only one of them is sleeping,
The fated one, the strong one, who has faith
In his dark gods. Gradually it grows light.
They will not live to see another morning.
What is the point, one wonders, in concluding
A story told once and for all? The carriage
Sets off down the road to Barranca Yaco.

The White Hind

From what back-country ballad of England's verdant land,
From what Persian miniature, from what mysterious realm
Of all the nights and mornings that our yesterday hides in its hand
Comes the snow-white hind that appeared to me this morning in my dream?
It would have been only an instant. I saw her cross the meadow
And disappear into the gold of a spectral close of day,
Airy creature made out of a little gleam of memory
And a little of forgetfulness, white hind that casts no shadow.
The deities and spirits by whom this curious world is ruled
Permitted me to dream you but not to have you for my own;
Perhaps in some meander that the endless future may hold

I shall find you again, oh white hind that for one instant shone.
I myself am a fleeting dream that lasts but a day or two,
But little more than the dream of a moment of whiteness and of dew.

Elegy for the Impossible Memory

What wouldn't I give for the memory
Of a dirt street with low adobe walls
And a tall horseman looming against the dawn
(His poncho long and frayed)
On one of those days on the plains
That has no date.
What wouldn't I give for the memory
Of my mother looking out at the morning
On the ranch at Santa Irene,
Not knowing that her name would be Borges.
What wouldn't I give for the memory
Of having fought at Cepeda
And seen Estanislao del Campo
Riding out to meet the first bullet
With brave and reckless joy.
What wouldn't I give for the memory
Of a great wooden door to a hidden villa
That my father pushed open each night
Before getting lost in sleep
And pushed open for the last time
On the 14th of February, 1938.
What wouldn't I give for the memory
Of Hengist's long ships
Weighing anchor off the sands of Denmark
To conquer an island
Not yet called England.
What wouldn't I give for the memory

(I had it once and have lost it)
Of a golden canvas of Turner's,
Immense as music.
What wouldn't I give for the memory
Of having heard Socrates
As, on the evening of hemlock,
He serenely examined the problem
Of immortality,
Balancing myth and logic
While blue death crept upward
From his feet, already numb.
What wouldn't I give for the memory
Of your having said that you loved me
And of not having slept until dawn,
Heartbroken and happy.

Relics

The Southern Hemisphere. Under its algebra
of constellations unknown to Ulysses,
a man is seeking and will go on seeking
the faint relics of that epiphany
vouchsafed to him, so many years ago,
on the other side of a numbered door
in a hotel, beside the timeless Thames,
that flows along as that other river flows,
the ethereal element of time. The flesh
forgets its sorrows and its happinesses.
The man waits and dreams. Slowly, vaguely,
he rescues a few trivial circumstances.
A woman's name, a whiteness, a body
by now without a face; the hazy half-light
of an evening of no date; the drizzling rain;

a few wax flowers on a marble slab;
and the low walls, the color a pale rose.

Elegy

Buenos Aires, 14 January 1984

Now it is yours, Abramowicz, the singular taste of death, withheld
from no one, which will be offered to me in this house or across the ocean,
on the banks of your Rhône, flowing fatally as if it were Time itself, that
other and more ancient Rhône. Yours too the certainty that Time leaves its
yesterdays behind and that nothing is irreparable or the opposing certainty
that the days can erase nothing and that there is no act, no dream, that
does not cast an infinite shadow. Geneva considered you a jurist, a man
of lawsuits and verdicts, but in every word, in every silence, you were a
poet. Perhaps this very moment you are leafing through the various books
which you did not write but imagined and gave up on, and which for us
justify you and in a way exist. During the first war, while men were killing
one another, we two dreamed two dreams that were named Laforgue and
Baudelaire. We discovered things that all young men discover: ignorant love,
irony, a longing to be Raskolnikov or Prince Hamlet, words and sunsets.
Generations of Israel were in you when you said to me one time, smiling, *Je
suis très fatigué. J'ai quatre mille ans.* This took place on the Earth; useless to
guess how old you must be in Heaven.

I don't know if you are still someone, I don't know if you can hear me.

To One No Longer Young

Now you can see the tragic mise en scène
With everything in its accustomed place—
Ashes and sword for Dido the sad queen,
The coin for poor blind Belisarius.

Why do you keep on looking for the war
In the old bronze hexameters darkly lit

When here they are, the seven feet of dirt,
The sudden hemorrhage, the open pit?

Here the plummetless mirror that will dream
And then forget the face of your extreme
And final days, is keeping you in sight.

Now the end draws near. It is the house
Where the slow hours of your brief evening pass,
The street that fills your eyes, day in, day out.

Robert Mezey, 1991

EUGENIO FLORIT (1903–99)

Conversation with My Father

Clearly you already know it
you already know it all
know it all clearly.
Because of this you know too
how I wish to tell it,
for while I speak I am recalling
as I sit here beside you:
I writing
and you silent beside me.

. . . Well, since you left
many things have happened . . .
Men have died and been born,
grown ill and recovered,
felt well, taken their
sup of soup, piece of fish,
got up, gone into the sun
like cats to the window.
Others do not get up
but remain stretched out
and die.
Die like you,
and others, men and women,
and all that you love
and all those who follow you.
Although many still live.
They keep living, despite weeping and mourning.
And one day they want to go
for a walk, to go to the movies,
to play the piano much as you do.
Not that in this way I bury you deeper;

but that, more living, they remember you more.
Because they live with you, with what you enjoyed
in your books. (Though I still
have in its grey covers, *Peñas arriba,*
which you left open
that day . . .)
And we all continue living
and you see, remembering you daily.
And we say: he liked this dessert,
and used to walk here, always in a hurry,
and once shaved off his moustache
and at once let it grow again.

. . . .

More than once I thought
how much you enjoyed
walking in these parts, to go to the museum
and there tell me about *Las Meninas*
and then gazing side by side at *La Duquesa de Alba,*
that Doña Cayetana de Silva
that your brother Pepe once brought
from the other side.
Yes, it would be fine
to wander again through so many rooms—except
the little French things of the 18th century, so silly,
and the English women with their buttery flesh.
And then go into the park
and sit down to talk at our ease
observing how at sunset the air
moves rippling the lighted waters of the pool.

You already know how the war came about
and how in it people died;
and how the war ended
and how the people's mania followed it

bent on destruction, killing
as if all the maceration of flesh were not enough.
And we learn nothing.
And it is sad to think that all this agony
could simply disappear
if man could learn to wipe the grin from his face,
and to say one good word, truly,
and wish, in fact, to make life noble.
But he does not want it, as you see.
What he wants is to follow
this overwhelming dance of death
which is not your death nor mine
—that is to say, death as it may happen
about the house, one that is met in slippers
or at most in the open country
or in clear water,
without the other, heaped up mountainous
in stinking fields and foul waters,
death which drops from the air
and comes from hiding
to crush bodies as if they were nuts
reap them as if they were heads of wheat.

Then there are other things:
the case of the atomic bomb,
to me, among ourselves, leaves me neither hot nor cold
—to the day it leaves me in eternity cold.
And that would be the last of my worries.
That which worries me most is to be blinded or maimed
unable to see a day full of sunlight
nor hold a rose in my fingers
for the eyes have fallen into a pit of darkness
the fingers remain dried up like burlap.
I say, that if we are to see, it means almost nothing to me.

But the inquisition of having to be seated
in those metal chairs or made of I don't know what,
with glass mirrors where you may not sit
which are on the walls and the window,
but mirrors where plates and cups are set
and glassware on the tables instead of wood,
so that you have to keep looking at the skirts of the ladies,
that yes, is more an inquisition than the bomb.
When you left, all of this had hardly begun,
but now . . .
I tell you I yearn to go into an old curtained house
with rugs on the floors
(but real ones, not those made of wood-fiber and synthetic silk)
and wide comfortable chairs
(so as not to be seated as if out of courtesy
on hollow metal stuck into our hams)
and lamps like those which thank God
I have at home
(and like those others
found in funeral parlors
or hotel lobbies, lamps, yes, which give light
but cast no shadow).
And the worst is that it pleases people to have it
this way, and there are those
who tear up a whole marble fireplace in their homes
to replace it with an idiotic artifact
embodying a thermostat and air control and
I don't know what else,
but which, since there is no visible flame,
gives off heat without light
and since there is no light there are no shadows
shadows for the half closing of the eyes
to quit reading and turning the page,
to quit reading with half vision

shadows to redirect the wavering eyes
and refocus them on the word
which awaits us at the end of the strophe.
(With all this, father,
you will say that I am growing old;
and you'll be right.
At my years I prefer
to go home and hang up my overcoat and hat,
and to take a cup of tea with lemon in it
or chocolate beside the window.
Since thank God I am not cold,
I tranquilly allow the cat
to do whatever he pleases.
And if the question of a cat hot or cold
is beside the point,
the question for us, you and me, and whoever else
is to pass the time reading.)

Let us turn to other things,
in my opinion, you are well off up there.
Did you finally go to your own Castilian land
as I thought you would?
You must have enjoyed meeting
so many friends
and stopped to talk with them
on some Cuban threshing floor at midday.
(There will be those who will think this an error
for they do not know of the little town that you loved;
where, as soon as I can, will go his ashes.)
But to change the subject,
you would be amused
to see how your son
the poet has turned painter
—of course only to put down mere nonsense.

Because, as you well know
—now I recall those little green mountains
and those blue skies that you painted in tempera
for the Nativity scenes you made for us at Port-Bou—
I say, as you know,
it is something very amusing
to daub a canvas with paint
without knowing whether it is going to be flowers or a gorilla.
With me it is mostly monsters
but I hope some day . . .

And with this hope I leave you for the time being.
It is late. You know I never leave you;
that to stop talking is not to quit you,
I take myself off, but still listening,
I am with you when I leave you . . .
I mean . . . that I do not go, leaving;
but let me finish this letter
though I am seated beside you forever.
For when I stop talking to you, I continue to talk.
Well, I am making a botch of it, but you
          understand.

                              William Carlos Williams, 2011

PABLO NERUDA *(1904–73)*

Ode to My Socks

Maru Mori brought me
a pair
of socks
that she knitted with her own hands
of a shepherdess,
two soft socks
you'd say they were rabbits.
In them
I stuck my feet
as in
two
jewel cases
woven
with threads of
twilight
and lamb skins.

Violent socks,
my feet were
two fish
made of wool,
two long sharks
of ultramarine blue
shot
with a tress of gold
two gigantic blackbirds,
two cannons:
my feet
were honored
in this manner
by

these
celestial
socks.
They were
so beautiful
that for the first time
my feet seemed to me
unacceptable
like two decrepit
firemen, firemen
unworthy
of that embroidered
fire,
those luminous
socks.

Nevertheless
I resisted
the acute temptation
to keep them
as schoolboys
keep
fireflies,
or the erudite
collect
sacred documents,
I resisted
the furious impulse
to put them
in a cage
of gold
and to feed them
every day
bird seed

and the pulp of rosey
melon.
Like discoverers
who in the forest
yield the very rare
green deer
to the spit
and with regret
eat it,
I stretched out
my feet
and pulled over them
the
beautiful
socks
and
then my shoes.

And this is
the moral of my ode:
twice beautiful
is beauty
and what is good is twice
good
when it is two socks
made of wool
in winter.

William Carlos Williams, 2011

MIGUEL HERNÁNDEZ (1910–42)

So Bitter Was That Lemon When You Threw It

So bitter was that lemon when you threw it—
with a hand as innocent as warm—
that it retained the rigor of its form
and the harsh, bitter taste by which I knew it.

My blood, roused by the yellow jolt that drew it,
rose to a fever from its former calm,
as if it had been nipped to quick alarm
when a long, rigid nipple bit into it.

But when I saw your smile—how I provided
amusement with your lemon to my chest,
and my dark thought so far from your perceiving—

inside my shirt the blood swiftly subsided,
and what had been that porous golden breast
became a sudden, sharp, bewildered grieving.

Rhina P. Espaillat, 2011

HÉCTOR INCHAÚSTEGUI CABRAL *(1912–79)*

Gentle Song for the Donkeys of My Town

Donkey—Saint Joseph's, and the coal-man's too—
sad vehicle that links the poor bastard
and the arrogant rich,
you whose ambling trot carries, in early morning,
the field hand's sour sweat
transmuted to fragrant fruits,
dark yucca, bright green plantain,
our native pepper,
and the delicate complex leaf
of coriander, large and small.

If the pregnant girl is nearly due,
let her go by donkey;
if the old man can barely take another step
because the earth is calling him,
let him ride the donkey;
if the child is too small
to take the milk to town,
it's all right, let him go by donkey. . . .
Mount of Saint Joseph and the small-town con man,
of the accordion player and the schoolteacher
whose hair has been gray these thirty years;
donkey that brings water,
carries precious medicine,
donkey whose infancy is sad and short,
and whose old age is long and sadder still. . . .

Young, you are all ingenuousness, soft eyes,
long shaggy pelt and gentleness
and wordless love
of the thin shade of acacia trees. . . .

Later, long fallen ears
dead as two useless husks
over your noble, heavy cloud of brow.

Later, the bitterness of each long trek,
burdens—too heavy—
bruises—dense and red—
and sometimes, in late afternoon,
the small white hand of a child
stroking slowly
your aching lower lip
where the thorn
no longer finds a foothold
for its single cleat.

And later still, bare open field,
thistles blooming yellow,
grass out of reach,
well-aimed stones,
pitched words,
sharp bone slowly piercing
your hairless hide,
a mass of prickly weeds
clinging to rump and feet and lower lip.

Donkey—Saint Joseph's, and the coal-man's too—
sad, slow vehicle that links
desperate country need
with the town's pretense of city life,
donkey whose infancy is useless and happy
and whose old age, like ours,
comes to its close
at the wide gates
of the other world.

Rhina P. Espaillat, 2011

OCTAVIO PAZ *(1914–98)*

Tomb of the Poet

The book
    The glass
The green obscurely a stalk
        The record
Sleeping beauty in her bed of music
Things drowned in their names
To say them with the eyes
        In a beyond I cannot tell where
Nail them down
        Lamp pencil portrait
This that I see
      To nail it down
Like a living temple
      Plant it
Like a tree
    A god
Crown it
    With a name
      Immortal
Derisible crown of thorns—
      Speech!
The stalk and its imminent flower
        Sun-sex-sun
The flower without shadow
        In a beyond without where
Opens
    Like the horizon
      Opens
Immaculate extension
Transparency which sustains things

Fallen
       Raised up
By the glance
           Held
In a reflection
Moons multiplied
             Across the steppe
Bundle of worlds
            Instants
Glowing bunches
Moving forests of stars
Wandering syllables
Millennia of sand endlessly falling away
                   Tide
All the times of time
        TO BE
A second's fraction
           Lamp pencil portrait
In a here I cannot tell where
           A name
Begins
       Seize on it, plant it, say it
Like a wood that thinks
          Flesh it
A lineage begins
        In a name
An adam
      Like a living temple
Name without shadow
        Nailed
Like a god
      In this here-without-where—
Speech!
     I cease in its beginning

In this that I say

        I cease

TO BE

      Shadow of an instantaneous name

I shall never know my bond's undoing

Ustica

The successive suns of summer,[1]
The succession of the sun and of its summers,
All the suns,
The sole, the sol of sols
Now become
Obstinate and tawny bone,
Darkness-before-the-storm
Of matter cooled.

Fist of stone,
Pinecone of lava,
Ossuary,
Not earth
Nor island either,
Rock off a rockface,
Hard peach,
Sun-drop petrified.

Through the nights one hears
The breathing of the cisterns,
The panting of fresh water
Troubled by the sea.
The hour is late and the light, greening.
The obscure body of the wine
Asleep in jars

---

1. Ustica is a volcanic desert island in the Sicilian sea. It was a Saracen graveyard.

Is a darker and cooler sun.

Here the rose of the depths
Is a candelabrum of pinkish veins
Kindled on the sea-bed,
Ashore, the sun extinguishes it,
Pale, chalky lace
As if desire were worked by death.

Cliffs the colour of sulphur,
High austere stones.
You are beside me,
Your thoughts are black and golden.
To extend a hand
Is to gather a cluster of truths intact.
Below, between sparkling rocks
Goes and comes
A sea full of arms.
Vertigos. The light hurls itself headlong.
I looked you in the face,
I saw into the abyss:
Mortality is transparency.

Ossuary: paradise:
Our roots, knotted
In sex, in the undone mouth
Of the buried Mother.
Incestuous trees
That maintain
A garden on the dead's domain.

Touch

My hands
Open the curtains of your being
Clothe you in a further nudity

Uncover the bodies of your body
My hands
Invent another body for your body

Friendship

It is the awaited hour
Over the table falls
Interminably
The lamp's spread hair
Night turns the window to immensity
There is no one here
Presence without name surrounds me.

Dawn

Cold rapid hands
Draw back one by one
The bandages of dark
I open my eyes
                        Still
I am living
                    At the centre
Of a wound still fresh

Here

My steps along this street
Resound
            In another street
In which
            I hear my steps
Passing along this street
In which

Only the mist is real

Oracle

The cold lips of the night
Utter a word
Column of grief
No word but stone
No stone but shadow
Vaporous thought
Through my vaporous lips real water
Word of truth
Reason behind my errors
If it is death only through that do I live
If it is solitude I speak in serving it
It is memory and I remember nothing
I do not know what it says and I trust myself to
How to know oneself living
How to forget one's knowing
Time that half-opens the eyelids
And sees us, letting itself be seen.

Certainty

If it is real the white
Light from this lamp, real
The writing hand, are they
Real, the eyes looking at what I write?

From one word to the other
What I say vanishes.
I know that I am alive
Between two parentheses.

Charles Tomlinson, 1968

JUAN MATOS *(b. 1956)*

The Illusion of Memory

On a phrase by García Márquez

The exile is not one man alone.
He is the man who departed and the man who arrived.
The man who departed, departed,
and left behind all that was left, which, being left,
nevertheless is not there.
Where?
His garden.
His school.
His people . . .
Where?
The man who departed, departed,
but those others . . .
Where?
The man who departed
departed alone.
Alone.
But with everything!

The man who arrived,
arrived, and with him, himself.
The man who arrived
came alone.
But in his eyes he brought everything.
Everything.
His life on his back.
The man who arrived
arrived, and with him, himself.
But he came alone.
Alone . . . only himself.

The Night Was a Pretense of Night

We, those we were, are no longer the same.
—Pablo Neruda

The night was a pretense of night
and you the simulacrum
of the woman I dreamed nightly
but I was not the man I had been that night
nor the one you wished for.

Like a slender necklace reduced to words
I slipped from your altar toward oblivion
like paper scribbled with poems that could not
fill the void in your breast or crown your waiting.

In this being without being—surf without sand—
I live without living, tormenting your heart
like death that gnaws but will not
finally sever the absurd and empty hours.

The night was a pretense of night
and I the not-I sent to punish you
and sentenced to the shipwreck and the pain
of being no more than the solitude of your nights.

Life was a pretense of life
and I the attempt unmade, the unforged
agonizing arrowhead—deep wound
forever unhealed despite its silence.

Rhina P. Espaillat, 2011

SWEDISH ▶

GUNNAR EKELÖF *(1907–68)*

"There exists something that fits nowhere"

There exists something that fits nowhere
And yet is in no way remarkable
And yet is decisive
And yet is outside it all.
There exists something which is perceived just when it is not
    perceived (as silence)
And is not perceived just where it is perceivable
For there it is exchanged (as silence) for another thing.

See the waves under the sky. Storm is surface
And storm our way of seeing.
(What do I care for the waves or the seventh wave.)
There is an emptiness between the waves:
Look at the sea. Look at the stones of the field.
There is an emptiness between the stones:
They did not break loose—they did not throw themselves out,
They lie there and exist—a part of the rock sheath.
So make yourself heavy—make use of your dead weight,
Let yourself break, let yourself be thrown away, fall,
Ship-wrecked on rocks!
(What do I care about rocks.)

There are universes, suns and atoms.
There is a knowledge carefully built on strong piles.
There is a knowledge, unprotected, built on insecure emptiness.
There is an emptiness between universes, suns and atoms.
(What do I care about universes, suns and atoms.)
There is a second viewpoint on everything
In this double life.

There is peace beyond all.
There is peace behind all.
There is peace inside all.

Concealed in the hand.
Concealed in the pen.
Concealed in the ink.
I feel peace over everything.
I smell peace behind everything.
I see and hear peace inside everything,
One-colored peace beyond everything.
(What do I care about peace.)

"The knight has rested for a long time"

The knight has rested for a long time
straight in the saddle
high in the mountainous land
so desolate that the eye hesitates
Wonderful stretches of smoky hills that never come near!
Beneath and far off his companions are chattering
The falcon waits on his breast
it has laid its head on his cheek

O strange tenderness in my heart!
—Then he raises his hand
and the bird flies out
away
He sits there and watches it climb
in gyres always higher and higher
He rests still straight in the saddle
when the night falls
Feared night!
Longed-for night!

"When one has come as far as I in pointlessness"

When one has come as far as I in pointlessness
Each word is once more fascinating:
Finds in the loam
Which one turns up with an archeologist's spade:
The tiny word you
Perhaps a pearl of glass
Which once hung around someone's neck
The huge word I
Perhaps a flint shard
With which someone who had no teeth scraped his own
Flesh

"So strange to me"

So strange to me
this rose, this thing delicately bursting out
this absent thoughtfulness
or light over a turned-away cheek . . .
As on a spring day
when you sense something and hold it firmly
an instant, a second
unchangeable
something that shall never turn to summer

Christina Bratt and Robert Bly, 1963

LARS GUSTAFSSON *(b. 1936)*

San Francisco Sailing Further Underground

When the light falls over the hills
they brighten like fire, for a last moment

the whole city drinks the light

The first white men who saw Alcatraz
found the island swarming with penguins

solemn comical birds that died easily.

The Chinese were called in by Morgan, ten dollars,
not as a wage but once for all

and they died like flies in their railworks
no Chinese women were allowed

but ten or eleven came in any case
all Chinatown from eleven Chinese wombs

and the sick young girls from Canton
were locked in the cellars to die

Kaiser Morton, Lord of the USA
protector of Mexico, donor of the Xmas tree in Union Square

there's verdigris along his epaulettes

he died easily one winter night

If you are quiet you can hear the Creoles dance

Schooners, galliasses, four-masters, barques
entire city quarters consist of sunken ships

which were filled with sand and anchored
in a sisterly manner close against each other

The whole Embarcadero rests on an underground fleet.

Pan American Building, Bank of America

the skyscrapers are standing on decks deep down

and under the earth that fleet is sailing on

Free Fall

year after year it goes on
sometimes it seems to slow up

but it never stops

here are big friendly trees
they're not waiting for me

in the yellowed grass of late summer
the flock of crows rises

violently,

as if they didn't want to be overheard

someone simply strokes my hair
and I am perfectly happy
for three minutes

then I go on falling

headlong

year after year it goes on

there is no hand to catch me

and that's all

Darkness

Round my other side
my averted side
my uninhabited side

Darkness in darkness
and in the inmost dark
something to wrestle with

strong enough to whirl me away like a leaf

Fragment

(A . . . confined, in the command module
on the first expedition to Jupiter

after thirty four weeks goes into orbit
round the biggest, most ancient planet.

Then for four seconds
he weighs as much

as the biggest bronze bell in Kiev
and doesn't know it.)

. . . .

(A vanishes

like a shining point into the terminator's giant shadow.)

A Poem on Revisionism

An uncertain fly
trapped in a night-express

still tries flying
and finds it succeeds remarkably

Having come from the southern to the northern end of the coach
a much wiser fly already

the train going faster and faster into the night

Robin Fulton, 1974

VIETNAMESE ▶

NGUYỄN BỈNH KHIÊM *(1491–1585)*

Ironic Apology

This annoying war. And I, comfortable in my horror of it,
content, safe, solitary, terribly concerned, of course.
My duty pledges me to my former lord
and I must keep my word, remain apart, aloof—
all an immortal can hope for. I should not have to face the world,
only sing a little, meditate, blend my soul with the universe.
This inconsiderate war. I must dwell on the word "contentment,"
a poet, an immortal, after all.
Anyone can be involved, of course.
How many people can choose fame?

Nguyen Ngoc Bich and Robin Morgan, 1967

PHÙNG KHẮC KHOAN *(1528–1613)*

On War

War, no end to it, people scattered in all directions.
How can a man keep his mind off it?
The winds dark, the rains violent year after year,
laying waste the land, over and over.
After all, a man can make up his own mind
whether to act or not. They cut each other's throats
for the world. I can't take much interest in it.
Who is it that moves the clouds and permits the sun to shine?
He speaks, he smiles, he goes on bringing peace to the world.

Nguyen Ngoc Bich and W. S. Merwin, 1967

TO HUU *(1920–2002)*

Road Sabotage

The cold moves from Thai-nguyen down to Yen-the
and the wind rages through the woods and the Khe Pass.
But I am a woman from Bac-Giang who does not feel the cold,
who feels nothing but the land, the land.
At home we have yet to dry the paddy
and stock the corn and chop the manioc;
at home we have quite a few children;
still, I follow my husband to sabotage the road.
Lullaby, my child, sleep well, and wait.
When the moon fades, I will return.

> Over the hills
> the moon squats, watching.
> The road is too long, the holes too shallow.
> Deeper, they must be deeper pits.
> Spades, shovels, hands, men, women.
>
> The rocks fall, the earth breaks.
> Deeper, they must be deeper.
> The soil smells rich in the darkness,
> the women compete with the men in teams:
> men, women, spades, shovels, hands.

You have grown skilled at this, but so have I.
The road is too long, the night too short.
The path curves, winds, twists,
yet we gash our trenches into its flesh:
pits for the French when they come this way,
beds for the French to lie in,
graves in the land for the enemy of the land.
Faster, we must go faster. Deeper, they must be deeper.
The wind forms ice on my eyes and blurs the moon.

No child's cry breaks the silence, only the hushed rhythm
of spades, shovels, hands, sabotaging the road.

Nguyen Ngoc Bich and Robin Morgan, 1967

TRU VU *(b. 1931)*

The Statue of the Century

I hammer the pain of separateness
into a statue to stand in the park.
Below it I carve a horizontal inscription
that reads: Soul of the Twentieth Century.

My statue spills no tears
for it has none left to spend.
My statue tells no stories
for what's the use of telling stories.

My statue: the soul of the century
with no halos above its head.
My statue: the soul of the century
with no phoenixes beneath its feet.

My statue in fact is bare, naked,
no banner in its hand.
My statue casts its shadow aimless, everywhere,
with stone eyes fixed on nothing.

    Nguyen Ngoc Bich and Robin Morgan, 1967

TỪ KẾ TƯỜNG *(b. 1946)*

That Painter in the City

1

in the morning you just wake up when that painter suddenly splashes
    a swarm of green leaves
every one of us we see the sun suspended in air
but not that painter
he insists on thinking it a ripe fruit
and so he paints on the citreous background
a strange perfume

2

when he turns mad and jumps on the sandbag to perform
the children crowd round and cheer
the painter draws a ripe grenade hanging from a branch
and he loudly proclaims to the multitude
everlasting peace
he also points out to everyone
a sunbaked corpse loitering on the fence
then he adds to it just a touch of remaining fresh blood

3

and when the blind bird is with child
he sketches on our eyes a pair of wooden crutches
and says here is enduring happiness
to illumine your blackened days

4

then the day we lie down
that painter again strokes a fresh green meadow
he says that's a cool and comfortable bed
and every morning

he adds innumerable fragrant blossoms
as we start to forget to breathe little by little.

Nguyen Ngoc Bich and Robin Morgan, 1967

ACKNOWLEDGMENTS

A special note of appreciation to the following authors' representatives for granting permission to publish their works in this anthology:

The translations of Anna Akhmatova appear with the permission of Mrs. Margarita Novgorodova and FTM Agency, Ltd.

"La rosa" from *Fervor de Buenos Aires* and "Buenos Aires" from *El Otro, El Mismo* by Jorge Luis Borges. Copyright © 1996 by Maria Kodama, used by permission of The Wylie Agency LLC.

Translation of "Chanson," "Les Amours XIII," and "Dedication of a Mirror to Venus" by W. S. Merwin. Copyright © 1949 by W. S. Merwin. Translation of "He goes, my lover," "Friends, I cannot deny," "Waken, my love, who sleep in the cold morning," and "At the voice of the enchanter" by W. S. Merwin. Copyright © 1952 by W. S. Merwin. Translation of "That the fevered breath attain relief," "Glorious Lord, fountain of clarity," and "High waves that shift and gather from the sea" by W. S. Merwin. Copyright © 1950 by W. S. Merwin. Translation of "Insomnia. Homer. Taut sails.," "Tristia," "We shall meet again, in Petersburg," and "Armed with the sight of the fine wasps" by W. S. Merwin. Copyright © 1972 by W. S. Merwin. All of the above are reprinted by permission of The Wylie Agency LLC.

Permission for use of "Three Fables from La Fontaine" ("The Scythian Philosopher," "Phoebus and Boreas," and "The Schoolboy, the Pendant, and the Man with a Garden") is granted by David M. Moore, Administrator of the Literary Estate of Marianne Moore.

Grateful acknowledgment is due the many sources that provided background information for the biographical notes in this anthology.

NOTES ON POETS

Anna Akhmatova. Considered in the pantheon of renowned Russian poets, along with Osip Mandelstam, Boris Pasternak, and Marina Tsvetaeva, she survived blacklisting by Joseph Stalin, and the imprisonment of her son under his regime, to become through her voice the conscience of Russia. The poems translated by Judith Hemschemeyer predate the revolution.

Anonymous Fourteenth-Century Poet. He was active in the late fourteenth century, writing a more obscure northern dialect of Middle English than his contemporary Chaucer, whose southern speech became the main source of modern English. He is referred to as either "the *Gawain* Poet" or "the *Pearl* Poet," from another poem accepted as by the same hand and surviving in the same manuscript not rediscovered until the mid-nineteenth century.

Guillaume Apollinaire. Born in Rome, he traveled through Europe before settling in Paris. After he returned wounded from World War I, his play *Les mamelles de Tiresias: Drame surrealiste* (The Breasts of Tiresias), produced in 1917, contributed to establishing the surrealist movement. His poetic works include *Alcools: Poèmes, 1898–1913*, edited by Tristan Tzara (1913), and *Calligrammes: Poèmes de la paix et de la guerre* (Calligrammes: Poems of Peace and War) (1918).

Jean-Antoine de Baïf. One of the French poets forming the Pléiade, after the influential group of seven Alexandrian poets (third century B.C.), he created new metrical patterns and a system of spelling based on phonetics. As royal secretary to Charles IX, he lived at court in Paris and, in 1570, founded the

Académie de Poésie et de Musique. In 1572 he published his collected *Euvres en rime* in four volumes.

Charles Baudelaire. French poet and noted critic of contemporary art, he also gained renown as the translator of Edgar Allan Poe. Considered an early modernist, his singular volume of poetry, *Les fleurs du mal* (The Flowers of Evil) (1857), published in several subsequent editions, remains a major influence on the work of poets in later periods.

Joachim du Bellay. A poet, critic, and member of the Pléiade group of poets, in 1553 he traveled to Rome as a secretary to his cousin Cardinal Jean du Bellay, where he wrote *Les antiquités de Rome* (The Ruins of Rome) early in his four-and-half-year residence. The sonnets of *Les antiquités* provide a glimpse of classical Rome from the point of view of the French Renaissance.

G. G. Belli. Though largely unknown in his lifetime, he authored 2,279 sonnets written in Romanesco, the dialect of the people of Rome. They give spirited, funny, frequently obscene accounts of life under the nineteenth-century papacy. Today, he is considered a major poet of the period.

Yves Bonnefoy. Trained as a philosopher, he is also an essayist, literary critic, and art historian as well as the most important contemporary translator of Shakespeare and other English poets into French. Described as France's greatest postwar poet, he has authored ten books of poetry, most recently *L'heure présente* (2011). His many honors include the Prix Montaigne (1978) and the *Hudson Review*'s Bennett Award for Literary Achievement (1988).

Jorge Luis Borges. An Argentine poet, short-story writer, essayist, and translator, he is recognized as one of the foremost literary figures of the twentieth century. He was director of the National Public Library and a professor at the University of Buenos Aires. He shared the first Prix International with Samuel Beckett in 1981.

Catullus. According to Cicero, he was of the "neoteric" poets who rejected the epic and its public themes in favor of using colloquial language to describe personal experiences. His poems survived in a single manuscript discovered in Verona around 1305 and then disappeared again but not before copies were made, one of which, with 116 poems, resides in the Bodleian Library at Oxford University.

C. P. Cavafy. A Greek poet born in Alexandria, Egypt, he worked at the Ministry of Public Works in Alexandria (1892–1922). He published little during his lifetime, preferring instead to circulate poems among friends. A short collection of his poetry was privately printed in the early 1900s and reprinted with new verse a few years later.

Christine de Pisan. Though born in Venice, she lived most of her life in Paris. As a young widow, she began writing in Middle French to support her family, thus becoming Europe's first professional woman writer. She composed poems on courtly love as well as polemical prose works. Eventually, she retired to an abbey and composed a long poem celebrating Joan of Arc.

Pierre Corneille. Widely acknowledged as the creator of French classical tragedy, he was one of the three great seventeenth-century French dramatists, along with Molière and Racine. He is best known for *Le Cid*, whose complexities regarding duty and honor typify the playwright's emphasis on psychological reaction over exaggerated action. A prolific playwright, he expanded the boundaries and raised the level of dramaturgy on the French stage.

Rubén Darío (Félix Rubén García Sarmiento). He was an influential Nicaraguan poet, journalist, and diplomat. As a leader of the Spanish American literary movement known as *modernismo*, which flourished at the end of the nineteenth century, he revolutionized poetry in Spanish on both sides of the Atlantic through his experiments with rhythm, meter, and imagery.

Giraut de Bornelh. A twelfth-century French troubadour of humble origins from the Limousin region, he would study in winter and travel from court to court in summer, giving his income to impoverished relatives and the church. In 1168 he went to the court of King Alfonso II of Aragon.

Joan de Guilhade. He was a low-ranking noble who made a living as a troubadour, apparently employing jongleurs to propagate his songs. Active in the mid-thirteenth century, the heyday of the Galician-Portuguese school, he was one of its most prolific and inventive poets, with fifty-four surviving *cantigas* that employ a number of original images and instances of irony.

Guillem Comte de Peitau. A powerful count considered the first of the Provençal troubadour poets, he was equally conversant with Arabic Spain and northern France. This tradition was carried on by his immediate successors, especially the ones in the courtly love tradition in the royal courts of his granddaughter Eleanor of Aquitaine, who continued the kinship with the Moorish kingdoms. Eleven of his troubadour verses are extant.

Gunnar Ekelöf. A member of the Swedish Academy (1958), he was a poet, critic, and essayist. In his first collection, *Sent på jorden* (1932), his poems were imbued with surrealism, whereas later work also reflected his interest in musical forms and Eastern mysticism. In his final decade, his Akritas trilogy explored the simultaneous experience of presence and transitoriness.

Sergei Essenin. A Russian lyric poet, he bemoaned the industrialization of rural Russia and the political unrest born of the Civil War and World War I, calling himself the "last poet of the village." He toured the United States with his wife, dancer Isadora Duncan. *The Collected Poems of Yesenin in English* was published in 2000.

Eugenio Florit. A poet, critic, and translator, he was born in Spain and emigrated to Cuba as a teenager with his family. He taught Spanish and Latin American literature at Barnard College from 1944 to 1969. In addition to his thirty-four volumes of poetry, his criticism included *Hispanic-American Poetry since Modernism* (1968).

Jean Follain. A French poet born in Normandy, he was a member of the group called Sagesse. The last of his nine volumes of poems was titled *Espaces d'instants* (1971). In 1970 he was awarded the Grand Prix de Poésie from the Académie Française for his life's work.

Bogomil Gjuzel. A founder of the Association of Independent Writers of Macedonia, since 1995 he has edited its bimonthly journal, *Naše Pismo*. Born in Èaèak, Serbia, he is a poet, prose writer, playwright, essayist, and translator. From 1999 to 2003, he was acting director of the Struga Poetry Evenings International Festival.

Johann Wolfgang von Goethe. Two works brought him early fame: *Goetz von Berlichingen* (1773), a play of Sturm und Drang (Storm and Stress), and *Die Leiden des jungen Werthers* (The Sorrows of Young Werther) (1774), his saga of unhappy love. He lived thereafter at the court of the Duke of Saxe-Weimar-Eisenach and held office in the Weimar government. His greatest work was *Faust*, a dramatic poem in two parts.

Fakhr addin Gorgani. He was an eleventh-century Persian poet.

Jorge Guillén. A Spanish lyric poet, translator, and professor who became a member of the Generation of 1927, the group of poets who commemorated the tercentenary of Luis de Góngora and were influenced by such European movements as symbolism, futurism, and surrealism. In exile voluntarily to protest the Franco regime, he taught Spanish literature at Wellesley College (1940–57). His major works are *Cantico* (1928), later expanded, and *Homenaje* (1967). He received the *Hudson Review*'s Bennett Award for Literary Achievement (1975) and the Cervantes Prize (1976).

Lars Gustafsson. He edited the Swedish literary journal *Bonniers Litterära Magasin* (1960–72), and, until 2006, he was a professor of philosophy and creative writing at the University of Texas, Austin. A prolific writer, he has produced, since the late 1950s, poems, novels, short stories, and critical essays. Among other major awards, he received the Swedish Academy's Bellman Prize in 1990.

Zbigniew Herbert. He fought with the Resistance in Poland as a teenager, and his poetry was formed by his experiences under both the Nazi and the Soviet dictatorships. He was coeditor of the poetry journal *Poezja* from 1965 to 1968, but he resigned in protest against its anti-Semitic policies. His books include *Report from the Besieged City, and Other Poems* (1983) and *89 Poems* (1998).

Miguel Hernández. A self-educated Spanish shepherd, he became a poet and playwright encouraged by the Generation of 1927 (see Jorge Guillén). He fought with the Republican forces against Franco and the Nationalists and joined the First Calvary Company of the Peasants' Battalion as a cultural affairs officer, reading his poetry daily on the radio. He died of tuberculosis in prison during the Franco regime. A bilingual edition entitled *The Selected Poems of Miguel Hernández* was published in 2001.

Krassin Himmirsky. In 1977 he served as chargé d'affaires of the Bulgarian Embassy in Washington, DC. His collection *Time Bomb: New and Selected Poems* was published in 1999.

Kakinomoto no Hitomaro. Probably from Nara, he may have been a court poet, an official, or a wandering entertainer. Among his surviving works are poems in two major period forms: sixty-one tanka and sixteen *chōka*. His poems can be found in the anthology *Man'yōshū* (Collection of Ten Thousand Leaves).

Homer. Although little is known of the great author credited with composing the *Iliad* and the *Odyssey*, the poems themselves are the measure of the writer. These epics served as the foundation of Greek and later Roman education and culture through the classical age and were the basis for Virgil's *Aeneid*. Their humanist influence continued under the culture and into the Italian Renaissance. With excellent contemporary translations, they remain the foundation of the classical canon.

Horace. A Roman lyric poet, he studied in Rome and Athens. His poetry ranged from epodes and satires to epistles and lyrics, and in his later verse he sought to adapt Greek meters to Latin. He once served as a scribe for the Treasury of Rome but lived most of his life on Sabine Farm near Tivoli, a gift of his patron, Maecenas.

Victor Hugo. Recognized as one of France's most celebrated poets, he is better known abroad in translation for his novels *Notre-Dame de Paris* (1831) and *Les Misérables* (1862). A leader of the romantic movement beginning in 1830, he also entered politics and was elected a deputy for Paris in the Constituent Assembly and, later, the Legislative Assembly. Opposed to Napoleon III's coup d'état, he lived in exile in the Channel Islands for nineteen years, where he wrote some of his most famous works.

Vicente Huidobro (Vicente García Huidobro Fernández). A Chilean poet, playwright, novelist, and journalist, he spent his formative years in Paris. He proposed a movement called *creacionismo*, stressing a fusion between the avant-garde and the ideals of Neoplatonism with the works of Ralph Waldo Emerson. With Apollinaire and Reverdy, he cofounded the Cubist magazine *Nord-Sud*. In 1925 he returned to Chile as a newspaper editor and presented himself unsuccessfully as a candidate for Chile's presidency. In 1931 he published his definitive work, *Altazor*.

Héctor Inchaústegui Cabral. Born in Baní, Dominican Republic, he was a poet, essayist, journalist, and playwright. One of his most significant works was a dramatic trilogy called *El miedo en un puñado de polvo* (Fear in a Handful of Dust) (1964).

Philippe Jaccottet. Born in Switzerland, he has long been a resident of France. In addition to translating German, Italian, and Spanish writers and poets, he has also written several books of literary criticism. In 2010 he was awarded the Schiller Prize, Switzerland's highest literary honor. In 2011 his collected writings were published as a volume in the distinguished Pléiade series.

Attila József. An important modern Hungarian poet attracted to Marxist ideology, his poems depicted proletarian life. Only seventeen when his first poems were published, he went on to produce six books, combining in his work the symbolist tradition with a concern for social justice. In 1936 he cofounded the review *Szép Szó*.

Erich Kästner. A German satirist, poet, and novelist, his 1931 novel *Fabian*, about Germany's lost generation, chronicled the last year of the Weimar Republic. Following military service in World War I, he became a pacifist and an opponent of totalitarian systems. He was arrested twice by the Gestapo in the 1930s for crossing the border to see his Swiss publisher. In 1957 he was awarded the Büchner Prize for literature.

Jean de La Fontaine. As a poet, he wrote fables considered masterpieces of French literature. From 1652 to 1671, he served as an inspector of forests and waterways, and, among other socially prestigious positions, he became a protégé of Nicolas Fouquet, the wealthy superintendent of finance. Whereas his fables—the first six of twelve books were published in 1668—hewed closely to the Aesopic tradition, he also drew on tales from East Asia.

Valery Larbaud. A major figure of twentieth-century French literature, he was a poet, novelist, essayist, and translator. With regard to the latter, he worked with James Joyce on the French version of *Ulysses*. *Sous l'invocation de Saint Jerôme*, his collected writings on translation, was published in 1944. The poem included here is the last piece, and only poem, in his collection of essays *Jaune, bleu, blanc* (1927).

Leconte de Lisle. A French poet born on Réunion Island off East Africa, he was a prominent member of the Parnassian movement, a group of nine-teenth-century French poets who favored restraint and objectivity in lieu of the excesses of romanticism.

Lope de Vega. An outstanding dramatist of the Spanish golden age, he was known as el Fénix de España (the Phoenix of Spain). Of his estimated 1,800 plays, only 431 are extant, and only 50 shorter dramatic pieces survive of the several hundred he wrote. He was born and died in Madrid.

Lucretius (Titus Lucretius Carus). He was a Roman poet and philosopher of the tumultuous first century B.C., who had a major influence on subsequent poets, particularly Virgil. Little is known of his life; his dates are based pri-marily on a brief notice in a chronicle compiled by Saint Jerome in the fourth century A.D. His *De Rerum Natura*, a didactic epic in six books, is the only surviving full-length exposition of Epicurean philosophy.

Antonio Machado. He was the leading poet of Spain's renowned Generation of 1898, young writers who declared Spain's moral and cultural rebirth follow-ing its defeat in the Spanish-American War (1898). His poetry was infused with the austere and dramatic landscape of Castile, where he lived. Exiled for sup-porting the loyalists during the Spanish Civil War, he crossed the Pyrenees by foot only to die a month later in France. His *Poesías completas* appeared in 1936.

Stéphane Mallarmé. A leader of the French symbolist movement, he pub-lished *L'après-midi d'un faun* (1876) and *Les poésies de S. Mallarmé* (1899), a slim volume containing his oeuvre of fifty poems. Writers and artists attending his Tuesday-evening salons, a center of Parisian intellectual life, were known as *les Mardistes*, after the French for "Tuesday."

Osip Mandelstam. Born in Warsaw, Poland, he emerged as a major Russian poet and member of the acmeist school that rejected the mysticism of symbolism in favor of concreteness of imagery and expression. He was arrested in 1934 and sent into exile for reading an epigram denouncing Stalin; later, after a second arrest, he died in a transit camp. His works include *Tristia* (1922) and *Stikhotvoreniya, 1921–1925* (Poems, 1921–1925) (1928).

Juan Matos. A Dominican Republic poet now living in Worcester, Massachusetts, he teaches English as a second language at the Goddard School of Science and Technology. He is a cofounder of Palabra, Expresion Cultural, in New York City and of Tertulia Pedro Mir, a poetry-reading series in Lawrence, Massachusetts. His latest book is *Del milagro de la espera* (The miracle of waiting) (2005).

Pero Meogo. He was a Galician poet active in the thirteenth century. All nine of his *cantigas d'amigo* feature a mountain stag, which has been interpreted as a symbol of male sexuality.

Gabriela Mistral (Lucila Godoy y Alcayaga). A Chilean poet and educator, she became the first Latin American to win the Nobel Prize in Literature (1945). She taught Spanish literature in the United States at Columbia University, among other institutions. Her *Poesías completas* was published in 1958.

Christian Morgenstern. A German poet-philosopher, he was a humorist with a whimsical imagination who manipulated word meanings and context in dislocated sentence structures to create clever satirical poetry. His two volumes in this genre are *Galgenlieder* (1905) and *Palmström* (1910). An interest in mysticism led him to the theosophical teachings of Rudolf Steiner.

Pablo Neruda (Neftalí Ricardo Reyes Basoalto). A Chilean poet, he served in his country's consular service in the Far East, Latin America, and Spain (1927–35). Both the Spanish Civil War and the murder of Garcia Lorca, whom he knew, resulted in his joining the Republican movement. In 1945, as an extreme leftist in politics, he was elected a senator in Chile. A surrealist, he revived common speech and bold metaphors in free verse. In 1971 he was awarded the Nobel Prize in Literature. *The Essential Neruda: Selected Poems* was published in a bilingual edition in 2004.

Nguyễn Bỉnh Khiêm (Trang Trinh, Hanh Phu, Bach Van cu si [White Cloud Hermit]). A Vietnamese poet, scholar, and prophet, he served the emperor, but, protesting corruption, he retired to his village and taught, among others, his half-brother Phùng Khắc Khoan (see below). His poems treated the simple life marked by a sense of fortitude. His long poem *Sấm Trạng Trình* (*The Prophecies of Trạng Trình*) has been compared to Nostradamus's *Centuries* for the truth of its prophecies. It includes the line "*Việt Nam khởi tổ xây nền*" ("Vietnam is being created"), an early use of the word "Vietnam."

Kostis Palamas. He was the first modern Greek man of letters, and his name gave the term "Palamic" to poetry of that period. He was central to the demotic movement to use vernacular language and founded the "new school of Athens," favoring restraint over romantic exuberance. He wrote thirty volumes, including epics, lyrics, and plays, and composed the words for the "Olympic Hymn," performed at the first modern Games in 1896. His funeral during the German occupation became a major symbolic event for Greek resistance.

Jean Passerat. A professor of Latin at the Collège de France, he wrote scholarly Latin works and commentaries on Catullus, Tibullus, and Propertius. He was one of the contributors to the "Satire Ménippée," the manifesto of the moderate Royalist party in support of Henry of Navarre's claim to the throne. Among the poems for which he is known are "Ode du premier jour de mai" (Ode on the First Day of May) and the villanelle "J'ai perdu ma tourterelle" (I Have Lost My Turtle Dove).

Octavio Paz. A Mexican diplomat, poet, and writer, in 1937 he attended the Second International Congress of Anti-Fascist Writers in Valencia, Spain. He was appointed ambassador to India but resigned diplomatic service in 1968 to protest the government's suppression of student demonstrators at the Olympic Games in Mexico. As a founder of two magazines devoted to the arts and politics, *Plural* and *Vuelta*, he continued his work as an editor and publisher. He received the Cervantes Award (1981) and the Nobel Prize in Literature (1990).

Peire Vidal. A celebrated Provençal troubadour, he was a favorite performer at the courts of France, Spain, Italy, Malta, and Palestine during the late twelfth and early thirteenth centuries. He combined rich and elaborate metrical forms with simplicity of expression, and his witty and humorous love songs and satires provide a fascinating insight into the courtly society of his times.

Phùng Khắc Khoan (Trang Bung). In addition to being a prolific poet with Taoist leanings, he was Vietnam's ambassador to China in 1597 during the Ming dynasty. He was proficient in Confucian studies and fortune-telling sciences, like his half-brother Nguyễn Bỉnh Khiêm (see above).

Lucio Piccolo. A Sicilian poet, Piccolo was also a brilliant pianist and an interpreter of Wagner. He had a close friendship with William Butler Yeats, and his style of poetry incorporates both the Sicilian baroque tradition and the themes and techniques of Yeats's symbolist poetry. In 1956 he published *Canti barocchi e altre liriche* (Baroque songs and other lyrics).

Dimitri V. Psurtsev. He is a professor of translation at Moscow State Linguistics University and lives in a dacha outside the capital. He has translated modern British and American prose and poetry from Steinbeck to Dylan Thomas and A. S. Byatt. In 2001 he published two volumes of poetry, *Ex Roma tertia* and *Tengiz Notebook*.

Raimbaut de Vaqueiras. Among the foremost Provençal troubadours, he was well traveled and conversant in several languages and dialects. He was knighted for bravery in battle by Boniface I, the Marquess of Montferrat, whom he served in the Piedmont region of northern Italy. Only seven of his thirty-five poems survive with music, including one for Boniface's daughter Beatrice, adapted from a dance melody played by a jongleur.

Richard I (Richard the Lionheart). King of England and a member of the Plantagenet family, he was the third son of Henry II and Eleanor of Aquitaine. He joined the Third Crusade in 1190 to recapture Jerusalem from

Saladin. He was captured and imprisoned during his return by Leopold II of Austria and released after payment of a ransom. Fond of poetry and music, he was nurtured in the troubadour culture of his mother's southern homeland. He became a lyric poet of considerable reputation among troubadours.

Yannis Ritsos. One of Greece's most prolific poets, he published 117 books of poetry in addition to several verse dramas and a book of essays. His poetry has been translated into forty-four languages. Owing to his leftist activities, he spent many years of his life interned in prison camps or in exile on Greek islands. He won the 1975–76 Lenin Peace Prize and other literary awards in Eastern Europe.

Francisco de Sá de Miranda. He was a Portuguese poet and dramatist who introduced Renaissance poetic forms to Portugal. The son of a canon of Coimbra, he grew up in the royal court at Lisbon and received a doctorate in law. His play *Os estrangeiros* (The Foreigners), ca. 1527, was the first Portuguese prose comedy in the classical manner, and his *Cleopatra* (ca. 1550) was probably the first Portuguese classical tragedy.

Sappho. Born on the island of Lesbos at a time of cultural flowering, she was a leader of the Aeolian school of lyric poetry. She contributed to the literary genre not only through her theme of love, but also with her emphasis on emotion, on subjective experience, and on the individual, marking her work in contrast to the epic, liturgical, or dramatic poetry of the period. Plato hailed her as "the tenth Muse," and she was honored on coins and with civic statuary.

Olga Sedakova. One of the most respected poets in modern Russia, she is the author of more than thirty books of poetry, essays, translations, and literary criticism. She is also a philologist and ethnographer. As a teacher in the Department of Philosophy at Moscow State University, she is influential as a thinker and essayist. She has been awarded the European Prize in Poetry (1995) and the Aleksandr Solzhenitsyn Prize (2003). She continues the distinguished line of philosophical poets.

Motomaro Senge. He was one of the better-known poets of pre–World War II Japan. His poetry is characterized by a simple, matter-of-fact style that reflects his fascination with nature and the commonplaces of everyday life.

Sophocles. An innovator of drama in classical Athenian culture, he was also a politician, priest, and military leader, and his musical accomplishments led to his recognition as a master of song. His most famous surviving works include the Theban plays—*Oedipus Rex, Oedipus at Colonus,* and *Antigone*—as well as *The Women of Trachis, Ajax, Philoctetes,* and *Electra.* He wrote more than 120 plays, of which only these 7 survive.

To Huu. Hailed as North Vietnam's poet laureate, he was born in Vietnam, French Indochina. An early member of the Communist Party, he joined the Vietminh in 1942 after imprisonment for his political views. When the country split in 1954, he was appointed deputy cultural minister in North Vietnam, inspiring party members with his propagandistic verse, meanwhile keeping other poets in line. He became deputy prime minister, but blamed for ill-fated economic reforms, he resigned in 1985.

Nuno Fernandes Torneol. He was a Galician-Portuguese troubadour in the thirteenth century.

Tru Vu (Tran Dai Binh). A poet of South Vietnam, he has taken the name of a famous eighteenth-century poet as his pen name. A precocious poet since his teens, he turned to painting and calligraphy after the Communist takeover of South Vietnam (1975).

Marina Tsvetaeva. A Russian poet, she was considered one of the most original silver-age poets of the twentieth century, bridging two contradictory strands of Russian poetry—symbolism and acmeism (see Osip Mandelstam). *The Tsar Maiden* (1922) is one of her best-known poems. Suffering from poverty during the revolution, she moved with her family to Berlin. Upon returning in 1939, her poetry was rejected by the Bolshevik regime, and translation was the only work afforded her. In 1941 her husband was shot for espionage and her daughter sent to a labor camp.

Tu Fu. A Chinese poet of the Tang dynasty, his early poetry celebrated the beauty of the natural world and bemoaned the passage of time. As a young traveler, he met the renowned Li Bai and flirted with Daoism; upon returning to Ch'ang-an, the capital, he resumed his conventional Confucianism. Later, as a government official, he was captured during the 755 An Lushan Rebellion. Thereafter, he wrote of humanity in the grips of war, mastering all poetic genres, especially the *lüshi*, or "regulated verse." He died on a riverboat.

Từ Kế Tường (Vo Tan Tuoc). A South Vietnamese poet, he wrote for many journals beginning in the 1960s. Following the Communist takeover of the country, he became a journalist writing for public-security organs. The *Tuoi Ngoc Magazine* is under his editorship.

Fyodor Tyutchev. The favorite poet of Leo Tolstoy, he wrote many lyrics about nature. During most of his twenty-two years abroad in the Foreign Service, he was posted at the Russian Embassy in Munich, where he immersed himself in Western culture and German philosophy and romantic literature, becoming personally acquainted with such figures as Heinrich Heine and Friedrich Schelling. Through the latter's philosophy, he saw the universe as an organic whole, animated by a single undivided life force. A collection of his poems was published in English as *Poems of Night and Day* (1974).

Giuseppe Ungaretti. A pioneer and leader of the modernist movement in twentieth-century Italian poetry, he was born in Alexandria, Egypt, of Tuscan parentage. He was a founder of the hermetic movement in the 1920s and 1930s that, influenced by French symbolism, believed in the mystical power of words. Following military service in World War I, he distilled the experience in two of his essential volumes: *Il porto sepolto* (The Buried Harbour) (1916) and *Allegria dei naufragi* (Joy of Shipwrecks) (1919). He accepted the chair of Italian literature at São Paolo University, Brazil (1936–42). In 1970 he was awarded the Neustadt International Prize for Literature.

Paul Valéry. He was a major French symbolist poet as well as an essayist and critic. His greatest poem is considered *La jeune parque* (The Young Fate) (1917). Perhaps his most striking achievement is his monumental intellectual diary (more than twenty thousand pages), called the *Cahiers* (*Notebooks*). In 1925 he was elected to the Académie Française. He spent the remaining twenty years of his life writing numerous essays on poetry, painting, and dance. The candlelit procession of his funeral was a national event following the liberation in 1945.

François Villon. Although he lived life on the seamy side, he is perhaps the best-known French poet of the Middle Ages. During his exile from Paris, commuted from a death sentence for killing a man, he fell in with a band of thieves, giving rise to his poems in thieves' jargon. Although he employed medieval forms of versification, his personal message placed him among the moderns. His works include the *Lais* (1456) and the *Testament* (1461).

Walther von der Vogelweide. He was a renowned German lyric poet of the Middle Ages, whose poetry emphasizes the virtues of a balanced life, in the social as in the personal sphere, and reflects his disapproval of those individuals, actions, and beliefs that disturb this harmony. The title *hêr*, which he was given by other poets, indicates that he was of knightly birth. More than half of the two hundred or so of Walther's poems that are extant are political, moral, or religious; the rest are love poems.

NOTES ON TRANSLATORS

William Arrowsmith (Orange, New Jersey, 1924–92). A founder of the *Hudson Review* and a classics professor, he was an eminent translator of Greek dramas. In 1980 he received the National Book Award in Translation for *Hard Labor*, by Cesare Pavese.

Paul Blackburn (St. Albans, Vermont, 1926–71). A prominent Black Mountain poet, he studied Provençal at the University of Toulouse as a Fulbright scholar and became a leading translator of Provençal troubadour verse. *Proensa: An Anthology of Troubadour Poetry*, selected and translated by him, was published in 1978.

Lorna Knowles Blake (Havana, Cuba, b. 1953). She teaches creative writing at the 92nd Street Y in New York and poetry craft at Sarah Lawrence College. Her first collection of poems, *Permanent Address* (2008), won the Richard Snyder Publication Prize from the Ashland Poetry Press.

Robert Bly (Madison, Minnesota, b. 1926). Following studies as a Fulbright scholar in Norway, he became a translator of Norwegian poetry. In 1967 he won the National Book Award for *The Light around the Body*. His latest collection of poems is *Talking into the Ear of a Donkey* (2011).

Louise Bogan (Livermore Falls, Maine, 1897–1970). She served as the *New Yorker*'s poetry critic for thirty-eight years; her books of criticism include *Achievement in American Poetry, 1900–1950* (1951). In 1955 she shared the Bollingen Prize in Poetry with Leonie Adams for her *Collected Poems, 1923–1953*.

Clarence Brown (Anderson, South Carolina, b. 1929). A professor emeritus of comparative literature at Princeton University, he learned Russian while serving with the Army Security Agency. He translated much of Osip Mandelstam's poetry and prose, and his biography *Mandelstam* (1973) won the Christian Gauss Award in Literary Criticism.

Olga Carlisle (Paris, France, b. 1931). Granddaughter of the Russian writer Leonid Andreyev, she gained notoriety for smuggling out from Russia and publishing seminal works by Aleksandr Solzhenitsyn. Her 1993 memoir, *Under a New Sky: A Reunion with Russia*, records later adventures there.

Dick Davis (Portsmouth, UK, b. 1945). He is professor of Persian and chair of the Department of Near Eastern Languages and Cultures at Ohio State University, from which he received the Distinguished Scholar Award in 2002. His most recent book of poems is *A Trick of Sunlight* (2006).

Rhina P. Espaillat (Santo Domingo, Dominican Republic, b. 1932). Having moved to the United States as a child, she writes poems, short stories, and essays in English and in her native Spanish and translates in both directions. Her latest poetry collection is *Her Place in These Designs* (2008). The Dominican Republic's Ministry of Culture honored her for service to culture.

Ruth Fainlight (New York, New York, b. 1931). Living in London, England, since age fifteen, her *New and Collected Poems* (2010) draws on thirteen collections spanning forty years, including translations from Portuguese, Spanish, and classical Greek.

Dudley Fitts (Boston, Massachusetts, 1903–68). Although he also translated works by Latin, Spanish, and Latin American authors, he is known for his translations from classical Greek, often in collaboration with Robert Fitzgerald, his former student at the Choate School.

Robert Fitzgerald (Springfield, Illinois, 1910–85). He served as Boylston Professor of Rhetoric at Harvard University and was a prolific translator of Greek classics. Awarded the Bollingen Prize in Translation for his verse translation of Homer's *Odyssey* (1961), he also translated *The Iliad* (1974) and *The Aeneid* (1983).

Kimon Friar (Imrali, Turkey, 1911–93). Although he moved to the United States as a child with his Greek parents, he remained in the Hellenic linguistic milieu, eventually becoming a translator and critic of modern Greek literature. In 1978 he received the Greek World Award.

Robin Fulton (Arran, Scotland, b. 1937). He has lived in Norway since 1973 where he taught at Stavanger University until 2006. His distinguished translations of Scandinavian poetry earned awards from, among others, the Swedish Academy. His own poetry books include *Coming Down to Earth and Spring Is Soon* (1990).

Emily Grosholz (Philadelphia, Pennsylvania, b. 1950). She teaches philosophy at Pennsylvania State University. Her latest poetry collection is a bilingual edition titled *Feuilles/Leaves* (2007), and her translation *Beginning and End of the Snow/Début et fin de la neige*, by Yves Bonnefoy, was published in 2012.

R. S. Gwynn (Eden, North Carolina, b. 1948). A poet known for his wit and complex verse forms, he is also a critic, editor, and occasional translator who teaches at Lamar University. His translations include individual poems by Gustavo Adolfo Bécquer, Heinrich Heine, Victor Hugo, Stéphane Mallarmé, and François Villon.

Michael Hamburger (Berlin, Germany, 1924–2007). In addition to translating German poets, he published the anthology *East German Poetry* (1973) and was awarded Germany's Goethe Medal. He wrote a critical work, *The Truth of Poetry* (1969), and his *Collected Poems* appeared in 1984.

Anthony Hecht (New York, New York, 1923–2004). A longtime professor of poetry at the University of Rochester, his book *The Hard Hours*, relating the horrors he encountered in World War II, won the 1968 Pulitzer Prize. A consultant in poetry to the Library of Congress from 1982 to 1984, he was also awarded the Bollingen Prize in Poetry (1983).

Judith Hemschemeyer (Sheboygan, Wisconsin, b. 1935). She is the translator of *The Complete Poems of Anna Akhmatova*, first published in a bilingual edition in 1990. The latest of her five books of poetry is *Lovely How Lives* (2010).

Johanna Keller (Ahoskie, North Carolina, b. 1955). Founding director of the Goldring Arts Journalism program at the S. I. Newhouse School, Syracuse University, she has written on classical music for newspapers and periodicals and published poems in literary magazines.

Galway Kinnell (Providence, Rhode Island, b. 1927). A 1984 recipient of a MacArthur Foundation Fellowship, he was Erich Maria Remarque Professor of Creative Writing at New York University. In 1983 his *Selected Poems* won both the Pulitzer Prize and the National Book Award.

Bela Kiralyfalvi (Nyiregyháza, Hungary, b. 1937). Having fled Hungary during the 1956 uprising, he was a professor of theater at Wichita State University where he taught dramatic theory, criticism, and script analysis. In 1974 he founded the National Playwriting Contest for students.

Carolyn Kizer (Spokane, Washington, b. 1923). Founder of *Poetry Northwest* in 1959, she edited the magazine until 1965. In 1964 she taught in Pakistan and that year won the Pulitzer Prize for *Yin: New Poems*. Her translations include poems from Chinese, Japanese, and Urdu.

Richmond Lattimore (Paotingfu, China, 1906–84). A translator of classical Greek literature, he taught Greek at Bryn Mawr College (1935–71). He is noted for his translations of *The Iliad* and *The Odyssey*, and he received the 1962 Bollingen Prize in Translation for Aristophanes's *The Frogs*.

Denise Levertov (Ilford, England, 1923–97). Identified with the Black Mountain school, her poetry engages humanist and sociopolitical themes like the Vietnam War. Her collection *Evening Train* (1992) was particularly lauded for its mature style, as was her posthumous book *This Great Unknowing: Last Poems* (1999).

P. H. Liotta (Burlington, Vermont, b. 1956). A professor of humanities at Salve Regina University, he published *The Wolf at the Door: A Poetic Cycle*, translated from the Macedonian of Bogomil Gjuzel, in 2001. As a member of the Intergovernmental Panel on Climate Change, he shared the 2007 Nobel Peace Prize.

Robert J. Littman (Newark, New Jersey, b. 1943). A professor of classics at the University of Hawaii at Manoa, he specializes in Greek literature, history, and the Greek Bible as well as Egyptian archaeology.

Charles Martin (New York, New York, b. 1942). He has published translations of Catullus, Ovid, and the Bhagavad Gita (with Gavin Flood) and an introduction to the poetry of Catullus. In 2005 he received the Award for Literature from the American Academy of Arts and Letters. The latest of his five books of poems is *Signs and Wonders* (2011).

David Mason (Bellingham, Washington, b. 1954). Among his many books are a memoir of Greece, *News from the Village: Aegean Friends* (2010), and a verse novel, *Ludlow* (2007), in which Greek immigrant characters play a prominent role. He was appointed poet laureate of Colorado (2010–14).

Daniel Mendelsohn (New York, New York, b. 1960). His books include *The Lost: A Search for Six of Six Million* (2006), which won the National Book Critics Circle Award and the Prix Médicis in France. He has also written a two-volume translation, with commentary, of the complete poems of C. P. Cavafy (2009). He teaches at Bard College.

W. S. Merwin (New York, New York, b. 1927). His poem "Meng Tzu's Song" appeared in volume 1, no. 1 (1948), of the *Hudson Review* while he was still a student at Princeton University. Twice awarded the Pulitzer Prize, he was poet laureate in 2010–11. His *Selected Translations* was published in 2012.

Robert Mezey (Philadelphia, Pennsylvania, b. 1935). Professor emeritus at Pomona College, he won the 2002 Poets' Prize for his *Collected Poems, 1952–1999*. He is well known for his translations of Jorge Luis Borges.

Marianne Moore (Kirkwood, Missouri, 1887–1972). A leading modernist poet recognized nationally by the early 1930s, her *Collected Poems* earned her the Bollingen Prize in Poetry in 1951 as well as both the Pulitzer Prize and the National Book Award in 1952.

Frederick Morgan (New York, New York, 1922–2004). A founder of the *Hudson Review* in 1948, he edited the magazine for fifty years. Among his eight collections of poems, he published *Refractions* (1981), composed entirely of his translations. He was made Chevalier de l'Ordre des Arts et des Lettres by the French government (1984) and was winner of the 2001 Aiken Taylor Award in Modern American Poetry. *The One Abiding* (2003) was his last book of poems.

Robin Morgan (Lake Worth, Florida, b. 1941). A poet, novelist, and anthologist, she is an influential force in the feminist movement. In 1999 she published *A Hot January: Poems, 1996–1999*.

Timothy Murphy (Hibbing, Minnesota, b. 1951). In 2011 he published three books of poems: *Mortal Stakes, Faint Thunder*, and *Hunter's Log*.

Kostas Myrsiades (Vourliotes, Samos, Greece, b. 1939). A professor emeritus of comparative literature and English at West Chester University, he is a distinguished translator and Neohellenist. He was the first American to receive the Gold Medallion (1995) from the Hellenic Society of Translators of Literature, awarded annually by the Greek government to a scholar from any country.

Nguyen Ngoc Bich (Hanoi, Vietnam, b. 1937). A founder of the National News Service for readers of Vietnamese-language newspapers worldwide, in 1997 he joined Radio Free Asia to direct the Vietnamese Service. In 1975 he published *A Thousand Years of Vietnamese Poetry*.

John Frederick Nims (Muskegon, Michigan, 1913–99). A former editor of *Poetry* magazine, he taught poetry at several universities. In 1990 he published two collections of poems, *Zany in Denim* and *The Six-Cornered Snowflake, and Other Poems*, as well as *Sappho to Valéry: Poems in Translation*.

Michael Paul Novak (Cicero, Illinois, 1935–2006). He was professor emeritus of English at St. Mary's University in Leavenworth, Kansas, where he taught for more than forty years. Among his publications were two books: *Sailing by the Whirlpool* (1978) and *Story to Tell: Michael Paul Novak Poetry* (1991).

Christina Bratt [Paulston] (Stockholm, Sweden, b. 1932). A professor emerita of linguistics at the University of Pittsburgh, she is the author of *Linguistic Minorities in Multilingual Settings: Implications for Language Policies* (1994).

Richard Pevear (Waltham, Massachusetts, b. 1943). He is a poet, essayist, and translator. Along with a number of works translated from the Russian, including Leo Tolstoy's *War and Peace*, in collaboration with his wife, Larissa Volokhonsky (see below), he has also published translations from the Italian and French.

Ezra Pound (Hailey, Idaho, 1885–1972). A modernist poet, Pound played a pivotal role in the imagist and vorticist movements. In 1949 he won the Bollingen Prize in Poetry for his *Pisan Cantos*, written while imprisoned by the US Army in Pisa for broadcasts deemed traitorous. He was eventually hospitalized in St. Elisabeths Hospital in Washington, DC, where he received many young writers before his release in 1958.

Jennifer Reeser (Lake Charles, Louisiana, b. 1968). She is primarily a translator of Russian and French literature, most notably the work of Charles Baudelaire.

F. D. Reeve (Philadelphia, Pennsylvania, 1928–2013). A noted Russian translator, in 2007 he gave the keynote address in Moscow at the International Conference of Translators of Russian Literature. In 1962 he escorted Robert Frost to a private meeting with Nikita Khrushchev. His novella–prose poem *Nathaniel Purple* was published in 2012.

John Ridland (London, England, b. 1933). A research professor in the English Department at the University of California, Santa Barbara, he came to the United States as an infant. In addition to poetry itself, he has a special interest in Australian and New Zealand literature. His most recent book of poems is *Happy in an Ordinary Thing* (2013).

Lawrence Rogers (Oakland, California, b. 1933). He teaches Japanese literature at the University of Hawaii at Hilo. In 2004 he was awarded the translation prize by Columbia University's Donald Keene Center for Japanese Culture for his book *Tokyo Stories: A Literary Stroll*.

Jerome Rothenberg (New York, New York, b. 1931). He began his publishing career in the late 1950s as a translator of German poetry. In 1959 he founded

Hawk's Well Press as a venue to publish collections by up-and-coming poets of that era.

May Sarton (Wondelgem [now Ghent], Belgium, 1912–95). From early sonnets published in 1929 to her last collection, *Coming into Eighty* (1994), she wrote more than twenty books of poetry, fiction, and nonfiction; a play; and several screenplays. In 1993 she was the recipient of the Levinson Prize for Poetry.

Peter Dale Scott (Montreal, Canada, b. 1929). He cofounded the Peace and Conflict Studies Program at the University of California, Berkeley, and was an antiwar speaker during the Vietnam and Gulf Wars. In 2002 he received the Lannan Literary Award for Poetry for his trilogy of books titled *Seculum*.

Lore Segal (Vienna, Austria, b. 1928). A noted novelist, translator, and author of children's books, her novel *Her First American* won an award from the American Academy and Institute of Arts and Letters in 1986, and her short story "The Reverse Bug" was included in *Best American Short Stories, 1989.*

Louis Simpson (Kingston, Jamaica, 1923–2012). Poet, editor, translator, and critic, he received the 1964 Pulitzer Prize for his collection of poems *At the End of the Open Road.* His volume of translations titled *Modern Poets of France: A Bilingual Anthology* won the 1998 Harold Morton Landon Translation Award.

W. D. Snodgrass (Beaver Falls, Pennsylvania, 1926–2009). He won the 1960 Pulitzer Prize for his first poetry collection, *Heart's Needle.* Though often called a "confessional" poet, he demurred, claiming his poems were simply personal. His *Selected Translations* won the 1999 Harold Morton Landon Translation Award.

A. E. Stallings (Decatur, Georgia, b. 1968). A 2011 recipient of a MacArthur Foundation Fellowship, she studied classics at the University of Georgia, Athens, and now lives in Athens, Greece. Her verse translation of Lucretius's *The Nature of Things* appeared in 2007 and a new collection of poems, *Olives,* in 2012.

Alan Sullivan (New York, New York, 1948–2010). In addition to his translation of *Beowulf* (2004) with Timothy Murphy (see above), his translation *78 Psalms of King David* was published in 2011.

Charles Tomlinson (Stoke-on-Trent, England, b. 1927). Poet, artist, and translator, he taught at the University of Bristol for thirty-six years and edited *The Oxford Book of Verse in Translation* (1980). His *New Collected Poems* was published in 2009. In 2001 he was made a Commander of the British Empire for his contributions to literature. Other honors include the 2001 and 2004 Italian Premio Internazionale di Poesia and the *Hudson Review*'s Bennett Award for Achievement in Literature (1993).

Larissa Volokhonsky (Leningrad [now Saint Petersburg], Russia, b. 1945). Together with her husband, Richard Pevear (see above), she translates Russian literature into English, including works by Leo Tolstoy and Fyodor Dostoyevsky. Their translation of a book by each author received the *PEN/Book-of-the-Month Club Translation Prize* (1991, 2002).

Craig Watson (Atlanta, Georgia, b. 1969). An assistant professor of English at Kennesaw State University, he has published both poems and translations from Latin in periodicals. He has also published essays on the painter Fairfield Porter.

Mary Jane White (Charlotte, North Carolina, b. 1953). She is a poet and translator who practices law at her home in Waukon, Iowa. Her first book, *Starry Sky to Starry Sky* (1988), contains her translation of Marina Tsvetaeva's long lyric cycle "Miles."

Richard Wilbur (New York, New York, b. 1921). Former poet laureate (1987–88), he is America's leading translator of plays by Molière, Racine, and Corneille, employing brilliant rhymes. His *Tartuffe* by Molière was awarded the 1963 Bollingen Prize in Translation. In 1957 he received the Pulitzer Prize and National Book Award for *Things of This World: Poems*. His most recent book of poems is *Anterooms* (2010).

William Carlos Williams (Rutherford, New Jersey, 1883–1963). Known as an imagist poet, he also practiced medicine in Rutherford from 1910 to 1951.

He shared the Bollingen Prize in Poetry with Archibald MacLeish in 1952, and his last book, *Pictures from Brueghel*, won a Pulitzer Prize in 1963. His Spanish translations, edited by Jonathan Cohen, were published as *By Word of Mouth: Poems from the Spanish, 1916–1959* (2011).

INDEX